Twilight of the Exiles

A Celebration of Goans And Friends

Cyprian Fernandes

Twilight of the Exiles A celebration of Goans and friends who were forced to leave East Africa and new friends.

© Copyright Cyprian 'Skip Fernandes 2020

Published by Cyprian Fernandes Pendle Hill NSW 2145
www.headlinesofmylife.today

Main cover image courtesy of Mitchell Krog

Twilight of the Exiles

Dedication

I dedicate this book to someone I have admired and respected for a very long time: My brother Johnny, David Joseph Fernandes to give him his full name. Throughout his life, he has tried to connect with as many people as possible who lived in Eastleigh (and the surrounding suburbs) Nairobi. He has travelled the world and wherever he has been to, he has tried to seek old friends. The folks that have been delighted most are the generation of my late parents. A lot of people in the world know my brother.

I AM ALSO INDEBTED TO: Maura, Johnny and Michelle Lobo, Maureen D'Mello D'Souza, Armand Rodrigues, Norman da Costa, Merwin D'Souza, Bill Pagano, the family of the late Ladis Da Silva and Asian Studies Center Michigan State University, Dr Sultan Somjee, Michael Krog Photography, Meldrita Laurente Viegas, Avila Laura Ramos, Paloma Fernandes. Joe Desa, Mel D'Souza, Walter Fernandes, Olaf Ribeiro, Claire Batchelor, Heather-Gail D'Souza, Diljit Bahra and too many others who helped in some way towards making this book possible. I am also indebted to the de Souza family for allowing me use of excerpts from Forward to Independence: My Memoir by the late Dr Fitz de Souza. Availabe on Amazon.

Main cover photograph by Mitchell Krog.

About the author

TWILIGHT OF THE EXILES IS the fourth book published by Septuagenarian Cyprian Fernandes, born and raised in Kenya. He was forced to leave school at the age of 12 and from that day onwards his life has revolved around words and writing. At 16-going on -17 he became a sports journalist and it was not long before he had begun the safari to becoming an investigative journalist, covering mainly crime and politics. He moved to England in 1974 and to Australia in 1979. He held senior positions on The Sydney Morning Herald's colour magazine inset Good Weekend and on The Australian. He was Editor of the St George and Sutherland Shire Leader and Communications Manager focusing on all aspects of engaging people inside and outside of an oil refinery fence. He specialised in emergency *response in dealing with the local community, local, state and federal government. He retired in 2009 and found sanctuary in an online blog which gave birth to the books he has published so far. The books have won over readers, many of whom he counts among his world- wide friends.*

The author in Rome

Contents

Dedication v
About The Author vi
Twilight Of The Exiles 1
Meldrita 9
Born To Run 17
Maura Lobo 22
Earth Angels 30
Paloma Fernandes 33
The Irish Goan 36
Ladis Da Silva 45
Zanzibar Goans Ladis Da Silva 49
Dr Fitz De Souza 59
Pio And Me 65
Maureen D'souza 71
Blaise 89
What The Blaises? 98
Jack Britto 104

Johnny Lobo 109

Valu! 117

Jose Marie Valentino De Abreu M.B.E. 117

The Birth Of St Teresa's 124

Anthony B. Almeida 137

The Prince And The Pomphret 144

Walter Fernandes 150

The Day Terrorists Attacked Our Home 154

Olaf Kenneth Ribeiro An Extraordinary Man 159

Kenya Lost A Warrior, Goans A Champion 163

Harold George D'souza 168

Ray Batchelor 175

Crescenti Fernandes 184

Steve "The Joker" Fernandes 193

The Longest Honeymoon 197

Tears Of A Daughter 204

My Dad And I 208

The Goan Clubs And Goan Culture 215

Bye Sis 219

Vicky Antao Lory 225

An Icon At The Centre Of Attention 229

John J. De Souza 234

Jack Simonian 238

The Talented Mr D'costa 245

Armand Rodrigues 250

The Bandits And The Alvarez Boys 268

The Bbc And Me, A Beautiful Love Affair 270

A Priest On The Run 275

Memories Of Days Gone By 281

Nicky D'mello 283

Eugene Pereira 288

Maureen Pereira 291

Justin Dourado 295

Bill Pagano 298

"Time*" At The Kilindini Bar! 307

St Francis Xavier Chapel, Malindi 313

'Half Crack' In Track And Field 318

John And Annie Gomes 323

Polly Fernandes 329

TWILIGHT OF THE EXILES

DEDICATE THIS book (could be my last unless ...) to all the people who were forced to leave their birth-mother countries because of the Africanisation program enforced by the newly independent nations. I call these people, myself and my family included the exiles of eastern Africa. Most exiles have adopted and adapted to their new homes and countries of the diaspora. There are some, however, who will never forgive the Africans, especially the Ugandan dictator Idi Amin, for virtually chucking them out. It was generally a quite brutal exodus for most, but Idi Amin was particularly savage in forcing the Asians out of their beloved Uganda. Others knew from the very start of the independence process that there was no place for them in African and that a day would come when they would have to leave. My family and I were of this mind hence we did not take up Kenyan citizenship. But you can't stop loving the yearning for the country of your birth. Sure, some of these countries are no longer 100% safe with a high crime rate and most people tend to say "thank God I live in Canada, Australia, New Zealand, Europe" or elsewhere. But that does not stop them from jumping out of comfy chairs screaming their lungs out, encouraging a Kenya victory on the track while watching it on television. Nostalgia binds us all and memory and nostalgia are stepmothers of a kind. We return at least once (or twice or three times, or whenever we can) to the old country and bask in its sunshine, feast on its cuisine and devour its fruit, and go on safaris in search of the Big Five Lion, Leopard, Elephant, Rhino, Buffalo and relive the dreams and memories of yesterday.

One of the key elements of these nostalgia safaris is to meet up with friends and family who remained behind. They have prospered and done well for themselves. A visit to the Nairobi Goan Gymkhana, a meet-and-greet or a "koroga" (cooking) party at the Nairobi Goan Institute or the Mombasa Goan Institute is always high on the travelling menu.

For a few days, or a week or two, or four, we live the life that we had become accustomed to before we had to leave. From the sidelines of the diaspora, most exiles wish nothing but the best for their countries of birth: safe cities and towns, a solution for the shanty towns and their people, elimination of political and monetary corruption. Most exiles remember one side of the colonial era with great nostalgia: good law and order. The other, colour-bar, exploitation of the African and the wholesale robbery of tribal lands and the crimes committed against the people of these former colonies, they would rather not think about. Most Africans have forgotten about the sad and ugly past. Similarly, like much of the nostalgia, Nairobi is wiping out with every new mega-structure, the bits that will now live in the memory of the aged (both exiles and the folks who live there) and soon all that reminds of the past in Nairobi will be there no longer. For a start, the exiles cannot recognise the new street names. Nor can we remember what was where in our youth or while we were adults. There are those who have cut the umbilical cord and have erased Kenya from all of their memory but bear no ill feelings towards anyone.

If there are no keepers of our collective and individual memory left alive, then we cease to exist completely, much more so than if we were remembered.

The ground is called laterite and is a clay which has been enriched with Iron and aluminium that has been developed over long periods by the heavy rainfalls and the intense heat. Sometimes the material is rock hard but when scuffed by vehicle wheels, it becomes a choking, red dust. The iron is the origin of the redness, it is a rusty red colour. – Jack Hill.

FOR a long time, I have been writing and talking about our East African DNA. Most Europeans will tell you of their love for their Kenya, Uganda, Tanzania... The histories of these countries' past are "in the blood." I have always interpreted that the critical element in the DNA is red dust which we breathed in, swallowed it with the raging wind or soaked our bodies with it helped along by those gorgeous rains. I have always loved that red dust from as long as I can remember growing up, first in the city of Nairobi and then in semi-rural (to start with) Eastleigh and its neighbouring environs. We walked mostly barefoot and if had the tennis shoes on, then there was probably a hole in each sole and the cardboard pieces had moved. I can still taste that dust on my lips and in my hair.

I am a child of the War years, WWII, that is. Already I have lost too many friends of my age group. In 20 years, I doubt if there will be anyone left who was born in the 1920s, unless they make it to 100. Along with them, we will lose some of those born in the 1930s and 1940s unless COVID takes them sooner.

In 40 years, there may not be anyone left who lived with us, grew up with us, worked with us, hunted and fished and picnicked and loved Kenya the way we did. It was always going to be the case of a broken-hearted melody.

Aha! I would hand over the collective works of our Kenya lives to the young adults (children of ex-Kenyan migrants of all colours) who live in Canada and have some idea about what their parents and grandparents' lives were like in that distant poetic land. A few live in the UK and yet others are strewn all over the world, especially southern Africa. A few live in Kenya; once were children, now grandparents and basking in the twilight of their lives.

In the meanwhile, I will sing her song, dance her beat, drink her juices, tea and coffee, and sup on feasts that often seem only distant memories when we were once free with wind in our hair, gentle breezes (kindly ghosts of Kenyans who died long ago) caressing my cheeks and TV screen in my brain is alight with those awesome memories of the children of the red ochre growing up shrouded by my mother Kenya.

A fellow journalist who has been writing quite a few obits and tributes of late asked me: "Who is going to write our obituaries?" Maybe no-one. Maybe by then, they might be out of fashion!

So, we will continue to celebrate those alive and sing and remember those that are no longer with us.

My forever Yesterdays

Soft, sweet, gentle things, kisses from a whispering Nairobi breeze on any evening. I remember one of the other loves of my life: Nairobi.

My friends, many colours, many thoughts, many dreams, trust, loyalty, poverty and riches, you don't count as money or wealth. Watching the world go by in Nairobi National Park or fishing somewhere, anywhere!

Having tea (or coffee) with a pretty girl at the Tea House of the August Moon opposite the Kenya Cinema.

What is it that psychologically tricks our taste buds into thinking that fruit and veg grown anywhere else other than Kenya lacks taste, aroma, that just plucked freshness, and just does not taste of that Kenya sweetness. And why is this particularly true of those gorgeous *matundas* (passion fruit) that I used to eat by the *kikapuful (basketful)* at one sitting topped off with a couple of slices of pineapple. And what about the *madafu* (tender coconut)? What is it about the Kenyan coast that makes them so different?

And all those (Indian) sweets, why do the *laddoos, barfi, gulab jamun* and *jelebies* (Indian sweets} seem and taste so different, the sweetness just right in the syrup, and laddoos moist but firm. Was it the water? Was it the air? Green mangoes with salt and chilli powder, red paw paws and yellow papaya. Days when Coke was a drink and Fanta orange was the prize. When girls smashed ripened pomegranate seeds on their lips or drank Vimto to make their lips red, centuries before they were encouraged to wear the "devil's colours" lipstick. They looked great au naturel! Grams and *jugus* (groundnuts) cooked in hot sand delicious, also charcoal grilled corn (maise) and yam chips (*muhogo yams*), the fruit pappetas and pocketsful of *jamlums* or *jamuns, seasonally abundant)* guavas (more salt and chilli), thick K.K.C. milk cream with a little bit of sugar or joggery (black jaggery), sweet potato cooked in the hot charcoal ashes, avocado with a little sugar or smashed in milk (or with ice cream, like *faluda*, Indian milkshake), thick masala tea, banana fritters and pancakes to die for ... so soft you never felt you ate them, sweetened balls of popcorn and white sugared grams, syrupy dried nut crunches, sugar and butter on hot chappattis, diwali sweets, Idd sweets, Christmas sweets, wedding sweets, Nirmala's halwa (who can ever forget that) sweet *mandaasi, irio, maharagwe,* skinny *muchusi* (curry) and the king of foods: ugali. Roasted bananas and delish banana fritters. Like kisses, soft, sweet pancakes with honey or fillings of grated coconut and joggery!

The fruit and vegie carts outside our homes each morning followed by the lullaby of the "*chupa na debe*" (bottles and cans) men! The happy-go-lucky *wabenzi* (wabenzi were Mercedes Benz owners) tiffin carriers who took warm, daily cooked food for the *bwanas* (Mr/menfolk in Swahili) in town.

Stern fathers who rarely spoke to their children and mums who fussed worse than mother hens and you only learnt to miss all that when they were gone but you loved them every minute of your life.

Music: Fadhili Williams and Malaika that opened a new world of music to the uninitiated. Bata Shoeshine Boys and Inspector Gideon and the Police Band who played us a new kind music with Kenya soul. Henry Braganza and the Supersonics, The Bandits, the Rhythm Kings, Cooty's bands, The Wheelers, Max Alphonso's amazing harmonica playing, Steve Alvares and his band and the talented Alvares family, classical, jazz, dance and pop.

Escape to Indian movies at the Shan, Liberty or Odeon or the wonderful family musical parties or those boisterous but wonderful Sikh weddings.

Basking in the midday sun, not too far from the hustle and bustle of the city, in the beautiful gardens where children ran wild like butterflies on Saturdays and Sundays where the family gathered for an Indian picnic made in heaven. My nostrils are still filled with the rich aromas! Dinner at too many Sikh restaurants or Punjabi snacks at tiny bars in the suburbs or roast chicken at the Sikh Union accompanied by four fingers of scotch paraded as two fingers, the fore-finger and the little finger. The gentle advice from my many Sikh uncles!

Puberty and growing up at all the social clubs, especially the Goan clubs, the music, the dances, the girls, the friends, the sports, the laughter and carefree, happiest times of my life.

Working at the *Nation*: the most significant moments of my life!

Lunch and drinks any Saturday at the Tropicana and their

brilliant salad tray!

Faluda (and Indian smoothie) at Keby's

The world's best samosas and *aloo bajjias* (potato marinaded scallops) at the Ismalia Café opposite the Khoja Mosque.

Maru's Cafe in Reata Road.

Kheema-mayaii (egg and mince) chappatis, delicious kebabs cooked fresh everywhere, the likes of which I have never seen or tasted again. Except maybe Hazel Nazareth's are equally delish and the first bite with a little juice from *dimu* (lime) or lemon quickly reminds me of home.

Quiet contemplation in the grounds of the Jamia Islamia Mosque or the Holy Family Cathedral.

Coffee with lawyers at Nairobi Town Hall

Coffee and snacks at Snocream Midnight rendezvous at Embakasi Airport.

The drives to anywhere outside of Nairobi: Mombasa, Karen, Nairobi National Park, Thika, Kiambu, Limuru, Naivasha, Gilgil, Nakuru anywhere, a million dreams. World's most splendid breakfasts at the Wagon Wheel Hotel Eldoret, Kericho Tea Hotel, Nakuru Hotel. The bathing of the mind at any game lodge: Watching that magical moment, the last nanosecond when dusk morphs into night. The first chorus of the night orchestra mixed with the grunting sighs of the animal kingdom going to *lala* (sleep).

Eastleigh, Pangani, Juja Road, River Road, Starehe, Kariokor, Dagoretti, Killeshwa, Parklands, Nairobi South C&B, Nairobi West, River Road, Park Road, Highridge, Forest Road, City Park, Nairobi Football Stadium, Mincing Lane, Nairobi markets, the churches, the temples, a million smiles.

Kariokor Market: The world's greatest *nyama choma* (barbecued meat) served with onions tomatoes, green coriander, pinch of salt, drop of vinegar and on the rare occasion a slice of lemon.

The bands, the music, the dancing, Swiss Grill, Topaz Grill Room, Equator Club, Sombrero, Starlight, Equator Inn, Jeans Bar, Caiado's Bar, Indian Bazaar, Museum, Ngong Racecourse.

Waited with panting nostrils each Easter to cover the East African Safari. I will treasure every single moment I spent in every game lodge, one of the best experiences of my life. Everyone should do it at least once. Hey, hey they told us: don't fall in love. Weddings must be arranged; the matchmaker must be allowed to earn her shilling or two. And for many, so it was. We brown skins had to stick to our respective communities and assimilation was out of the question. We were conditioned to accept that to the point it became part of our D.N.A. A few broke the taboos and were instantly marooned in a world far from the rest of us. We did not see anything wrong with that. It was the time, it was the place, and it was the custom. We were many religions, many faiths, many customs, many traditions and we each kept firm with that which we honoured our fathers and mothers for. We respected each other's boundaries and did our own thing. Yet, we got along, played sport together, even socialised in small proportions and we were no strangers to each other's houses when we were children. We had little or nothing to do with the whites socially. For one thing, they lived on the other side of town and we were familiar with their airs and graces or thought mistakenly perhaps that we might not do the right thing. Anyway, they were not a part of our world and we did not even give it another thought. It was the same with Africans. Although we did not know it at the time, this was the British conspiracy of separate development at work. It did not bother us. Some of us even enjoyed and revelled in the lie that we were better than our fellow Indians who were a class below us, according to the white people we served. The African was a savage, they told us.

There were no suicide bombers tearing people to shreds, no inter-communal riots, great marches of protests, boycotts, blackmail, street brawls and all that is ugly and all around us today. We have known what it is to be alive and free, free enough to feel the wind in our hair, hope in our hearts and love in our souls. were human, for the most part, could be as calm, cool and gentle as the climate itself. good. Well, not until the Mau Mau freedom army started fighting for the return of their land and colonial sent in the bomber aircraft, their soldiers, their police, their home guards and a team or two Indians who assisted.

Meldrita

The Queen of Track and Field

The years between 1950 and 1966 were the golden years of Goan track and field in East Africa, especially in the sprinting and middle-distance events. The Kenyan coastal capital of Mombasa produced the best Goan sprinters of all time, led by the late 1962 Commonwealth Games sprint double gold medallist, Seraphino Antao. These fleet footed Goans included Avila Laura Ramos, Albert Castanha (the man who should have gone to the Games but faltered in the trials), Winnie D'Souza Singh, Joe Faria, Juanita Noronha, Pascal Antao, Alcino Rodrigues, Jack Fernandes and a few others. They were all potential medal winners. But this story is about one of the most determined athletes of her time: the extremely shy and humble Meldrita Laurente Viegas. She was born in Mombasa on January 16, 1939, the second of four children. Greta, her older sister, lives in Goa. Her younger brother, Stafford Laurente, lives in Brantford, Ontario, Canada, and the baby of the family, Lauriette D'Souza-Lobo, lives in Toronto. Growing up, Meldrita often felt like the middle child who had to excel elsewhere to get the attention her siblings enjoyed.

Her father John Delphin Laurente was a civil servant with the British Colonial Civil Service (Revenue Department). At the time, the British Government relied on an army of Goan civil servants, sent to virtually every corner of the country, to keep things well-ordered. As a result, Meldrita's family lived in Meru (Central Kenya), Eldoret (Rift Valley) and Kilifi (the Coast) before finally settling in Mombasa when Meldrita was 12 years old.

Her mother, Maude, always tried to minimize the impact of this nomadic life on the children. She sent the kids by ship to Karachi, Pakistan, to live with her parents for two years. A young Meldrita remembers hearing bells for the Angelus from the local church and playing bones and ball (a game featuring pig bones and a tennis ball) on the stairs of her maternal grandmother's home.

Maude also sent the kids to live with her sister Charlotte and her family in Nairobi, while her husband was working in Eldoret, a Kenyan frontier town founded by South African Boer migrants. While in Nairobi, Meldrita went to the Dr. Ribeiro Goan School in Parklands for two years. Her aunt Charlotte was very strict and had a structured routine for her three children and their three cousins. She taught the children how to share. Table manners were high on the priority list. Meldrita missed her parents very much. Her frequent requests to return home finally wore her aunt down, and she was sent to Eldoret to be reunited with her parents. The persistence and determination she showed at a young age would serve her well as she matured.

The family finally ended up in Mombasa, which was much smaller than Nairobi but larger than other places the Laurente family had called home. When they moved to Mombasa, there was a natural period of adjustment. Meldrita went to the Goan (Sacred Heart) School. She found it difficult to make friends as most of her peers had their own social circles, which were largely closed to newcomers. The Goan community there was plagued by the old prejudices of the caste system.

Meldrita was not the kind of youngster who would let these sorts of things affect her. She played rounders, netball, and badminton, and participated in track and field in an attempt to fit in. Interschool participation in track and field brought her great success. She felt a sense of belonging with her track and field family. Later, she continued training and competing while she attended teachers' college and after her teaching career began at the Goan School at the age of 20.

Maude was a huge supporter and was always present when Meldrita ran at the Mombasa Municipal Stadium. John did his part by keeping the evil eye at bay and relishing in her accomplishments. After most meets, John would take Meldrita up to the terrace of their apartment building to take out *dishth* (evil eye). This ritual involved circling dried red chillies and alum around her head and burning the chillies in a charcoal fire thereafter. The burned alum was thought to reveal the faces of those casting the evil eye. The stench of burning chillies is pretty awful. But that was the tradition in those days.

Initially, Meldrita trained at the Goan School. Later she was a member of the Coast Teachers' Training College team. Mr. Loadman, the principal, took a keen interest in her. After Teachers' Training College she returned to the Goan School to teach. She coached the track and field team at the school and selected three girls to run the 4 x 110 yards relay at the Coast Championships with her. She trained with Ray Batchelor at the Mombasa Municipal Stadium. (Ray Batchelor revolutionized Goan sport at the Coast. He was perhaps the only one (or one of a very few) who broke the Colonial colour bar by working and socializing with Goans. He was also the man who coached Antao to gold.) Among those who trained with Meldrita under Batchelor were Seraphino Antao (sprints, hurdles), Albert Castanha (sprints, hurdles, high jump), Alcino Rodrigues (330 yards, 440 yards) and Joe Faria (sprints), Bruno D'Souza, Fathiya Hinaway (hurdler), Ann Sanford (relay team) and Irina Ribitzski. Meldrita has fond memories of Ray. After light jogs and warm-up exercises, he would ask her to run up the stadium steps with her knees as high as she could get them. He told her that this would help improve the length of her strides. She remembers him giving the athletes tins of Milo. He insisted that they eat two hours before a meet. When Meldrita first competed against Winnie D'Souza Singh, Winnie defeated her in the 100-yard dash in a close finish.

That was a turning point for Meldrita. Winnie hadn't broken the Kenya record in the race, so Meldrita set her eyes on the record. It motivated her er to train intensely. She had become accustomed to winning and never wanted to be second best again.

She never lost to Winnie again. Meldrita broke the Kenya record at the Kenya Championships in Kisumu and the record (11.4 secs) stood for many years. The success she enjoyed fueled her training, and she remained the champion for a number of years. The Queen of Track and Field had been crowned. Meldrita saw success in other events as well. She broke the Kenya record for long jump at the Coast Championships and held the record of 17 feet 5.5 inches for several of years. She held the Coast record for the 220 yards (26.5 secs), and she usually ran the anchor leg of the 4 x 110 yards relay.

Meldrita was recognized for all her contributions to track field and field when she was named the female Athlete of the Century at the centenary celebrations of the Mombasa Institute in 2001.

Every win was followed by "a feed", a celebration at Blue Room in Mombasa that would always include faluda and samosas.

Meldrita stopped participating in track and field after she got married. Her husband, Menino Viegas, worked for the Kenya Railways and was based in Voi (relatively close to Mombasa) for many years. The family returned to Mombasa in the late 1970s. Meldrita played field hockey with the Mombasa Institute, and she encouraged her four children to play as well.

Meldrita, Menino and their four children moved to Canada in 1983 and experienced a huge culture shock. Meldrita, who was very involved in the lives of her children, had to come to terms with leaving the children at 7 am and not seeing them again until 5 pm. Not having any house help was also a huge adjustment, as it made the day longer and there was less time for leisure. Meldrita and Menino had left all their friends behind, and they both found it difficult to find employment. Getting around the city required making allowances for significant travel time. However, in time, things improved tremendously. Meldrita and Menino found work, the kids thrived and ultimately went on to university. There was much to cherish.

Meldrita participated in the GOA (Goan Overseas Association) Sports in the first summer after her arrival in Canada. She finished second in the 100 meters. She had to take pain killers to be able to participate as she was experiencing right hip pain. The pain eventually overcame her desire to compete. Furthermore, she didn't like being second best! Three hip surgeries have sidelined her completely. She now officiates at track and field meets.

Meldrita and Menino are presently enjoying retirement and are very involved in the lives of their nine grandchildren. They have wonderful memories of lives well-lived.

Meldrita in Toronto today

Born to Run

By Laura Ramos

My sprinting career began ever since I could walk. I had four brothers. For four years, I seemed to be an embarrassment to my older brothers, as I was shy, awkward, and spoke only Portuguese, Kiswahili and understood Konkani. They kept running away from me anytime I tried to tag along. I had no friends and always hid behind my mother when her friends visited us. So, I spoke very little and became a good listener and learned by rote. My greatest joy was to run, climb trees, and playboy games – gilly-danda (India game), marbles, seven tiles and whittling wood to make toys. I could make catapults from scratch and dabbled in kite making.

Four years later, my third brother was born and two years after him, a fourth, sealing my destiny to become a tomboy and a tough one, too. The first day in school, I was a misfit. I cried when I had to leave my brothers, and take my place in the kindergarten class, with a stern teacher at the front. I began sniveling non-stop, until the teacher got fed up, seized my hand, and marched me to my older brother's class. He was embarrassed and angry but seemed ready to protect me if anybody made fun of the situation. I wowed then, that I would never embarrass any of my family again. So, I shut my mouth and absorbed every lesson. That year, I took the first prize in English and loved it. School became fun, and learning became my 'best friend'! My classmates noticed my skills in Physical Education and sports. I had a trove of good friends, some of whom I keep in touch with to this day.

In 1960, my father, who worked for the Medical Department, was transferred to Mombasa where he worked at the Government Hospital on Salim Road. It took him about 30 minutes to get to work from Hobly Road. My brothers were enrolled in the Goan School in Ganjoni and I was enrolled at The Star of the Sea School on Salim Road near the Goan Institute. My school was co-ed from Kindy to grade 7. I graduated with a grade I Cambridge Overseas Certificate. I then studied at the Coast Teacher Training College. It was here that I had the chance to play netball, and gymnastics was a part of Physical Training. Two years later, I was selected by the Principal of the Arab Girls' School to teach at the newly opened facility specialising in Physical Education. The students had never been to a public school before, and they were faced with many challenges and a close eye was kept ensuring strict Muslim rules were adhered to. Many were natural athletes and welcomed the protection of high school walls so they could remove their 'burkas' (head and body cover) and participate freely in all physical activities.

In my teens, I joined the Coast Athletic Club run by coach Ray

Batchelor. Albert Castanha, Seraphino Antao, Pascal Antao, Alfred Viana, Phila Fernandes, Joanita Noronha and Meldrita were some of those that trained with me. I took part in the 100m 200m sprints as well as the shot put, long and triple and high jumps.

After school, I corrected student work and prepared lessons for the next day. Then I walked with my sports bag 800 yards away to a track next to the Goan Institute Club sports field. All alone, I warmed up doing stretches, then practiced starts and sprints ending with jogs and cooling down exercises. By 5:00 pm. I would remove my spikes and walk to the club pavilion where my fellow field hockey players were gathering for practice. There, I formed two teams and began practicing skills needed to be competition ready. By now there was a group of male experts to help with coaching. I then went to the nearby badminton courts to work on game skills for singles, doubles and mixed doubles. I followed these routines most weekdays. I travelled to other states for competitions and to play against rival teams. I was selected as Sportswoman of the Year 1962.

I met my husband, Lama, in 1960 when he came from Dar-es-Salaam after East Africa and other states got their independence from Britain. He played football and field hockey for St. Mary's School in Bombay and for the Goan Institute in Dar-es-Salaam. It was destiny that brought us together. It was a difficult time as many government workers were losing jobs to indigenous people. Lama proposed and I accepted, determined that we could begin life together anywhere. He went to Dar-es-Salaam to work in the private sector and after finding an apartment, we set our wedding date and were married in April 1964. By this time, Lama was working for Alitalia Airlines. We made two trips to Rome with our first and then two boys. I worked as a teacher at a model school attached to the Teacher Training Center where I met Helen Alpert. We became good friends until she finished her contract and returned to America.

In 1969, we were allotted green cards to immigrate to America after a 4-year wait. Our trip to France took hours. From Paris to New York 8 hours, where we were snowed in for two days. At the home of Lama's Italian friend based in NY "Mummy, look! It's Christmas!" yelled my oldest, seated at the window. He had seen a Christmas card with a picture of drawn curtains opening to a snowstorm. After two days, the plane took off on the flight to Los Angeles and then to Santa Ana, California. As I stood with my family at the door of the plane, I had an indescribable feeling of peace and freedom, the warm sunbathing us with hope. Our friend, Helen, greeted us with open arms. We had kept in touch and when she heard that we were going to settle in NY, she had written, "That's a concrete jungle! Come to California." She had set up our apartment down to flowers in vases with a group of friends.

Lama got a job with Western Airlines a year later (a 45-miles, one-way commute to LA). I went to college at night, working part-time at schools to pay for it. We made time for tennis and badminton. We have kept up a schedule for workouts at the gym. We talk about the past with nostalgia with many friends that have settled here, not only from Africa, but from Bombay and Goa as well. We meet many in Toronto at reunions of the Goan School. Thanks to social networks, we keep connected. Many have passed away, but the yen to make the connections is alive!

Laura on the winner's podium, one of many!

Maura Lobo

Our journey with Saint (Mother) Teresa

I am humbled and feel truly blessed to have been in the presence of Saint (Mother) Teresa. As I gaze at her little statuette on my desk, I hear her voice saying "my girl (as she affectionately called me) look deeply into my eyes and see God's compassion, feel the warmth radiating from my heart and know God's love, feel the strength in my hands for these hands do God's work".

Our journey with Mother began in the late 1970s when Mother was visiting Kenya. Wilfred Maciel, a family friend, invited Johnny and I to hear Mother speak at the Holy Family Basilica Cathedral in Nairobi. We had six children at the time but decided to take our eldest daughter Mary Ann who was nine years old with us. Our first images of Mother were of a petite dainty nun, cloaked in simplicity. She spoke of her order of the Missionaries of Charity and their work among the poorest of the poor in Calcutta and around the world, poignantly reminding us that we too had to take responsibility for our poor people in Kenya. She said this was the reason she had come to Kenya, to open a home at Huruma. Our little girl Mary Ann was listening very attentively and without me noticing, reached into my purse, pulled out a 100 Kenyan Shilling note, walked over and handed Mother the note, saying, "Mother this is for the poor". Mother reached over to her saying, "God works in mysterious ways, thank you my child" and continued, "if this little child can do so much, how much more can we do together for the poorest of the poor?"

In the 1980s, we began helping the Salesians of Don Bosco. The original small group of priest and brothers led by Fr. Tony D'Souza had left India to start their mission in Kenya at Upper Hill. We adopted most of them into our family, invited them to our home, cooked meals for them at their home. We also helped in dealing with the Government ministries, organised fetes, and fundraising events to build the Shrine. Our three daughters sang in the choir and our three sons organised youth rallies. My mother, Mary Lobo, seemed to be like a mother to all. Jerry, our third son, volunteered to work with the priests and brothers doing various tasks around the church, later driving them to the missions around Kenya, as they were unfamiliar with the terrain in the northern frontier. They affectionately called him "Brother Jerry". A great honour the Salesians bestowed on me was to ask me along with Cardinal Maurice Otunga, to lay a scroll dedicating the Shrine to Mary Help of Christians their patron, in the foundation of the current Shrine in Upper Hill, Nairobi.

In the late 1980s, we met up with Mother again at Huruma. When we arrived at Huruma, we were taken to a small room by the chapel. Mother came in, greeted us and we began with a prayer. In Mother's presence, I always felt a sense of comfort and peacefulness. She spoke about the work they did at the home and how they welcomed volunteers to help in the service of the poor. While Mother spoke, I noticed her keenly looking at both of us. Mother ended with a prayer, wished us well and left the room. While heading to our car, one of the sisters called out to us and asked us to accompany her as Mother wanted to speak to us again. Mother said she recognised our faces as the parents of the little girl at the Basilica. Mother had a fantastic memory.

She asked us about our family. We told her at length. We also told her of our work with the Salesians of Don Bosco. She listened, smiled, and said, "This is divine providence, God has brought you to me." Mother asked us if we would be interested in becoming her first Co-workers in Kenya. We would lead a group of volunteers under this banner. She explained what was involved. We accepted. Mother was delighted at our acceptance and gave us a copy of the mandate of the International Co-Workers of Mother Teresa. She then took us for a brief tour of her home, gave us her blessing and we departed. She mentioned she was leaving for Calcutta the next day and would send us a letter of appointment. It arrived shortly after our visit.

Mother Teresa delighted with donations of baby cots for the children

We set to work calling a few friends to join our family as Co- workers of Mother Teresa. We shared the simple mandate as Mother had shared it with us: visit the home to work as often as we liked; once a month prepare a simple meal of rice, minced beef with green peas, potatoes and carrots (no spices), bread and fruit; while serving meals, hand out plates to each person with dignity; feed those that could not feed themselves, pre and post meals spend time talking and engaging with the older people or playing with the children; and end each visit with a prayer in the chapel. Among the ladies in our group, it was mostly Olga Fernandes and Maria Rebello who cooked the large quantity of rice once a month and I cooked the beef mince at our respective homes. All the families within our group would drive over to spend time with the people, serving and feeding them. The dedication and commitment from our Co-worker group was remarkable.

Our Co-workers ending our time with a prayer led by Maura in the Chapel at Huruma

In 1988, the International Co-workers of Mother Teresa were meeting in Paris for the Fourth Chapter. Having a growing family, I told Mother while I would love to attend, I could not afford it. Knowing what an enriching experience this was to meet others doing similar work. Since I was the only link in East Africa at the time, Mother reached out to Margaret Calles, our connection in South Africa and mentioned my predicament. Margaret had visited Kenya previously to work with us and stayed in our family home, so she knew me well. She operated a travel agency in South Africa and very kindly arranged a ticket for me to fly from Nairobi to London. I felt so fortunate. In London, I was able to briefly meet my three brothers and their families before staying for one night with Ann Blaikie the first layperson to volunteer with Mother in Calcutta and the founder of the Co- workers of Mother Theresa, who lived in Surrey. Early the next morning we departed by ferry to Calais and onwards by coach to Paris. It was a fantastic chapter in Paris where we got to meet global links and learn through talks and videos what work the Co-workers were doing in their respective countries. There were dignitaries, religious and lay guest speakers also invited. On the third day of the conference, two co-workers asked me to join them over lunch for a quick trip to the Basilica of Sainte-Thérèse of Lisieux. The Basilica turned out to be 200 kilometres away and with the horrendous traffic, took 3 hours to reach. The Basilica was inspirational and equally stunning both architecturally and decoratively, but we ended up missing the entire afternoon of the conference. The next day when I saw Mother, I told her I was sorry to have missed the previous afternoon to which she smiled and replied, "My girl, how lucky you were to visit the Basilica, I wish someone could have taken me."

In 1990, Mother was happy with the work we were doing in Kenya and wanted us to share this with her other homes in Africa. She appointed Johnny and I as International Area Links for East and Central Africa.

There was no fundraising allowed in Mother's name or the name of the Missionaries of Charity, as Mother always believed when a need arose, God provided. We established a group of benefactors who generously gave money as well as donations of supplies, medicines, and other necessities for the home. Mother opened two more homes in Kenya; one in Kibera for men and the other in Otiende for children. Huruma became a home only for the elderly. Our co-worker group also grew to 50 in number, and we were able to service each home with our meals once a month. Mother had always told us before you begin your service of the poor, remember to begin with a service in your own home, with your family, then radiate it outwards to the community, especially the less fortunate.

We often exchanged letters with Mother in those pre- internet days. Every time she came to Kenya, we went to the airport to meet her as Johnny had arranged special permission from the Immigration Minister Mr Kwinga to meet Mother at the plane and escort her out of the airport. Through one of our benefactors, we were able to arrange a small plane to fly Mother from Wilson Airport to Suguta (to start her mission) and Johnny accompanied Mother on that trip. She had a warm relationship with my mother, Mary Lobo, and referred to her as "her older sister". She knew each of our six children by name and often asked after them. By then, Jerry our third son, was in the U.K. and John our eldest had emigrated to Canada. Mother was familiar with James our second son who supported us a lot with our work at the homes and our three daughters Mary Ann, Melita and Michelle who were always by our side when we visited and worked at the homes.

In 1993, we emigrated to Canada. While happy to be reuniting with our three children - John, James and Mary Ann who preceded us, it was with heavy hearts that we relinquished our responsibility of leading the co-workers in Kenya. We passed the baton on to our original co-workers and friends to continue the work we began. In 1994, Mother called for a dissolution of the formal international co-worker organisations around the globe fearing they had become too institutionalised and called instead for the volunteers to return to their grassroots origins. Around that time, many of our original group of Co-workers also began leaving Kenya for new lands. We continued to keep in regular touch with Mother. Her last letter to us was in November 1996 and sadly, she died in 1997. Today, Mother is a Saint, and in closing I echo my original sentiment, we are truly blessed to have personally known and worked alongside Saint (Mother) Teresa in service of the poor.

Johnny and Maura Lobo in Canada

Earth Angels

#Wingsoflove

"Mother Teresa's goals were based on a simple commitment of unconditional giving to change the world one person at a time. She inspires the work of the Earth Angels."

The Earth Angels team (Kenya) Paloma Fernandes, Marion D'Souza, Renee Rodrigues, Sharmila Braganza and Kalpu Shah are a group of women based in Nairobi, working to help abandoned, physically and mentally disabled, orphaned and the poorest of poor children, living in orphanages and homes run by non-governmental agencies as well as assisting with educational needs for these children. They are assisted by a team from Canada Fleming Viegas and Elaine Fernandes Vitor.

Their simple beginnings started over a decade ago when they helped to organise a Christmas celebration at the Mother Teresa Home at Otiende, near Nairobi in 2008 which was a refuge for children abandoned due to their physical and mental disabilities. They discovered many other homes and schools that were in dire need of help. The team's reach has grown tremendously and can reach all the Mother Teresa homes in Kenya as well as 15 homes and schools for orphaned, underprivileged, physically and mentally challenged, abandoned, HIV positive and Albinism in Nairobi, Machakos, Athi River, Lukenya, Eldoret, Naro Moru, Samburu and Kisumu and provided them with wheelchairs, mattresses, stationery, clothing, assorted food items, sanitary pads, mosquito nets as well as many other items.

They also run a daily feeding program for St. Stevens School in Githogoro slums, which they built and can provide breakfast and lunch for 200 children. Their monthly feeding program reaches over 12 homes, mostly in Nairobi and Machakos. Their quarterly feeding program includes the Halcha women's group in Samburu and the Namayiana Women's Group in Kajiado. These women run self-help groups and educate and feed about 200-300 children.

In keeping with the theme of putting a smile on the faces of our special children, they have Christmas parties for the children of Mother Teresa Otiende, Mother Teresa Kasarani, Vincentian Prayer house and most recently for almost 600 street children at the Mother Teresa Home in Huruma.

Education is key to commitment as the Earth Angels and they have sponsored the continuing education of nearly almost 20 children. They provide exercise books and stationery to 18 schools across the country annually. During the COVID Pandemic, the Earth Angels were able to reach over 4000 families in Githogoro Slums, Tana River, Hola, Kilifi, Kwale, Nyatike, Ruiru and Baringo amongst others.

In Kilifi and Kwale and Tana River, the Earth angels were able to buy 15,000 kgs of cassava, 2500 coconuts, 3000 mangoes from farmers and distribute to vulnerable families. They also supplement these donations with mosquito nets, blankets, sanitary pads, masks, cooking oil, wheat flour, maize flour, rice, soap and other assorted items reaching over 2500 families.

In Nyatike Migori, the Earth Angels provided 200 vulnerable and older people with food rations including maize flour, wheat flour, porridge flour, sugar, salt, soap, cooking oil, rice, beans, Long- Life milk as well as blankets and mosquito nets. Phase 2 of the project is underway to provide mattresses as well as food rations for another 300 families affected by the COVID pandemic.

In the slums of Githogoro in Nairobi, the Earth Angels team were able to reach 800 families with the emphasis on pregnant, elderly, HIV positive and vulnerable people with food rations for three weeks including maize flour, wheat flour, rice, sugar, cooking oil, bar soap, porridge flour, soya, assorted vegetables as well as masks. They were also able to provide 500 buckets for storage of water during this time. As the numbers of those affected keep increasing, the need for assistance is rising at a tremendous rate. The Earth Angels Team will carry on looking at ways to assist the needy.

PALOMA FERNANDES

Paloma Fernandes has been the CEO of the Cereal Millers Association for the past 13 years. The Cereal Millers association represents the large-scale grain milling industry comprising of varied wheat, maize, and other cereals millers in Kenya with a reach over 35 million consumers in Kenya.

Her primary responsibility is stakeholder engagement with Government bodies and NGOs for issues about food security, food safety, food taxes, tariff barriers within the region. She makes recommendations and offers feedback on Government food- related bills. She regularly meets with relevant Government ministers.

She is primarily involved with aflatoxins, (Genetically Modified) GM food technology and fortification in the food industry. She is committed to providing safe and affordable food to consumers.

Paloma is a former Vice Chairman of the Goan Institute Nairobi where she managed to increase hiring revenues and also bring families back to the club. Paloma has been the lead coordinator of GI's famous talent show dubbed GI Got Talent for the past three years, with more than 100 participants and over 400 guests at the shows. Paloma introduced the Free Seniors Christmas function at the GI as well as the first DIVA night in a bid to encourage families to come back to the club. She was also the coordinator of the Grand Christmas Raffle, raising money for the club's festive activities.

Paloma founded Earth Angels Welfare 15 years ago. She is a qualified Economist, Administrative Manager and Systems Analyst with a BA in Economics. She completed the Corporate Governance Course administered by the Centre for Corporate Governance Kenya attaining 1st position out of 68 fellow directors and CEOs from the region.

The Earth Angels team

The Irish Goan

AM indulging myself just a little and you will forgive me for doing so. I write about my once pukka Irish friend who with his twilight headlights on is more than most of us in the diaspora. They have had an apartment in Bardez, not far from Calangute but nicely hidden from the tourist gaze.

He loves his food hot and swears that any food cooked without those red demons from Goa should be barred for public consumption. There were times when we went out to dinner in Sydney and he would always put a timely two fingers into his top pocket and snick out a packet containing finely chopped red chillies. His number one dish was Goa's natural central heating and tongue warmer, Sorpotel. He has cooked a few times. The first was when he and Harold George D'Souza and a few mates were organising a New Year's Eve Party. Harold and Mal were actually the kitchen hands and not the chefs (they will claim otherwise). I have got it on good authority that the chef was actually Harold's late mother. The girls would not fib, would they. Anyway, the Irish chap has never raised the issue again, so I say let sleeping pigs lie ... somewhere.

It was not so long ago that Rebecca and Tony, Tony and Lucinda, Harold and Hazel, Mal and Margaret and one or two other friends would meet at least one Friday or Saturday each month for dinner. COVID has smashed that up but I also think that age is wearing us down a bit. Driving those few kilometres without a friendly driver is simply not worth it because you cannot drink and drive. The Friday Club which has not met since February or March is another victim of the COVID. One or two or three or even four are recovering from this and that and the rest are twiddling their thumbs and remembering the good old Friday drinks at the Baulkham Hills Bowling Club. Is this the end of the famed Friday Club, I hope not. Certainly, Leslie Scott, Andrew Scott (if he can catch a ride), Loy D'Souza and I would be raring to go. Drake Shikhule, fired by his successes in the medical marijuana business, has been ringing around, urging a meeting of the club. I am confident that once the prison walls come crashing down and we are all freed from the

A young Mal Ferris

COVID prisons, we will have a full quorum.

Back to my Irish friend. The small group of Moira villagers who used to celebrate the village feast with the help of their friends began dwindling after Sheila and George Pereira left this earth.

Sheila was a powerhouse. She was always the belle of the party, the feast or the dance. For the senior citizens, she used to get up on a table and sing and dance her heart out.

Since no one was coming forward, my Irish friend let some rumours fly like the kites, suggesting that he might lead the Moidekars. Goodness gracious me! The spark that lit that storm was nothing like the annual bushfires the eastern part of Australia is victim to each year in Summer. Suddenly people were invoking the saints, others were seeking out Goans who used to deal in matters of disht (evil eye) and this and that. Needless to say, my Irish friend was well and truly hammered. Shame really because he is a very special, hardworking and generous man.

My Irish friend was once Vice President of the Goan Overseas Association of NSW. He was simply brilliant especially since he increased the profit from the sale of alcohol to the point where the association's coffers were bulging with healthy profits. However, on one occasion he did go home with a lot of skin off his back missing and he was suspected of having huge scratch marks running from his shoulder to the buttocks. A relation had taken him to task for overcharging for a glass of lemonade. If I remember correctly, he was charging $1.50 for a glass when the two-litre bottle cost only $2 from Woolies. Big overheads, he was explaining to anyone who would listen. However, jokes aside, he was one of the best workers the association ever had in the days when we could run our bar and most committee members were hands-on as opposed to hands-off and armchair drivers.

In the end, his enthusiasm and collective financial ignorance by some drove him out of the association. The committee of Harold George D'Souza invested the association's funds in stocks and shares. No sooner had this been done, there were raging volcanoes erupting everywhere. The committee was torn to shreds at an extraordinary general meeting and had to undertake the sale of the shares. Today they would have been worth quite a bit, maybe even a million. Not only would they be worth so much but in the intervening years just think how much we would have received in tax paid dividends. The association could have given free functions twice a year along with the children's Xmas party. Never mind, we live and learn.

On the other hand, the naysayers were strong in making the case that investing stocks and shares could bankrupt the association. What was their thinking! Most of the funds were invested in the big banks if they went under, so would the country. Try telling the doomsayers that.

I think I have met M&M in Goa on two or three occasions. If memory serves me right, the last time was in 2009. My sister Flora and her family and I had been to Sri Lanka and had come to Goa for Christmas. We were living in Salcete and M&M were in their Arpora sexy apartment. They paid for an apartment for me and came and picked me up and in no time, I was nestled in a pretty nice place. We did anything and everything but the most essential thing was dinner. We would check out the restaurants and their respective chefs in the morning and try and see if could find a menu to our liking even if the things we were asking for were off-the- menu. Most restaurants obliged because they were familiar with M&M. One of the first things they did was to bring all their grog and shelf at my place. The reason is that, at my place, there was a pretty little swimming pool. No one swam in it, at least I did not see anyone swimming in it. So, after dinner, we would sit by the pool, solve all the world's problems and then before the sun peeped out, we would hit our respective beds. Their nest was just five minutes away.

Oh, by the way, for brunch we to Mal's favourite little café for samosas and other Goan pastries. He just can't get enough of them. Well, neither does anyone else coming from outside of Goa.

It turned out to be a delightful week. The night before they were going to drop me to Salcete, we agreed that alcohol that night would be limited to war-time rations: a couple of sips and that was that. Single Malt, of course. While they were there, I felt a pinch in my left shoulder and put it down to the late shower that I had had that evening and thought nothing of it and went to bed in pretty good spirits. As the night wore, the pain continued and increased until around 5 am, I thought I was in trouble. So, I rang my Irish friend and told him to come quickly and take me to the hospital. Being in no fit state to drive (I don't how he did that, a secret horde of nightcaps?) he suggested that I go and see a mutual friend in my block of units and ask him to ask his doctor to come and see me in this emergency. I did that but his doctor told him that he stopped making house calls a "century ago".

Rang M&M up again and they there in 10 minutes and we headed for a clinic in Baga. They duly processed the ElectroCardioGram and we waited for the result which came about 10 minutes later: "Sorry," said the girl. "Our ECG machine has broken down. Please go to our other clinic in Calangute." We shot off faster than a rocket heading for the moon. We went through the ropes and got the same result: Machine broken down! Was it me, my body breaking these machines, can't be!! This time they told us to rush to their private hospital in Mapusa. When we got there, it was a completely different world.

I had this test and that test, this blood test, this X-Ray, that ultrasound and that other X-Ray. It was all clockwork, no waiting. Minutes later, I was talking to the Cardiologist/Surgeon. He said I had a blockage in one of my major arteries and he needed to put a stent in it. I asked if he could give me some medication that would look after it for the next day or two while I returned to Sydney that day or the next. He said: "You might want to take a chance, I won't." That was that. For some reason, my credit card did not have a PIN but M&M said they would pay for it. I suggested that they go back to my place because there was enough money in a stash there. Anyway, minutes later, I am on my back watching a TV while a cardio team is discussing various aspects of delivering the stent. Several minutes later I am in lalalalalal land.

When I eventually wake up, I am in a state of hell. Hell is not always fire red, it can be pitch black, too. Worse, the thing that worried me most was that I had no idea where I was. Took me a while to figure it out and turn around to discover the gizmo little lights around the bed's headboard. I also finally located the buzzer which as just an inch or two away, and virtually on my body. After I had done the pressing thing, two Goan nurses appeared.

They were speaking in Konkani but I could not hear too well.

One of them said something to me, and I said, "in English please."

"What is the problem? Are you in pain? Do you need anything?"

"I need some light. Where am I? I know I am in a hospital but where in the hospital?

"In the Intensive Care Unit." "Why is it so dark?"

"It is designed to calm our patients who may be recovering from major surgery."

"Can I get some light, any light?"

"A few minutes later, the other nurse returned with a little oil lamp and a candle".

I fell asleep again with the oil fumes assuredly in my nasal passages.

Next morning the boss of bosses, the owner, arrived on his rounds, dressed in his General Manager attire, along with his gold watch. I insisted that they get me out of that black hellhole of Mapusa. Eventually, they got me into a private room. The best thing was that my sister was able to bring me some decent Goan food.

The next morning, I left for Benaulim and later that evening for Sydney via Mumbai. We had to buy new Business Class tickets for my niece and me.

When we got to Sydney, the initial carrier refused to refund the price of the ticket but I headed for mediation at a tribunal in Melbourne. Lasted 10 minutes. I simply made the point that this man sold us the tickets but did not deliver the product. Got our original money back. Meanwhile, the insurance refunded the business class tickets because the cardiologist gave a certificate saying that I was asymptomatic. And the rest is history.

Back to my Irish friend. He used to own two log cabins on a small mountain not too far from Sydney's wine country at Eaglereach. Someone had the bright idea to buy a mountain (well not quite, but big,

1000, acres) and sell plots for the construction of eco-lodges under strict licence. So, we used to go up there regularly. It was the life of the other Reilly. Lots to drink, lots to eat, great walks and plenty to please yourself. The only problem was that when the rest of us were having such a good time, he would be busy doing this, that, or something else. He would stop in time for lunch or dinner. Both events were long because everyone brought one, two, or three dishes and he would barbecue this or that. Breakfast was huge. I have to confess the drink had the better of me on a couple of occasions. And then I never had another drop. My Irish friend married a beautiful Goan girl. He met Margaret at a Catholic Club in London while he was in training with Tesco in 1967. They got married in September 1969. How the hell did an Irish Tesco manager get to marry a Miss World could have been girl? They have three children and five grandchildren. I rang him up the other day and told him I needed to interview him and he told me to "bugger off", with a few smiles and sniggles.

After he quit Tesco, he went out to work for himself, selling bacon, sausages and whatever else he could lay his hands on. It was hard yakka but that was nothing to him. After a year, he bought an old Co-op Building in North Wales. Then started producing his own-branded prepacked food. In the end, he was the boss of a major meat factory, turning over a considerable amount. The family then sold out to migrate to Australia. That was a blessing for us.

An exceptional couple, we are all truly blessed. I could not wish for a better pair of friends. I am blessed, yet again. By the way, he will swear to anyone who cares to listen that he is pure Irish right down to the last drop of Guinness. In a moment of whimsey, he might admit the Goan part of him is mainly curries, pastries and feni.

Mal on top of his world in Sydney with his daughter Leonie, atop of the world famous "coat hanger"...Sydney Harbour Bridge

Ladis da Silva

LADIS DA SILVA (1920-1924) was a gifted artist, began and excelled with oils, watercolours and acrylics. He made a name for himself when he moved to pen washes and renderings which are often mistaken for woodcuts. He is also a well-known and respected writer. He was the founder member of the Zanzibar Arts and Crafts Society. In London, 1941, he founded the Goan Arts Society. He was a member of several notable art societies in the UK. I know of two exhibitions in Kenya: the first at the Catholic Parochial School and the other at the Donovan Maule theatre. He emigrated to Canada in 1968 and specialised in Native Indian and Inuit Art. His published works include Through a Doorway in Zanzibar, The Americanisation of Goans, An Island Kingdom, Legendary Chandor: Seat of the Kadamba Dynasty in Goa.

WAS born in a fairly well-to-do family in Zanzibar in 1920. Zanzibar is an island off the coast of East Africa. Many writers, authors like Sir Richard Burton, Sir John Kirk, W.H. Ingram, Krapf, Speke, Sir Lloyd Mathews, Dr Livingstone, Sir Arthur Hardinge, L.W., Hollingworth, have, in their books and autobiographies, called this island the "Spice Island" or the "Emerald Island" of the Indian Ocean. The island is bordered by golden sands, surrounded by a deep blue Indian Ocean, a few atolls, fringed with the romantic coconut palm trees. I used to paint these scenes in colour from my young age ... and even inspires me now.

Like Darwin's Galapagos, the island is rich with the tropical flora and fauna. History has blazed this into international recognisance from the fifteenth and sixteenth centuries. Navigators like Vasco da Gama, Luis Da Camoes, Affonso de Albuquerque, and several others, as we have already read previously, found their sea route from Europe to the Indies, invariably they all made Zanzibar their calling place for food, fuel, water and repairs. Explorers like Dr Livingstone, Stanley, Speke, Sir Richard Burton, also glamorised this place. Very close to our heart is our patron St Francis Xavier, who landed in Malindi on July 28, 1542, and a detailed account of this was given to me previously. There still exists a chapel in Malindi where he said Mass when the Portuguese fleet was at anchorage there. Quite a number of Goans who went to Mombasa from Zanzibar made it a point to visit Malindi and see the chapel and Vasco da Gama's lighthouse. I have visited the chapel and the nearby graveyard several times.

The famous buccaneer Captain Kidd is said to have sought refuge around Zanzibar, Pemba and the surrounding islands, to hide from the British, who were looking for him. It was also rumoured among the natives that Captain Kidd had buried his loot and treasures on some of these islands around Zanzibar and Pemba. Treasure hunters from various nations are still searching for these lost treasures. Many of these treasure trove hunters claim they had found a map drawn by the buccaneer himself and still continuing their endless search for the treasures. Some have ventured as far as the Seychelles Island.

Zanzibar in those early days was the "nerve" and "earning" centre of East Africa. It eventually became a "spending centre", as it grew more and more prosperous in its trade and commerce. With the British setting up their administration headquarters in conjunction with treaties signed with the Sultan of Zanzibar, they had the privilege from the Sultan to use Bet-el-Ajaib, meaning the "House of Wonders" for this purpose. This magnificent palace on the Zanzibar seafront is a very impressive edifice and was built during the reign of Sultan Said Bargash in the years 1870-1888. Beit-el- Ajaib is a palatial mansion and towers above all the other buildings. It has a clocktower which is used as a look-out tower for incoming and outgoing vessels. From this town, one can see for miles and miles in all directions. The architecture of this palace is unique in that it is in the English style and it is supported by massive pillars and has a few old cannons at the entrance. In addition to this, it has an antiquated elevator.

Whilst on the island during my young days it was rumoured by the natives and the Arabs that the Sultan built two other palaces, which were all connected to Beit-el-Ajaib by secret passages; the palace on the left with a small, enclosed park was used by his harem and later became a school for Arab girls. The main palace of the Sultan was built at the seafront on the extreme left of Beit-el-Ajaib. The natives also said that Sultan Bargash killed all the artisans and skilled workers who built this famous palace as he thought in the whole of East African there was no building to compare it with … and he did not want a substitute to be built. He was proud of his outstanding achievement and wanted everyone to know about it.

The British utilised the Bet-e; -Ajaib for several years until the "revolution" by Africans which overthrew the Arabs.

The British had the offices of the Secretariat and Establishments, the Treasury, the Audit and several other sections of their administration housed in this palace. Renovations were made and telephones installed during my time. I can well imagine what it was like in those early days when the British did not have any such facilities! I also recall how visitors to Zanzibar never left the island until they took a guided tour of the Beit-el-Ajaib. Since the Palace could not house all the administrative offices of the "Customs" and "Wharfage", "Passages", "Shipping" etc were accommodated in other palatial buildings not too far away from the main palace.

All key positions in the British Administration Offices were held by the old English "bards" and "lords" and "barons" and ex- civil servants from the India British Government. These ex-civil servants were transferred from Indian to East Africa, as they had the experience and expertise in running an administration. In Zanzibar, however, they had to reorganise everything from scratch.

Being in Zanzibar, I had the opportunity to learn several languages (oriental and occidental) and, naturally, the African. I learnt Kiswahili, the native language of Zanzibar, since my birth. This proved invaluable to me in other parts of Africa. Thereby I acquired a lot of information about Zanzibar, its history, legends and folklore, East Africa and the coastal kingdoms from natives and Arabs. Kiswahili is claimed to be originally a Bantu language and primarily used as a dialect by the Wahadimus of Zanzibar. As the years passed, with different nations ruling the East coast of Africa, or trading in slaves, spices, ivory etc, it slowly assimilated a rich tinge of the Portuguese, Persian, Arabic, Indian and even the English language. The intermixture brought about a rich, pleasant and very courteous language which reminds us of the French language. Kiswahili to this day is being used through Eastern Africa. I have formed my own opinion about this rich, exotic language … it is full of finesse and courtesy, which was the result of Indian and Arab influence of several years.

Since the Arabs had made East African their permanent home and did not want to return to Oman and Muscat in Arabia, they had no choice but to learn the native language. They came in contact with the natives on their plantations and in trade and commerce, slave trade, and so it was inevitable that happened. Strangely, Arabic which was their mother tongue was seldom spoken, even in their homes, where the women and the slaves spoke only Kiswahili. Arabic was spoken at royal *barazaas* at the Sultan's palace and very few special occasions.

ZANZIBAR GOANS LADIS DA SILVA

From "Zanzibar," by L. Da Silva, 1983, Journal of South Asian Literature, Vol. 18, No. 1 [GOAN LITERATURE: A MODERN READER (Winter, Spring 1983)], pp. 258-265. Copyright 1983 by Asian Studies Centre, Michigan State University. Reprinted with permission.

TRY AS I MIGHT, I found it immensely difficult to trace the arrival of the first Goan in Zanzibar. The best I can recollect is when I was once invited by some sheikhs near Chukwani Palace, close to a Polytechnic School, and shown a grave by the seafront It had an Arab inscription on it and although age-old, it was in fair condition, even though some of the sides had fallen off with the rain and the storms. I was told by them that this belonged to the first Goan who arrived in Zanzibar more than 100 years prior. He had lived there, worked there and died there. Both Arabs and the natives were descendants of people who lived during his time and got the story from generation to generation. I cannot discount this story as I do know that Goans had come from the east coast of Africa long before any white man had done so. Evidence of this is there because of the trade between India and East Africa.

From historical records I have, I am prepared to state that Goans emigrated to East Africa some 125 years ago. Many Goans land in the port of Mombasa in Kenya earlier and were employed as civil servants in Kenya and Uganda. Kenya history tells you that the first district commissioner's Chief Clerk was a Goan. The above facts are partially substantiated in the memories of Sir Arthur Hardinge, the Consul General in Zanzibar, who wrote: "A Goanese clerk was engaged in the Health Office in the year 1894."

At this time, East Africa was under the government of the British Samaraj. This is one reason why Goans were given preferential treatment in the civil service. We are well aware of the fact that when in Bombay, Goa and Greater India, that had studied English and the three Rs, and were therefore well qualified to be civil servants under the British Raj. During this period Indian currency was used in East Africa. I vividly recall that was the currency during my time in the 1930s ... rupees, annas, pice.

The judiciary, too, ran on the British system. They had Indians, Goans, Parsee lawyers, while the magistrates and the justice of the peace in the Appeal Court were all Britons. They had adopted the Indian Acts in their Hansard. The Arabs had their system in addition to this, their customs and traditions were age-old. They had *khadis* (judges) who dealt with minor cases and *mudhirs,* i.e., district commissioners who were appointed in different suburban areas and remote villages to run and settle the local native affairs. I must say those days all respected the law.

Goans had a rudimentary knowledge of accounts, storekeeping, inventory, customs-clearing, shipping and various other jobs. It is recorded that this was the reason why they had no problems in securing posts with the British, throughout their (the British) stay in East Africa.

During German times in Heligoland (then called Tanganyika), they called the Goans "Goanese" who were classified as a separate race in the population census. The Germans in Tanganyika (now Tanzania) considered the Goans very special people, and because of this, they were accorded preferential treatment. Goans were popular in sports, they were good musicians, honest and industrious.

These are the traits the Germans like in anyone. The European General Hospital in Dar-es-Salaam, the main port of Tanzania, had a special wing for the Goan community. Other ethnic groups were allotted a portion of the Nation Hospital.

Most of the early Goans who travelled abroad arrived without their families as they were single. They felt that they should travel first to a foreign land, tap the sources, see what it was like, secure a job position, earn some money, and if everything was well and favourable they would bring their wives or their families (or return to Goa and find a suitable bride). In those early pioneering days, there were rumours in India and Goa, that "Africa was a White Man's Grave" like West Africa … that there were cannibals, malaria, tropical diseases, wild animals, and an environment that was full of difficulties. There were further told that all these took a heavy toll of foreigners. Therefore, it needed some pluck for the few who ventured out as adventurers. These would, of course, include our dear parents who had the grit to do what they did. (Generations will always remain grateful for that and more)

In those days travelling abroad was done by steamship or by dhow. The BIA (British India) ploughed through the Indian Ocean regularly once a month, except for the monsoon season, when the ocean was treacherous with storms and tempests.

Passaged cost a fortune. Because of this, it was not common for some Goans to travel to East Africa by the big Cutch Dhows, for which they paid a negligible amount of money. I recall the experiences of some of our Goans had travelled by dhow during my young days.

I understood from them it was no fun travelling by dhow in the high seas for a couple of months … in sheer discomfort, unsanitary conditions, and eating lousy Indian spice food that was half-cooked. There were no vegetables, no fruit or other amenities of life one could expect. With the storms, the heavy swells of the ocean brought about seasickness ... it was something unbelievable

...a terrible experience overall. Goans, generally speaking, who are used to a life of comfort and ease, would find this a nightmare. I have travelled with the British India ships through the Mozambique channel during monsoons and know that even this bad enough for a heavy tonnage steamer. One ship, Clip Fountain, that sailed before us, sank in the storm.

When shipping was scarce, Goans and Indians would travel from Zanzibar to the mainland to Dar es Salaam or Mombasa by dhow. They also travelled by dhows to the sister island of Pemba.

When the Goans landed in Zanzibar there were few people of their ethnic group around. These had come earlier. Because of this, they would voluntarily come forward to help any new arrivals. Since of most of these were single men, and Arab mansions were huge, these bachelors preferred to live together in a "mess" (expressed in North America as "rooming" or "sharing an apartment"). The new migrants were then assisted in procuring suitable jobs, and this was done through their compatriots who were in good graces with the British Officials. I was given to understand that they had no difficulties in doing so as the Briton like the Goans.

Living together, learning from each other, cooking, washing, playing cards (flush or poker) was fun in those early days. More than anything, speaking Konkani, their mother tongue among themselves was not unusual. The most amusing event was when they got together on a special festive occasion and had a few drinks. Eating their Goan delicacies, which each tried to cook in their way, interspersed with the Goan music of *mandos* and *fados,* they cracked jokes in Konkani, English and Portuguese simultaneously. At this time, they had managed to obtain the services of a native servant whom they taught to cook and do some of the household chores. Labour was cheap then. Even when the servant stole food and drinks every day, the bachelor took this with a pinch of salt ... life was fun ... it was no point griping. When the Goans got into their revelries, eating and drinking and talking gibberish, the natives often wondered whether they were in their right minds or scatter-brained. However, the servants got used to this routine life. Even the English had this hotch-potch at their parties.

Beyond this, the Goans did not go overboard, although it was known that a few had Arab and native mistresses ... but these stray cases.

Several Goans had learnt to speak Hindi when back home and this knowledge was put some good use in East Africa with the local Indian traders. I guess this was one reason my brother and I went to an Indian school to learn Gujarati, a little Marathi and Sanskrit, before joining the Mission high school.

In a small Goan community such as this, other than their parties they had practically no other social life at all. So, they resorted to playing cards or organising bachelor parties to have good fun. At these parties, they sang their folks songs and played the violin, a favourite instrument of the Goans. A Goan plays musical instruments by notes and not by ear. This was achieved through private tuitions and schools, learning the Konkani "Masters". At all their parties they never missed drinks. This was must and to a large extent, it still is. I guess we got this trait from the Portuguese. It was not an unusual sight to see bottles of Johnnie Walker which, in those days, cost Rs. 1.50. They had lots of Portuguese wines, *mandel, cajel, urrakk, granjeau* from Goa. Goa sausages arrived by ship that touched ports every month. Let it be remembered that in those days the island of Zanzibar was a free port and good were allowed to come duty free.

Despite all these expenditures, I know that there were well able to save some money to send home. This is how they managed to bring their wives and their families to East Africa eventually.

Occasionally the British officials invited them to the English club after a friendly, hockey, cricket or soccer game to have drinks and meals (maybe). This strengthened their relationships in the office. Many a Goan was promoted because his boss knew him better after meeting him at sports or at socials.

The Arabs and Swahilis and other ethnic races that lived there were friendly. In fact, Zanzibar was known to be the friendliest place in the whole of East Africa. Slowly Arabs and the natives started inviting them to their parties at home, where they would partake of their rich, spicy sumptuous and scrumptious meals. Of course, the absence of their women at these parties was conspicuous, and no alcoholic drinks were served in their homes. This had a religious significance for them.

Goans who were early pioneers in East Africa had good knowledge of English and Portuguese languages, plus a few other languages they had picked up here and there while doing several jobs abroad. Portuguese was spoken only within their circles and was of no use in official circles or business. I can safely adduce that the Portuguese language did help them immensely with the vocabulary in English, as has been in my case.

Goans likewise adhered to the age-old Hindu man-made caste system wherever they went. But as time passed, with so many problems, in various countries, this system was ironed out. The elimination of this scourge is a boon, as we are all human.

Some of the Goan clergy and Catholic Church in Goa then made no effort to eradicate this cancerous, pernicious system. To the contrary, some walled-in it and promoted it. However, in alien countries they have emigrated to, they cannot afford this anomaly. I have been told by people wherever I went on my travels that, as Catholics, Goans should be ashamed to even mention the caste system.

We heard the good side of the story of Goans in Zanzibar, and now we have to turn to a chapter on how they survived going through initial stages as new immigrants. The tropical heatwave, cholera, dysentery, yellow fever, malaria, smallpox, blackwater fever, bronchitis, pneumonia, and several other tropical diseases took their toll. I know of a few that paid the prices and whose graves are in Zanzibar and Pemba. Civil Servants were at timed compelled to be transferred to the island of Pemba, which was noted for malaria and blackwater fever. I have travelled there several times by the local Arab ferry steamers *Al Said* and *Al Hathera* and have witnessed the conditions there. I have made it a point to also visit the graves of friends who succumbed to blackwater fever and were buried there.

Malaria was very common in Zanzibar and no one slept on any of these islands without a mosquito net at night. Zanzibar and Pemba, as you will note, are malarious because of the mangrove swamps, thick jungles, clove and coconut palms. During the monsoons, it rains incessantly and these heavy rains form puddles and pools, where mosquitoes breed. The government took every possible measure to either control it or eliminate it in those days. I know this for sure because of several friends I had in the Health Office on both islands. There was a belief that neglected malaria brought about blackwater fever, which caused high temperature and the passing of blood urine. Hospitals, dispensaries and various medical facilities in those days were limited. And dispensaries and various medical facilities in those days were limited. And the few that existed were crowded every day. It was a ritual for everyone who lived on both islands in those days to dose him with quinine daily.

Few Goans ever wanted to go to Pemba, but gradually several Indians, Arabs, and European civil servants and hospital personnel commenced going there and eventually settling down, including my uncle Martin D'Silva who worked in the hospital, retired, went to Goa and died there. Goans who went to Pemba worked in hospitals, as lawyers, court clerks, businessmen, bakers, tailoring concerns, grocery shops, etc. Pioneers such as these paved the way for many others who followed suit, undaunted despite several difficulties and obstacles they had to encounter.

Geography plays a paramount role in emigration. Only those living close to convenient ports in India, like Karachi, Bombay, Goa, were likely to make the long and arduous trip by sea. Consequently, as described before, these were not unskilled labourers as were the coolies and manual labourers who built the East African Railways (Kenya-Uganda to start with) or, for that matter like the settlers in South Africa, Mauritius, Madagascar, Fiji, and the West Indies. We should not forget that these coolies were recruited by indenture for work on sugar cane, banana, clove, tea and coffee plantations. Those that were brought even for this purpose made their respective countries rich with their sweat and toil, to collect the harvest for sale to the rest of the world. We cannot deny even those groups of coolies who stayed and settled earned their money honestly. Their children were well-educated and enhanced the whole structure of the countries they lived in. Most of the indentured coolies were sent back to their homelands after their contracts expired.

We will come back to the subject of the missionaries, as they played a very important part in our Goan lives when they encouraged our children to go to their missions, schools and convents. Missionaries those days identified each and every member of the congregation by name and made it a point to visit each and every parishioner at least once a year to bless their homes. This was an old Goan custom and perhaps a custom and tradition in Christendom. They would try and get better acquainted with the family, inquire about the children, their education, personal welfare, and take more interest in everything that has happened in the community. This was not resented by the Goans; as a matter of fact, it was welcomed, since the missionaries learnt our ways, customs and characteristics. All in all, we could say that in those days we had meaningful relationships between the Church and individual Catholic families. We must admit that a priest or the clergy was practically a member of the family in those days.

The missionaries knew that the ancestors of the Goans were converted by St Thomas and St Francis Xavier, and because of this, they respected the Goans.

Turning to Goans in Zanzibar and East Africa it is recorded that they eventually brought their families to live with them. Those who were single went back on overseas leave (which was granted under the British) and brought back their brides. All this happened after they had worked for some time, saved some leave, and were in a position to rent a place and live independently. I can envisage that this was no easy task for those early settlers. It should not be overlooked that before they brought their families, they initiated them as to what to expect and what not to expect in East Africa. We should find some consolation that our ancestors and parents did agree, after listening to the tales of their husbands, to take their chances in a new country.

The arrival of the families meant that the number of the community had increased considerably. Our Goans are noted to be good organisers, and as there appeared to be a requisite need to find a meeting place for the families to gossip and share their ideas, their joys and sorrows, they formed small clubs and institutes. In Zanzibar, we had the Goan Institute, and on special occasions and feast days, the Goans gathered at a rented place to dance, eat and drink to the melodies of the Goan band. As time went on, they collected sufficient funds to buy a suitable building which would be permanently theirs. Here they had a library, arranged indoor games, concerts, socials, literary societies and sports. This was the first Goan Institute. Goan Institutes were set up in all the main cities and townships of East Africa.

All this was a novelty to the other ethnic groups and is small wonder that they too slowly organised their clubs.

Without warning came the Revolution in Zanzibar on January 12, 1964, thus bringing to an end a long reign by the Omani Arab Sultanate. The revolution was so swift and quick that there was no time for reprisal.

And so, the Asians and with them, the Goans migrated to the mainland. Most of them migrated to Mombasa and Nairobi. Others went back to their homeland in Goa.

The wheel of Destiny slowly turned and with it came changes all over East Africa. These were sparked by revolutions, rebellions from the armies and the people. They wanted their countries for themselves ... Africa for Africans ... they wanted all the amenities that other ethnic groups had such as homes, cars, good food, clothes, farms, land, and above all jobs that the foreigners had supposedly taken from them. It was the birth of Nationalism, Africanisation and self-determination for the natives of Africa.

Dr Fitz de Souza

Death of a Kenyan freedom fighter

THE former Deputy Speaker of Parliament, MP for Parklands, solicitor and a fighter for Kenya's freedom died in London on March 23, 2020. He was 90. He is survived by his wife Romola, and children, Veena (Justin), Maya (Prashant), Roy (Aisha), Mark (Antke) and his many grandchildren.

Dr de Souza was a lawyer and a politician by design. In 1943, after finishing his secondary school education in Zanzibar, he headed for

Magadi in Kenya where his parents worked. He was inspired by Mahatma Gandhi to become a lawyer and "carried within me a burning sense of justice on behalf all those to whom it was denied." He would graduate as a barrister from Lincoln's Inn and do his PhD at the London School of Economics. London at the time was spawning young fighters for freedom from many parts of the British Empire/Commonwealth.

In Spring 1952, Fitz returned to Kenya "an idealist, determined to fight for equality for all Kenyans, for the rights of the underdog and the underprivileged, to oppose colonialism and to bring about socialism, fairness, and independence for the country". He never faltered. The Fitz I knew was not an extrovert (although Fitz was never short of a word or two) but never slow coming forward or making a stand on a particular belief when the occasion demanded it. Unlike a man he greatly admired, the softly spoken but sometimes flamboyant Pinto, Fitz, as his legal training had ingrained in him, considered all the risks and put his case firmly and without emotion. A politician but he was born a lawyer.

At the height of the Mau emergency Jomo Kenyatta, Bildad Kaggia, K'ungu Karumba, Fred Kubai, Paul Ngei and Achieng Oneko were charged with membership and management of the Mau Mau. The six men came to be known as the Kapenguria Six as the trial took place in Kapenguria.

Fitz de Souza was the right man in the right place. He brought the defence team together and it was led by Denis Pritt included H.O. Davis (Nigerian), Chaman Lal, Achroo Kapila, Jaswant Singh and Fitz de Souza. The trial is remembered for all the wrong reasons: The judge was allegedly paid off, as were the many witnesses and chief manipulator was the then Governor of Kenya, Sir Evelyn Baring. However, it was during this period that Fitz impressed Jomo Kenyatta and their friendship remained forever.

It was during the trial that Kenyatta told Fitz: "I am not the leader of the Mau Mau; I do not believe in violence. I believe you can achieve your goals without violence. But in any political party there are always some who believe you have to go further, you have to fight, and I know who they are – they are my friends, they are in this party (Kenya African Union), they are with us all the time. But I am not going to do the job for the British Government and expose them and fight against them."

"The British would like (Africans) to fight with each other and make this into a semi-civil war; they are killing our supporters and we were killing their supporters, and I am not going to allow that at all. I know what I want, and they know what they want, our objectives are the same…."

Kenyatta's regard for Fitz was so high that he asked Fitz to take his place at the second Lancaster House Conference on Kenya's independence. Kenyatta sat behind him. No one complained. Kenyatta trusted him implicitly.

Fitz told me often how Kenyatta pressed him to buy choice farms from the exiting colonials. In fact, President Kenyatta wanted to "give" him four or five farms. Fitz explained that he could not accept the generous gift because he was not a farmer and that the land should be given to people who deserved. Then Fitz was offered the position of Attorney-General, a Cabinet position but Fitz was quite happy in his role as Deputy Speaker of the parliament.

His book *Forward to Independence, My Memoir*. The *Nation* newspaper in Nairobi serialised large chunks of it. It is a historical document if only because it provides an honest eyewitness account of the politics, politicians and the truth behind was once only conjecture. I have always had this nagging feeling that there was much more that he could have revealed but being the lawyer that he was he chose not to. Similarly, Mahatma Gandhi converted him into socialism which he tried to practice as best he could but like so many others in the Kenyan tapestry were swept up by capitalism, honest capitalism which is considerate of others. Among other things of note the book outed:

The former South African-born Bruce Mackenzie (Minister for Agriculture) as an Israeli and British spy who was always short of money and was allegedly assassinated by Uganda Idi Amin via bomb disguised as a gift which blew up the plane aboard which Mackenzie was returning to Kenya.

Charles Njonjo introduced Tom Mboya to Fitz (they had known each other for many years) as the man most likely to succeed. Charles Njonjo was not interested in the defence of the Kapenguria Six.

He provided an eyewitness account of the shouting match between Pinto and Kenyatta in the grounds of Parliament House. He advised his friend to tone things down, even suggesting that Pinto did not have the support to take on President Kenyatta.

Fitz de Souza was also an astute businessman.

I must confess my slight bias in that I have always regarded him the greatest Kenyan Goan I have been privileged to have known. While he was with us, he enriched our lives even though we may not have been aware of it. In his death we are diminished, some more than others.

Hilary Ng'weno (one of the fathers of modern Kenyan journalism) on Fitz de Souza's fantastic memory: "*I had never met an elderly person who could remember so many details of his past. I would ask the same question after a few weeks and he would reply almost in the same words and phrases he had used before. He was remembering personalities and events of the years before and soon after Kenya's independence in 1963 and Fitz was not just remembering events touching on his life. He was remembering Kenya's history of which he was one of the great makers. The story you read in this book (Forward to Independence) is not a story just about Fitz. It is a story about the foundations of the Kenya nation. And it is for that reason that I feel strongly that Fitz Remedios Santa de Souza will forever remain a legend for many Kenyans.*"

Rest in Peace, my friend.

He became a lawyer and a politician by intent. He explains in his book Forward to Independence "As I set sail for Zanzibar the war in Europe was coming to an end, yet India's future lay still unresolved. By now a keen and devoted disciple of Mahatma Gandhi, I had decided to spend my life fighting not only for the freedom of India, but Goa too, and carried within me a burning sense of justice on behalf of all those to whom it was denied." He met and was greatly influenced by Pio Gama Pinto, who was destined to become the first politician to be assassinated in an independent Kenya. While de Souza admired Pinto's brilliance in political strategy and planning, in the future, it would be the student advising the teacher, especially in the day's before Pinto's excesses in challenging Kenya's first President, Jomo Kenyatta.

Above everything else, Dr de Souza had the integrity and astuteness reserved for the best legal minds. I watched him in his role of Deputy Speaker of the House every day for many years Kenyan Parliament Press Gallery. Both he and the Speaker of the House, Sir Humphrey Slade, were always respected even by a sometimes boisterous if not unruly Parliament. The call to "order, order" was heeded with good grace.

He was also an astute businessman with a gift or quickly assessing an opportunity and grasping the moment. Another blessing was his brilliant memory even in his later years, and his memoir *Forward to Independence* is testament to this. It is also the single most eyewitness expose of everything, everyone and every event Dr de Souza witnessed from the earliest days of Kenya's struggle for independence, early independence and post- independence about the achievements, the sins and the crimes. *Forward to Independence* is a gift of truth to the people of Kenya who longed for just such an explanation of some of the things that were done in the corridors of power or political conspiracy. Dr de Souza was a fly on many such walls.

The expose is brilliant, history has laid bare and for want of repeating myself, allow me to turn your attention to Fitz de Souza's earliest recollections of Pio Gama Pinto.

Pio and Me

By Dr F. R. S. De Souza

MY train arrived at Nairobi Railway Station at 8 a.m. one morning in February 1952, after five years as a student in the United Kingdom. There was no one to receive me. Indeed, I was not expecting anybody. My parents lived at Magadi and I was hoping to give them a surprise. I left my suitcase at a shop in Government Road and walked to the office of the Kenya Indian Congress, I had never met Pio. However, he had once written to me in London asking for information about some books he wanted to buy.

His welcome was very warm. I felt I had somehow known him for years. We immediately began discussing the problem of East Africa, and how we could help in the struggle for independence. We had much in common. To begin with, we were both almost penniless and terribly dressed. We were at ease with one another and our ideas of independence and socialism were similar. We must have talked for three or four hours. It was lunchtime and he invited me to lunch with him, at a place which was then the most expensive and luxurious that non-Europeans could go to. Our meal cost us about Shs. 3/- each.

We returned to his office and continued our discussions. I read the speeches of past Presidents of the Indian Congress, of the President of the Kenya African Union, Mr Jomo Kenyatta (as he then was) now our President, I was very impressed, and from then on we worked closely together. At about 6.30 p.m. he asked me what I was doing about accommodation. He invited me to stay with him and I readily accepted.

He shared a small room with three others in Pangani in a house run as a "mess" by a large number of his friends. He insisted on giving me his bed and slept on the floor for the next few days until I went to see my parents in Magadi.

His work in Kenya politics is discussed by other friends, but I know, and history will record that Pio had a hand in the preparation of most of the memoranda and statements issued by

K.A.U. in those days. He often used to sit up to 5 a.m. in the Congress Office drafting political papers in the nationalist cause.

For all this he never expected payment. His reward was in the contribution he made to the struggle. He never looked for personal credit. A couple of years later when he was the Editor of the "*Daily Chronicle*", the Royal Commission on Land asked for evidence and there was no one to put forward the African case for all the leaders were in detention. Pio resigned his job, and for three months read the voluminous Carter Commission Report and other documents on the land issue and took statements from Kikuyu Elders and others. He then wrote out, and personally typed and cyclostyled, always working into the early hours of the morning, the 200-page Kikuyu Tribe's Memorandum as well as Memoranda for other individual Mbaris in the Central Province. Pio never told anybody about his work. I sent a copy of this Memorandum to Mzee Kenyatta at Lodwar. He was so impressed that he suggested we publish the Memorandum but for lack of funds, the work was never done.

One day during our discussions Pio suggested that we should do something in East Africa to assist in the Liberation of Goa. I was a little surprised and told him that while I was very sympathetic to the liberation of Goa, and indeed of the rest of the world, I thought that as we were East Africans we should confine our activities to East Africa. We might dissipate our slender resources and there was also the risk of being misunderstood, even by our friends. He explained that as a student and young man in India he had taken an active part in the struggle for the liberation of Goa. He had actively assisted in the formation of the Goa National Congress and had escaped from Goa only when police were searching for him with a warrant to arrest and deport him to an island off West Africa. It was our duty, he suggested as socialists to assist all liberation fronts. Even if we did not now consider ourselves Goans we had names such as De Souza, Pinto, etc. which could be used with some effect. Portuguese colonialism was as bad as any other.

This Goan organisation in East Africa was being used by the Portuguese whose constant propaganda was that Goans overseas - even the educated ones supported the regime and were happy with the Portuguese. Pio had already started a Goan vernacular paper in Nairobi *"The Uzwod"* to arouse feeling against Portugal. Pio was, unfortunately, arrested before we formed the East African Goan National Association in 1954. Mr J. M. Nazareth, Q.C. was elected President, and I was one of the Vice-Presidents. The association did good work, but the Portuguese colonialists soon got to work with their fellow colonialists in Kenya and banned the organisation. The work of the organisation, however, continued. We were pleasantly surprised to see the great amount of support we had throughout East Africa, particularly from educated Goans. It was impossible for us to stop functioning, even if we wanted to. Contacts made with organisations and individuals in Bombay and Goa flourished. Of necessity, work had to be secret as the Portuguese Consulate and its stooges constantly sent dossiers on all of us to the Special Branch. As usual, they labelled the lot of us "Communists" as that seemed the easiest way to get us suppressed.

A few years later, in 1960, only a few months after he was released, Pio formed the East Africa Goa League. This time the Portuguese Government did not succeed in persuading the Kenya Government to ban it. Nationalists were already much stronger in Kenya. He led a delegation to see Mzee Kenyatta at Maralal. The government had persistently refused him permission to see Mzee Kenyatta but allowed an

East African Goan League delegation to visit him without asking for the names of the members of the delegation and was quite shocked when Pio arrived at Maralal as the leader!

In May 1961, a delegation from the Goa led by Prof. Lucio Rodrigues and Dr Laura D'Souza arrived in Kenya. Largely under the pretext of singing Goan songs and reciting Goan literature, they instilled some form of self-respect and dignity into East African Goans, many of whom had hitherto been loyal and servile servants of the British Crown. They were amazingly successful.

Hon. Tom Mboya, General Secretary of KANU and Hon. Muinga Chokwe, Coast Chairman, accepted an invitation to attend a Conference on Goa in Delhi. Tom Mbova was, I was later told by Goa Nationalists, extremely eloquent at the Conference. His forthright speech telling India and its Government that it hardly had a right to attempt to liberate Africa when it was afraid to liquidate Portuguese Colonies within its own country made a deep impression on Pandit Nehru and influenced his decision to liberate Goa.

Pandit Nehru then organised an International Seminar on Portuguese Colonies. Perhaps his mind was already made up to liberate Goa - he was testing reaction among friends. Among those who attended were Mr Kaunda from Zambia, Mr Nsilo Swai and Pio Pinto. All the delegates urged military intervention to liberate Goa. Pio was particularly active and passionate in canvassing support for the liberation of Goa as a start to crack the bastion of Portuguese imperialism everywhere. He had told me he thought a few violent and passionate speeches would convince Pandit Nehru to risk the criticism this action would arouse in the West.

A few months later, Mrs Lakshmi Menon arrived in Kenya, and it was obvious that the liberation of Goa was very much in the offing. Pio and Mr Chokwe even offered to organise an international volunteer brigade to assist, but this was not necessary. Goa was liberated by the

Indian army. The cowardly Portuguese just fled. Hardly a shot was fired. The only Indian casualties were two officers who went to accept the surrender of Aguada Fort after the Portuguese had raised a white flag and were killed at almost point-blank range

Pio, his brother Rosario, Peter Carvalho and I were invited to take part in the victory celebrations. Pio met many old veterans of the campaign - whom he had not seen since he left India in 1947. Most of them begged him to return to India. They wanted him to be their leader and it was obvious that he had many friends and a good deal of support wherever he went. But he declined. He said he was born in Kenya, and Kenya was his home. While he still had a soft spot for Goa and India, Kenya would be the home where he would work and die

Pio then went to New Delhi and discussed Goa with Pandit Nehru and officials of the Indian Government. He took advantage of the opportunity to ask Pandit Nehru for assistance to start a nationalist paper in Kenya. Panditji gave him funds with which Pio began the PAN AFRICAN PRESS LTD. which publishes "Sauti ya Mwafrika" (Voice of Africa), "Pan Africa" and the "Nyanza Times". Most people in Kenya believe that the funds for the press came from China. In fact, the original funds came from India. Naturally, India had to keep quiet about it then. Now that we are a free country, we can tell the truth to the world.

Back in Kenya, he worked on the launching of movements for the liberation of Angola and Mozambique. With Chokwe, he formed the Mozambique African National Union in Mombasa in 1962. Many of the delegates to the inaugural meeting had travelled hundreds of miles to be present. But the British Government banned the organisation and it faded away, but Pio had formed valuable contacts with Mozambique nationalists

Later Pio worked very closely with F.R.E.L.I.M.0. and the Committee of Nine of the O.A.U. and often visited Dar es Salaam to assist them. A few weeks before he was assassinated, he told me that his ambition was to resign his seat in Parliament and retire to Lindi or Mtwara on the Mozambique border to assist the freedom fighters actively. His friends would not let him go - they argued that he was needed here. He never lived to help the struggle in Mozambique. But he died with his boots on.

Maureen D'Souza

The safaris of my life and family

HECTOR D'MELLO was born in Mombasa, Kenya on October 20, 1920. His father was Pedro Caetano D'Mello, of Saligao, Goa, and his mother, Hortencia Crasto D'Mello, of Ucassaim, Goa.

My grandfather was already in Kenya in his late teens or early twenties. He was a founder member of the RGI (Railway Goan Institute), in 1906 (?). He worked for the East African Railways and

Harbours headquarters in Nairobi. Many Indians were employed in the administrative offices of the Railways. Many others worked in the colonial civil service. Goans were readily hired because they were Christian, because of their ability to speak English, their honesty and their hard work. Thousands of Indians also had come to Kenya to help build the railway from Mombasa to Nairobi, then on to Kisumu, and finally, to Kampala. During the construction to Nairobi, hundreds lost their lives from mosquito- borne diseases and other such illnesses, and unfortunately a few fell prey to the man-eating lions of Tsavo.

Grandpa must have gone back to Goa to get married in around 1915, and then the couple made their way to Nairobi. Their two older sons, Joe and Hector, were born in Nairobi, and the youngest, Edwin, was born in Goa, a few years later.

Dad went to the Catholic Parochial School in Nairobi. He liked school, but a short time later, having spent around ten years in Kenya, my grandmother and the two children returned to Goa. Granny had a house built in a pretty spot near the hills in Saligao, a place that had a spring flowing from rocks, where people went to bathe in the hot, dry summer months.

I know that my dad went to the Escola Primaria Official de Saligao, a building which stands today, in the centre of Saligao. He then went to St. Joseph's High School in Arpora, a school with a very good name in those times. It must have been tough for dad and others who had to walk miles across fields and paths to get to and from school each day. But that was normal.

Dad went to Bombay once he finished school, to study Accountancy, and shorthand and typing skills, required in the offices in Kenya. Once he had completed his course, he returned to Kenya.

Dad joined what was later to become the East African Railways and Harbours on December 3, 1941, (St. Francis Xavier's Feast Day, he always reminded us). During the 31 years that he worked for the Railways and Harbours, dad had many perks and incentives. He, and eventually the rest of the family, got housing wherever he went, free train rides between Kampala and Nairobi or Mombasa, trips around Lake Victoria on a ship. He also received six months home leave or long leave every four years, with a voyage paid for each of the family members, to India and back and 18 days of holiday each year.

When he started, being young and a bachelor, dad worked in some of the comparatively remote areas for short periods of time.

Kikuyu, Limuru and Changamwe were some of them. Later, he worked only in the larger towns and cities.

As far as I can remember, I think Dad returned to Goa to see his mum around 1945, and then again in 1949. It was during this holiday that he met and married my mum.

OLIVE D'MELLO was born in 1930, in Kabale, Uganda. Her father's name was Luciano Sabastiano Paolo des Dores e Sousa, and her mother was Arminda Amelia Maria Regina Francisco D'Sousa.

Her parents had come to Africa around 1924, and mum and four female siblings were born there. Mum was the middle sister. Their brother Oscar was born in Goa, some years later.

After a few years in Kabale, mum's two older sisters Linda and Beliza were left behind with their maternal grandma when the family went to Goa on holiday, and mum and the younger sisters went back to Africa, to Soroti, Uganda this time. Mum does not remember this period well. She says she kept an eye on the younger siblings while their mother did the cooking.

However, not too long after, my grandma and the three girls moved back to Goa, where her last child, a son was born in 1938. My grandfather continued living and working in Uganda, until one year, while returning to India by ship, he had a stroke and was paralysed on his right side. He lived on with the family for many years with this disability.

My grandma was a very hard working and enterprising lady, and upon hearing how good life was in Belgaum, India, she decided to make a journey there and check out the place herself. She found that the climate was excellent, the schools were very good and there were many Goans living there. She rented a large flat and returned to Goa.

Granny made the journey to Belgaum by bus, a whole day's journey at the time, with her husband, the children and all their possessions, including an African Grey Parrot. She lived there for the rest of her life.

To earn some money, granny kept boarders (older students who required accommodation). She was an excellent cook and pickle maker and kept everyone well fed and happy. All her daughters acquired her cooking skills.

Mum did her schooling in Belgaum, at St. Joseph's, which still exists today. She and her siblings had to walk several miles each way to and from school. If it rained heavily, they were given bus fares. When the girls were older, they had bicycles. Wartime was problematic, food items were rationed and mum says that instead of rice they sometimes ate ground corn and jaggery instead of sugar.

When Mum was 18, the family went to Goa to attend the wedding of her eldest sister Linda in February 1949. At the reception, mum was spotted by a matchmaker who subsequently went to my dad's parents with a proposal. Mum says she was not told anything before but was taken along (like a goat she says) to my paternal grandparents' house. After some small talk, the two sets of parents moved to another room, and mum was left, embarrassed no doubt, twisting the corners of her handkerchief! I guess dad was in the room too. Soon the deal was done by the parents. A date for the engagement was fixed for a few days later and the wedding would happen seven weeks later.

People nowadays, particularly the young are shocked about arranged marriages, but at that time, that is how things were done, and in most cases they worked. Mum and Dad were married for 33 years.

Dad and Mum were married on April 26, 1949, and soon after, they sailed for Mombasa. On arrival in Mombasa, they stayed in a hotel for a few days. Later they moved to railway accommodation. From then on, they changed homes and locations each time dad got a promotion or transfer. It was something they eventually learned to take into their stride and that would add to the excitement of living in Africa and allow us to make more friends in clubs, schools and workplaces. Friends or their offspring who we still keep in touch with all over the world. In all, we must have moved houses 15 times in 23 years. I went to seven different schools.

It must have been difficult for mum living in Makupa, Mombasa. She was a young lady, who did not know the language (Swahili) and had no friends. But she soon made friends and amongst these remembers a Mr and Mrs Pinto. Mrs Pinto was very good at smocking and mum learned to smock. She already knew a little bit of sewing, knitting and embroidery from the nuns at her school in Belgaum. Dad bought her a sewing machine, and that together with cooking and housework kept her busy all day. Later, until at least the age of ten, I always had beautifully smocked dresses made by mum, and so did my sister, and my cousins.

They had barely lived in Makupa for one year when Dad was posted to Athi River, an hour from Nairobi. Life was even more difficult in this place, with no friends at all, no Asians or Europeans to speak English to and only the indigenous people whose language mum did not know. It was at Athi River that mum conceived her first child. They had no form of transport and when mum went into labour, they had to hitch a lift in the meat van, belonging to the local butcher. My brother Deryck was born at the Alice Beaton Maternity Home in Nairobi. Life was lonely, but mum and dad often had company on Sundays when the Braganza family, Marcus, Nora, Alice and Theo, Daisy and whoever could fit into the car would bring some cooked food and come to see them and spend the day with them. Thankfully, they were there for under a year.

Dad's next transfer was to Nairobi. They lived in Railway quarters, not too far from where the Nairobi Goan Institute (GI) was later built, and they had many neighbours. I was born there, in a maternity home run by a very motherly lady called Mrs Badier. These were dangerous times in Kenya. The Mau were fighting for the return of their ancestral lands in the Central Province. The land in question was taken from them by the colonial government. There were attacks and trouble everywhere, and dad, while returning from work on his bicycle one day, had the bike snatched from him by a group of men who threatened him and told him to run away before they attacked him!

Our social life centred around the RGI, and As Social Secretary or Sports secretary, Dad accompanied a group to visit the Mombasa Goan Institute, in August 1952. It was now time for dad's six months' home leave, or "long service leave" as it was called. We headed for Mombasa by train, by ship to India, including a stop at the Seychelles islands.

Our time in India was spent partly with my grandparents in Saligao, my grandparents in Belgaum and one month in a rented house at the beach in Calangute, Goa. Usually, other families who travelled on the ship with us planned which month they would do this and so during that month at the beach, the adults could get together in the evenings on the beach and the children could run around and play games. We would sit in a large circle in the moonlight and sing songs. The beaches were full of beautiful shells in those days, sadly it is not so anymore.

On our return to Africa, dad was posted to Kampala, Uganda. I think I was about five then. Our first house, in an area called Nasambya, was a terraced single floor house with a small front garden. There were lots of children from other parts of India to play and with I picked up bits of several Indian languages. I can still get the gist of what people are saying in India, without being able to say if it is Hindi, Marathi, Gujarati, Urdu etc.

We became members of the Kampala Goan Institute, where we met many people and soon had many friends. I went to a nursery school run by my Aunt for about one year and later, Deryck and I went to the Norman Godinho School mainly frequented by Goans and have lots of fond memories of the place. Kampala was great. Everywhere you looked was lush and green and there were many beautiful gardens. We were within easy reach of Entebbe and the Botanical gardens there. We also went on picnics with other families to the sandy lakeside, where we had a lot of fun. Kampala was also close to Port Bell on Lake Victoria, where a small passenger ship used to regularly dock. The ship went around the lake and also docked at Kisumu in Kenya. My Uncle Edwin lived there and so we went to see him from time to time.

We to Jinja on the shores of Lake Victoria, the Owen Falls Dam is beautiful. There is a monument there honouring John Speke, the British explorer who found the source of the Nile. I regret very much that we were never able to visit Murchison Falls National Park in Uganda.

It was soon time to move again. This time the transfer was to Nakuru, Kenya.

Nakuru was a pretty little town in the Rift Valley, about 136 kilometres from Nairobi, along the stunning escarpment. It has a very mild climate because of its high altitude. There was a Goan School there and a Goan Club, and we soon settled down and made friends. Our house was a large semi-detached bungalow with a garden on three sides. Dad took to gardening and grew the best tomatoes I have ever eaten.

From the house, the land sloped gently down to Lake Nakuru, the pink lake as we called it, because of the blanket cover of elegant flamingos all year round. When something alerted them from time to time, flocks of them rose like fluffy pink clouds, circled in the sky, and came down again! What a sight!

The Queen Mother visited Nakuru in February 1959, and there was a lot of excitement, as we children lined the roadsides under the pretty purple jacaranda trees to wave our flags as she passed. Sometime in 1959, there was severe civil unrest in the Congo, and trainloads of European refugees escaped to Uganda and Kenya, before flying home. A lot of us went to the station to give them bags of eatables and clothes because they had nothing, some, not even a shirt on their backs.

Soon it was time to head for India on Dad's long-service leave. On the ship, our accommodation was in the hold which had been turned into a giant dormitory, with rows of bunk beds. We would nip up on deck to play and get a breath of air. Mum got into her bed on the first day and emerged on the last, as she suffered terrible seasickness. A *thali* (tray of food) would be brought for each of us for lunch and dinner.

To my great excitement, Dad told me that we were going to make a stop at the Seychelles, and that we were going to be met by friends from Nairobi who happened to be there. As we neared the islands, little boats with colourfully dressed natives came out to greet us and sell us beautiful objects made from Tortoiseshell and also large ripe mangoes and other fruit. We were shown around the beautiful island and taken to our friend's home for lunch.

And then it was time to board the ship again, for our onward journey. There was another surprise, we were going to change ships in Karachi, as our ship was not calling in Marmagoa. So, once again we had the opportunity of seeing another place, this time a big city and spending the night there, before boarding the Lurio, a Portuguese ship, for the final leg. We were out of hold and into a cabin.

We had a cabin on this ship, but although we had a dining room for our meals we had to queue up at the galley on deck, with our plates to collect our food. Drinking water was not served at the table, only Tinto, a light Portuguese wine, even for children. We soon got to our destination.

It was lovely to be in Goa, to enjoy the tropical fruit, the fresh fish, the sweetmeats, to go and meet friends, go to the colourful markets and in general have a wonderful holiday. We spent a month at the beach in Calangute, where other families from East Africa had also rented a house for the month. The houses were furnished, but granny Insisted that she needed all the kitchen equipment like the coconut scraper, the grinding stone, pots and pans and large copper pots to hold fresh water drawn from the well in Calangute. All this kitchen equipment together with a sack of rice, coconuts, and spices were loaded on to a bullock cart and took a whole day to get to Calangute, a journey which by car took us fifteen minutes.

Our month soon passed, it was now time to go and visit my grandma in Belgaum. We took the train chugging along slowly around the Ghats from Margao to Belgaum. The scenery of the mountains and Valleys was stunning, as we left the flat palm-filled coastal lands of Goa. The Dudhsagar waterfalls, which the train passes at seemingly arms-length, was breathtaking.

I loved Belgaum because I got to ride in horse carriages called tongas. Sometimes, I went along the roadside with granny, to stop village vendors on their way to market, and buy their fresh vegetables. I remember that granny got 100 eggs for 1 rupee! I was most impressed. She did have a large family to feed, and we children were encouraged to eat two eggs each for breakfast.

Soon, it was time to return to Nairobi. After the voyage, once again we got a train from Mombasa. It left in the evening and got to Nairobi the next morning. We were up early to sit by the windows and look out for wild animals as the train went through the great plains of Kenya. Ostriches ran along the side of the train as if in a race. Giraffes continued grazing as if nothing was happening. Impala and Thomson's gazelles and other animals were plentiful but, of course, there were no lions nearby, and unless you were lucky no elephants either. Perhaps that was just as well. I must qualify my statement about lions, there may have been some not far away, but we didn't see them. When the railway line was being laid some decades before, many Asians and Africans had lost their lives when man-eating lions entered the enclosures where their tents were and took the poor sleeping men away, one at a time. The book the '*Maneaters of Tsavo*' was a story about the lions. The maneaters were finally killed, but not before they had killed several workers and one British officer.

In Nairobi, I soon started at my new school, the Catholic Parochial School in the centre of town in Nairobi and Deryck went to Dr, Rebeiro's Goan School in Parklands. We were not at that house for long when we moved to yet another one, a bigger one this time. But this move was not going to last long. A few months later, Dad was sent on a temporary transfer to Uganda. Mum had just got a job at the South African Mutual Insurance Company, and Mum and Dad decided not to uproot us all. So, we remained in Nairobi and dad would go to Kampala for six months. We had to move out of the Railway house to a private one. Dad's transfer lasted much longer and so we moved into two different places with mum. We did see Dad when he visited, or if we went to Kampala on holiday. In the meanwhile, my sister Christine Ann was born. About six months later, Dad's position was confirmed and we moved to Kampala once more to be together again.

In the next four years, we moved three times, each time to a bigger and better house. Our last home was the best. Detached with a lovely garden all around, pretty flowers, and fruit trees such as mango and avocado. (The row on which this house stood and two other rows with large homes and buildings owned by Asians were raised to the ground when President Idi Amin years later, wanted to enlarge the gardens around the Parliament building in Uganda)

I went back to my first school and had to do an extra year there before going to secondary school because Kenya had seven years in primary school, but Uganda had 8. The friends I made in that school are still in touch with me now thanks to a classmate who got us together over the internet a few years back. It is lovely to be able to reminiscence and catch up with everyone.

In 1962, Uganda celebrated its Independence Day. Dad was President of the Kampala Goan Institute at the time and he and Mum were invited to the big celebration at Nakivubo Stadium.

President Milton Obote took over from the British. The Duke and Duchess of Kent and other dignitaries were present. Mum had to wear a long black dress and long black gloves, and Dad, a smart black suit. I went to the dress rehearsal with my Aunt and Uncle. There were fears of violence on the big day, which thankfully did not happen. I loved the flag with the Crested Crane and the melodious anthem.

It was at more or less this time that I made friends with Helen a little English girl who lived down our road. Soon Helen's mother got chatting to me and expressed her admiration for my sister's pretty dress. I encouraged her to come and meet my mom and talk to her about it. Mrs White ordered dresses from mum for her colleagues' babies (she was a teacher in a school) and mum got together a group of her friends who wanted to learn how to make the beautiful pastries, cakes and pies Mrs White excelled at, so that they could learn from her.

In 1965, I was to begin at secondary school, but dad was due long service leave once more, so we informed the school that I would be joining a little later in the year, and we left for India.

By now Dad's position in the Railways meant that we got first-class compartments on the train from Kampala to Mombasa, and, on the ship, we now had cabins. We could use the library, and the board games room, and we had many privileges, like using the dining rooms for our meals and being waited upon in style.

In Goa, being a teenager, I was delighted that granny had a transistor radio in her house, so I could listen to the Beatles and Rolling Stones, Cliff Richard and Elvis Presley, and sing along at the top of my voice. Granny thought the Beatles were a mad bunch of screaming kids. Where were the lovely waltzes and tangos and the likes?

Soon we were heading back to Africa. To my delight I was put on the list for the adult seating in the restaurant, together with mum and dad, as I was a teenager and did not have to eat with the children. There was an English nanny to babysit while the parents had their dinner. But Mum and Dad had a couple of friends on their table, and as there was one space on the table next to theirs, I was put there by the Maitre De. Imagine my shock when three officers walked to my table for dinner on the first night. I wanted to hide! I had no idea about using the multiple pieces of cutlery and crockery, etc. However, all three men were very nice to me and included me in some jokes and exchanges of interest. Much to my embarrassment, however, if I finished before they did and wanted to leave the table, they would all stand up and bow!

The Captain had a cocktail party for those in the upper deck (cabins), and a couple of nights later the passengers had a concert for the Captain and some officers. We spent a lot of time rehearsing so that it would be perfect. We were all sad to leave the ship when we docked at Mombasa. We got on the train for Kampala. It would take two nights.

I joined Kololo Senior Secondary School. I was happy to meet some of my old classmates there. We had a few European and American teachers and had to get used to their accents. I think our Maths teacher was Mr Kenneth; our French teacher was a French national. Our science teacher was an American man. They generally came through the Volunteer Service Organization.

One of our teachers was a very young, pretty Indian lady, who had just returned after completing her studies in the UK. She encouraged us to form a youth club. The date was set for our opening party and imagine my great sadness that it happened to be my farewell party, as Dad had just been transferred yet again, this time back to Nairobi.

We arrived in Nairobi in April 1966. We got admitted into secondary schools, Deryck to Dr Rebeiro's School in Parklands, and I at St. Teresa's Girl's School in Eastleigh. The next three years were delightful years and the friends I made in that school still meet in London from time to time, to celebrate and catch up 50 years later. There must be about 40 of us from our year group.

We were always members of the Railway Goan Institute and met up with friends there at weekends. Towards October of 1968, Dad was elected President of the club, and accepted willingly. Unfortunately, he had to resign early in 1969 as he was transferred to Dar es Salaam. My 'O' level results were out and I was going on to do my 'A levels". I had to change schools together with a handful of my classmates. We went to the Pangani Girls School, which used to be the Duchess of Gloucester school.

I could not go to Tanzania with mum and dad and had to stay on to pursue my studies. Deryck too, had to stay on as he was working as an apprentice engineer at Wilson airport.

I had a wonderful two years. My social life centred around the club and we took part in rehearsals for a concert for the 60th anniversary of the RGI. My Sundays were spent with other girls at the Nairobi racecourse, selling tickets at a booth, but earning pocket money. I loved going to the racecourse as I saw all the fashionable ladies in their latest outfits and pretty hats walking around with their smartly dressed partners. It encouraged me to buy fabric and paper patterns and make my fashionable dresses, without spending much money.

At school, our sports teacher encouraged us to go for a three- day camping trip out in the wilderness. We had experienced mountain climbers from the Outbound school on Mt Kilimanjaro, giving us lessons on climbing and abseiling. It seemed to be daunting at first but worked out to be great fun once we got the hang of it.

Soon things began to intensify at school, we sat our 'A' level exams and then had to wait for three months for the results. I aimed to study Fabric Design at Nairobi University. I never got to do that because just before the results came out, my life and my plans would change dramatically forever.

During the three months, I got a job at a glamorous dress boutique over the Christmas and New Year and then as a receptionist at a dental studio, at the Hilton in Nairobi. The most traumatic day in my life began like this. It was March 4, 1971, and my brother Deryck came home that evening very excited that he and another friend had together bought a car, a Volvo, from a mutual friend. He said that it was in excellent condition and that it had a powerful engine and body. That evening, friends invited a bunch of us to dinner at their home. Excited about the new car, six of us decided to go there in it.

After an enjoyable evening, we set off for home. Deryck and I were in the back, each sitting by the window. In the middle were two friends and the same in the front. We were young, our friend was driving fast and as we were on a dual carriageway, it did not occur to us that it could be dangerous, because the road seemed clear. As we rounded a big bend, however, there was an accident right in front of us that blocked both lanes and, because of a road divider, there was nowhere we could go. We hit the divider and the car overturned several times. We were now on the other side of the road. Cars coming up in the opposite direction, who had a clear path seconds before, were now faced with a terrible situation which resulted in a six-car pile-up.

Six people died on the spot including Deryck and Avena. And Samuel (Shafu) our third friend in the back, who was severely injured, unfortunately, died in hospital two days later. I was in hospital for six weeks with a fractured pelvis and several cuts on the head and left arm.

When I got out of the hospital, I did not want to live in Nairobi anymore and moved away to Dar es Salaam where dad and mum and my sister Christine lived. The accident had changed the lives of many, forever.

The only nice thing that happened to me was that because of my pelvis I was walking with crutches, and that meant that rather than travel by train, I had to take a flight to Dar es Salaam. It was my first ever flight, and I was excited. As luck would have it, I met someone on the plane whom I knew, he worked as an engineer for some airline I think and so as we flew over Kilimanjaro he managed to get the Pilot to invite me into the cabin to get the most stunning view of the mountain from the top with its snow, like icing on a cake, and a few minutes later a view of the exquisite Tanzanian coastline, the white sandy beaches, and the coconut palms down to Dar es Salaam.

With the loss of their only son, my Mum and Dad had suffered a huge blow, and it would take a long time for things to get anywhere near normal again. Dad was nearly 51 and the second in charge of the accounts section of the East African Railways and Harbours. He could have easily carried on, but instead, he decided to retire and move to Goa. Dad had completed 31 years with the same company he had risen step by step to the top of his sector.

We left Tanzania in May 1972 on a beautiful ship, calling at Mombasa, and then on to Goa, in India. Many families boarded the ship at Mombasa, many of them trying to flee from Uganda before the Amin administration got worse and worse and expelled all the Asians with no time to take any of their belongings with them.

I had teenagers of my age on the ship and we had a lot of fun together. We took part in a concert organised for the Captain who threw a cocktail party for all the passengers, and one night he even invited dad, mum and I to his cabin for a drink. It was an enjoyable evening, Dad and mum adapted slowly, but well, to life in Goa. We had brought our VW car with us which was an advantage then and It was with us until this year 2020.

Dad managed to enjoy his retirement for ten years before he sadly left us at the age of 62. Mum is blessed with relatively good health and was independent until two years ago, doing her wonderful cooking for all of us and her great grandchildren. She was 90 on October 14, 2020. As I write this, Mum is peaceful and serene in a home for the aged in her ancestral village in Aldona, Goa. She uses her smart phone very well and keeps in touch with people all over the world. I look back on a whole century and more of the lives of our family members and hope that this little account will serve some younger generations to understand what life was like for us in the nineteen hundred in our marvellous East Africa.

Standing left Angelo Fonseca (Goan Gymkhana), Hector D'Mello (Railway Institute), A R C Mascarenhas (Nairobi Goan Institute, I have not been able to identify the fourth gentleman. The Kenya Goan Sports Association Sports Committee with M R D'Souza hockey Gold Cup which was run by the Kenya Hockey Union.

Twilight of the Exiles

BLAISE

EVERAL Goan cricketers who stood out in the annals of the game: Antao D'Souza and (late) Wallis Mathias who played Test Cricket for Pakistan, Dilip Sardesai the Indian Test Cricketer, C. M. Gracias, Johnny Lobo, Michael Texeira, Alban Fernandes, Lawrence Fernandes and Blaise D'Cunha. The late Sardesasi played 30 test matches for India between 1961 and 1972. Dilip who hailed from Margao opened the batting and his run tally includes significant innings against the West Indies and England. For me, Blaise D'Cunha was special. He stands shoulder to shoulder with Sardesai and Wallis Mathias (batsman) and Antao D'Souza (medium pacer) for Pakistan. Both men also attended St Pat's in Karachi. Blaise's name is cemented in any list of top 11 cricket players from Kenya or East Africa as a whole.

Some of the outstanding Kenyan cricketers who were Blaise's teammates included: Jasmer Singh, Gursaran Singh, Ramanbhai Patel, Chandrakant Patel, Derek Breed, G.B. Jhalla, Don Pringle,

D.W. Watson, Mehboobali, Basharat (Basher) Hassan, Zulfilkar Ali, Ghafoor Ahmed (with a little help from Alihusein Namajee).

Of course, there are many, many more I could have added.

His name sits proudly in the roll of honour of the former Suleiman Verjee Indian Gymkhana (Nairobi Gymkhana) players, his favourite club and some of the great men he played club cricket with and against. He is now 93 (October 2020), generally in good health, resides in London and, as with all of us with age, getting frail. To this day, he has the respect and admiration of anyone who saw him anywhere in East Africa, Pakistan or India. I feel really, good now and will feel even better once I have finished writing this tribute. For more than 20 years, I tried to track him down. It was not until a few days ago that his son-in-law, Joe Desa, got in touch with me. He had just read the Johnny Lobo story featured in my blog. I am very indebted to Joe Desa for an immense amount of help with this story.

This is the story of a determined personality, who overcame adversity from polio and a snake bite on his thumb. The polio gave him a permanent limp and the snake bite was a blessing gave his spin bowling a unique and secret edge.

In Karachi, Blaise found a sports heaven at the Karachi Gymkhana Club and St Pat's school, which produced many hundreds of fine sportsmen and women. He was only 14 when he started but it was not long before he had made the school team. What's more, he was soon making some pocket money bowling to the senior batsmen in the nets.

From a clipping: "Blaise D'Cunha, one of the finest bowlers the school produced: vice-captain (it was not long before he was captain) of the school team, represented Sind province in the Festival Match against Maharashtra." He played Ranji Trophy cricket, inter-provincial school cricket at Delhi and Calcutta. "A very steady bat. A student at the school who is master of the willow."

"Blaise D'Cunha also proved to be a deadly bowler."

"Hardly 18 years old, with a little coaching will turn out a first-class bowler."

"A bright century by Blaise D'Cunha was the outstanding feature of a match between St Pat's and Pakistan Wanderers. The clock saved the Wanderers from defeat."

Blaise answered a few questions with the help of his son-in-law, JOE DESA:

Please give a brief insight into your early life: My father had secured a position as a Steward whilst in Goa, India, for East African Railways in the early 1920s; along with my mother and siblings, we moved to Masindi, Uganda, where I was born on March 24, 1928, one of 10 siblings. I was baptised Bras Agapito Lucas D'Cunha and was affectionately known to family and friends as Blaise.

My father's contract with East African Railways expired in 1932, unable to secure any new employment in East Africa, we returned to Goa.

He subsequently secured a position as a steward at the Karachi Gymkhana Club, in Karachi, Pakistan in 1935, where we resided on site, having the 'run' of the grounds as kids.

How and where did you learn to bowl?

I was a 'regular' in the sports fields, wherever and whenever feasible, initially playing Cricket, batting and bowling for fun as a pastime, later on as my bowling techniques improved, bowling to established cricketers who played for the club, additionally overseas touring players, practicing for upcoming club and national and international matches, earning monies (they put coins on the stumps and if I bowled them, I got the coins)

I attended St. Patrick's High School in 1937, where despite my handicap; I excelled at sports, high jump, where I was school champion and especially, Cricket.

I represented the St. Patrick's cricket team from the age of 14, playing local and national venues, including travelling to New Delhi, and the Brabourne Stadium, (Bombay) Mumbai, winning the Cricket Championship of India. I was part of St. Pat's Goan cricket team, some of whom went onto international and Olympic recognition in their own right from 1944 -1948, I played in the Ruby Cricket shield. We were winners for five years, Jack Britto (later Pakistan Hockey Olympian, also played in Malawi) was the Captain. Later, I took over the captaincy from him. I played for Pakistan under 18s in Lahore in 1948

When I was 22, I left Pakistan and returned to East Africa, taking a transfer from National and Grindlays Bank in Karachi, settling in Nairobi, Kenya.

I started my cricket career in Kenya, playing for Suleman Virjee Indian Gymkhana Cricket Club.

Before the independence of Kenya, Uganda and Tanzania, I represented East Africa, when the 'union' went their separate ways, I chose to represent Kenya. I was selected for the Kenyan/East African cricket tour of South Africa in 1956 against the non-white team and the subsequent return tour in Kenya in 1958.

I retired from international Cricket in 1965 but played for my club until 1967 and I took up table tennis in 1968 and soon represented Kenya.

What was so special about the way you bowled?

At a very young age, I contracted polio, which at the time was not initially medically diagnosed, affecting my left leg, leaving me with a pronounced limp. It limited my physical ability; determined not to be 'left out of the group', I adapted my skills to suit.

A snake also bit me on my right thumb, which is still evident today. I found that the enlarged thumb helped me with the spin.

How did he learn to bat? Were you a batsman or a bowler?

I was a bowler first and foremost. I was very lucky to have attended St. Patrick's High School in Karachi and at the time, there was a fantastic crop of very talented young men who excelled in sports, especially Cricket and hockey. Some of my compatriots included Orlando Ferro, Simon, D'Souza, Douglas Thomas, Michael Braganza, Gulam Razza, Jack Britto, Stanley D'Souza.

Who was the most difficult batsman to bowl to?

There were numerous. Too many to name individually, each one with exquisite technique and ability.

Who are cricketers you remember to this day?

Again, numerous. I played against the very best in my heyday. No one particular player above the very many superb, gifted and talented I had the pleasure to have played with and against.

(However, he does recall playing against the mighty West Indies, including the Three W's, Frank Worrell, Everton Weekes and Clyde Walcott in Kenya in the 1960s)

Is there one cricket performance that you can remember?

The Kenya tour to South Africa was ground-breaking in its time, apartheid was in place and strictly being enforced.

I also enjoyed playing snooker.

What he learnt in Karachi, perfected Blaise as an all-round cricketer at club and national level.

While the triangular Kenya/Uganda/Tanganyika matches were well supported, it was the annual Asians v Europeans which was probably the star match of the annual calendar. Blaise had a starring role in most of them, if not all. For example, in 1952, Kenya beat Uganda by 254 runs. In the first innings, Kenya scored 214 (Shakoor Ahmed 58, DW Dawson 58). Uganda scored a measly 87. Kenya in their second innings scored a further 190, thanks mainly to Dawson 78 and a spirited 39 by Blaise. It inspired one reporter to write: "D'Cunha was giving first-rate support and it is surprising that he warranted such a position as No. 11). In the second innings, Uganda capitulated scoring only 63. Blaise had match inning figures 7-53.

He also did it against Tanganyika in 1954. He skittled them out for 60 in the first innings taking 6-24 and followed it up with 5-37 in the second for a 233-run thrashing. Reaching that bowler's milestone of 100 wickets in a season was never too much trouble for Blaise. On one occasion (1955) while playing for Non-Official Asians against Asian Officials, he achieved the mark by taking a total of 10 wickets in the match. However, it was the Asians v Europeans where he shone equally with the bat and ball. If he was deadly as a spinner, he was even more so as a daring batsman. There was no, tap-tap, pussyfooting with Blaise, rather more calculated carnage as soon as he got his eye in. He cut, drove, and smashed the ball to all corners of the ground. When needed he could be relied on to save the team by hitting a quick 40 or 50 (in 50 minutes or less) or 100. He was ferocious and it was always a delight to see him in action. Once the Asians found their form, they won five or six consecutive matches to reduce 19 match tallies to 10-9 to the Europeans.

He fared well against all visiting teams, but it was the tour of South Africa that remained memorable for him. For one thing, he met and played against the coloured Basil D'Oliviera, who at the time should have played for South Africa but was not allowed to due to apartheid. Nonetheless, the Kenya Asians side was unbeaten and quite rightly the South African man had warned of Blaise as the dangerman with bat and ball.

JOHNNY LOBO, national and club teammate: I met Blaise at the National Bank of India (now Kenya Commercial Bank KCB) in Nairobi around 1947.

He told me he was from Pakistan and that his brother was the Manager of N.B.I. in Kericho. I immediately connected that they were from Moira in Goa the same village that I come from.

We spoke about Cricket at length and then I asked him if he would like to join us for a match against the Nairobi Club which he agreed to do. The match was N.C. vs Kenya Goans, and I was Captain for that game. Nairobi Club won the toss and chose to bat. In the early part of the innings, they looked solid at 60 for no loss and so I decided to bring in Blaise.

T.M. Bell who had already scored 50 was facing Blaise and on the third ball was clean bowled. The next man was also cleaned-bowled. I have never seen cricket players running to the pavilion to change and come back as umpires just to see Blaise bowl. In the end, he took 10 wickets all of them clean bowled.

RAMESH SETHI, former club cricket teammate: I played alongside Blaise in the Kenya Commercial League when we represented the Education Department. I used to travel from Nakuru. We won the Commercial League often because of his bowling. He was almost impossible to read. With R B Patel, we used to run through most batting line-ups. Our best win was against Barclays Bank when we scored 444-4 and bowled them out for 128. It was a memorable game for me too, I got a career-best 239 not out. Initially, I played for the RGI, then for the Railway Asian Institute and two years with the Sikh Union before joining the Indian Gymkhana. He was a master spinner, very accurate and had a huge googly, which accounted for batsmen who couldn't read it and were bowled when they left the ball gentleman with a wicked sense of humour. I can still picture his bowling action, with a characteristic limp in his run-up.

1951-52 Asians v Europeans: standing: N U Diwan (umpire) Kul Bhushan, Peshavaria, A Raoof, Johnny Lobo, Om Kumar, Chaggan, EJ Cohen (umpire). Seated: Gaffoor, Chandrakant, Ramanbhai (Captain) Harbanslal, D'Cunha

1958-59 Asians v Europeans Seating: Gafoor Ahmed, Chandrakant Patel, Ramanbhai Patel (captain), Harbans Singh (President of Kenya Cricket Association), Blaise D'Cunha, Gursaran Singh, Mehboob Ali. Standing: Higgs (umpire), Halim, Shashi Patel, A Aziz, R.B Patel, Robert Bresson, V.V. Bhandari, Harshad, N U Diwan (umpire)

What the Blaises?

By NORMAN DA COSTA

Put a red ball in his hands and Blaise D'Cunha instantly turned into a magician, a conjurer of tricks. This performer did not pull-out rabbits from a hat, but he baffled the best with his spin. Would that ball go straight, turn left, or right? Or would it be the trick ball in his repertoire: the dreaded googly. Only D'Cunha knew. In his younger days, he mesmerised batsmen in Pakistan. He then took his act on the road to Africa where he left an indelible mark in Kenya, Uganda, Tanzania and South Africa. D'Cunha was one of three Goans who made a name for himself in Pakistan along with Wallis Mathias and Antao de Souza, who were both capped by Pakistan (more on them and others below).

Charlie de Souza, one of Uganda's finest all-rounders who played against Blaise on several occasions, had the highest regard for the Kenyan. "When he first arrived, he was almost unplayable," said de Souza. The batsmen were unable to read his googly and, in their panic, they would surrender their wickets. Blaise also had a great match temperament and was a thorough gentleman."

After a long and stellar club career with Suleiman Virjee Indian Gymkhana, a club that fielded the likes of ace all-rounder

G.B. Jhalla, Ramanbhai Patel and Jawahir Shah, the spinner joined the Railway Goan Institute, a club better known for producing world-class field hockey Olympians including the late great Alu Mendonca who was also a fiery pace bowler. It was here at the RGI where I got a closer glimpse of this cricketing giant from close up instead of the press box. Due to polio at a young age, Blaise had a limp but that did not stop him from delivering a whirring ball. The ball hummed in flight. We, in the field, had to be on our toes all the time. While many batsmen fell to catches in the slips or the boundary, our wicket-keeper Cecil Fonseca, had a field day whipping off the bails for a stumping. One of Blaise's endearing qualities was that he was down to earth. There were no airs about him and he reminded me so much of Muttiah Muralitharan, the Sri Lankan superstar, who also spun his way to greatness. I met and covered the greatest spinner of all time for the Toronto Star and he was so much like Blaise – simple and genuine. Murali, of course, had a bent elbow and many felt this gave him an unfair advantage. Blaise had a bad leg and a huge right thumb as a result of a snake bite. But that did not deter him from also being a first-class high jumper. Apart from his exploits on the field, he was a joy to watch on the table. Yes, table tennis. He combined with Jarnail Singh, another multi-talented sportsman, to win several doubles titles and go on to represent Kenya. I once had the misfortune of being drawn against him in an earlier round of the Kenya Open. Needless to say, D'Cunha moved on in straight sets without breaking a sweat.

But back to Cricket. While Blaise was initially selected for Kenya and East Africa for his bowling, he quickly reminded the selectors that he could be relied on to bash that ball in the event the top order failed. In the annual Asians versus Europeans clash at the SVIG ground in 1955 D'Cunha and Jhalla played havoc with the Europeans in a runaway 255-run thrashing. Blaise carved out an unbeaten 100 as the Asians posted 251 for nine and in reply, the Europeans managed a meagre 215 thanks to fast bowler Jhalla claiming five wickets. In the second knock, Asians piled on 191 for seven declared and the Europeans hit the showers early after being dismissed for a meagre 72 thanks to Jhalla, who pocketed four for 27 and Blaise captured three for 28. That same year this outstanding all-rounder completed a haul of 100 wickets for the season with 15 centuries to boot. My buddy John Noronha, a former Ugandan who now resides in Canada and who I consider the local Wisden for his photographic memory and general knowledge of the game, provided me with details of some matches where Blaise had a significant impact on the outcome. One was in December of 1958 at the Nakivubo Stadium in Kampala.

"Kenya put up a modest total of 174 with Blaise the second- best scorer with 38. He then went to work on the Uganda lineup and skittled them for 68. Blaise took seven for 32 that included four ducks. The Uganda batsmen could not figure out his googly. Blaise went on to score a very useful 37 in the second innings to lead Kenya to a narrow 21-run win."

He tormented Uganda on two other occasions. In the first match in 1952, he took two for 35 and five for 23 to lead Kenya to a massive 254-run win. In 1954 he again struck with figures of five for 27 and five for 56 in a 128-run Kenya win." Tanganyika also felt D'Cunha's sting. In 1957 in Dar es Salaam, he sent the home team packing for 86 with him capturing eight for 28 (three clean bowled, two legs-before and two caught and bowled. He followed that up with knocks of 35 and 44.

After a star-studded career with the SVIG where the clubs hoisted several trophies, D'Cunha joined forces with his old buddy Johnny Lobo, one of only a couple of Goans to crack the Kenya Asian line-up. When Blaise landed in Kenya, he met Johnny who invited him to join Kenya Goans for a Sunday contest against Nairobi Club, considered the plum fixture during pre- independence days. It was the country's top European club and always put out a delectable lunch and tea spread. Goan clubs loved the hospitality at this venue and the Royal Air Force. At the RAF a bottle of beer could be purchased for 25 cents and a tot of hot drinks was the same price. No wonder few Goan cricket or field hockey player got home sober. Against Nairobi Club, the home team was off to a flyer with 60 without loss when skipper Lobo introduced his ace in the bag. D'Cunha teased and tormented the home team by capturing all the ten wickets and his reward was possibly an extra cucumber sandwich. Blaise had arrived and the rest is history.

RGI was the cream of the Goan clubs and among the early stars were star batsmen Maurice Gracias and Batu Noronha, Piety Fernandes and fast bowler Mendonca. The other stalwarts in later years included Darell Carvalho, Jarnail Singh, Charlie Ferrao, Sunil Sarkar and Teddy Gomes, a classy batsman who narrowly missed being picked for Kenya Asians.

The club played in the premier Kenya Cricket League and faced the likes of the legendary Basharat Hassan, Mehboob Ali, Zulfikar Ali, Akhil Lakhani, Narendra Patel and a host of other top-notch cricketers regularly. In 1968 the club with seasoned players such as Lobo, Fonseca, Darell Carvalho, Charlie Ferrao, Sydney Machado, Donald Gonsalves and Sunil Sarkar embarked on a fairytale run in the KCA Knockout tournament, coming within a hair's breadth of knocking out Sir Ali Muslim Club, the odds-on favourite for the trophy, out of the tournament. RGI struggled to 90 for eight before Fonseca tore the SAMC bowling to shreds by scoring a sensational 95. With Blaise in the lineup, it appeared RGI's Cinderella run would continue. But the RGI skipper made a tactical error in not using his ace bowler at critical times and SAMC survived what would have been the biggest upset in Kenya cricket annals. Wicketkeeper Naseer Butt and all-rounder Emery Jones combined to avert disaster. Emery, batting at No. 6 scored 33 and Butt at No. 7 got 56. "We usually never got to bat as our top order was so good," Butt told me from London. "When I came into bat, Emery told me 'just play straight' as I was having a tough time figuring Blaise's leg-breaks and googlies. Blaise was a spinner of the highest quality and we barely managed to win. After the game, Blaise came up and congratulated me. He was a very good person. A great cricketer" added Butt.

TOPS IN EAST AFRICA

Kenya had one great Goan all-rounder – Blaise D'Cunha. Tanzania countered with Alban Fernandes. Uganda led the way with three who could walk into any East African squad and they did. Fernandes was a fiery opening bowler and also a batsman who could clobber the ball. Fernandes also captained Tanganyika's field hockey team in several international matches and he was disappointed his country failed to qualify for the Olympics. Uganda produced the bulk of the best Goan cricketers in Africa. Several represented Uganda including all-rounder Lawrence Fernandes, Charlie de Souza and Michael Texeira. I never did see the late Texeira in action but every Ugandan sportsman speaks of him in glowing terms. Texeira played in the '50s for the Kampala Goan Institute, the Goans in the triangular quadrangular tournament and also the national team. The other classy batsman during his time was John (Chuck) Sequeira. Texeira's feats with bat and ball are legendary and he was always an automatic choice for East Africa. "His batting was a pure delight to watch," said Alu Mathias, a former Ugandan international batsman. In a triangular match against the Europeans in 1953 Texeira smashed 50 in 20 minutes and that "was a record for a game of that stature," said Mathias. Sequeira weighed in with 133 for a huge victory. "He was a fast bowler and confused batsmen by varying his pace." He will always be remembered for his 10-wicket haul against K.S.C. The European club was dismissed for 143 with Texeira taking all 10 for 42 runs. The Goans, behind a superb unbeaten 107 by Celly Dias, another Uganda cap, scored 157 for four. Lawrence was simply brilliant. A stone-walling opening batsman whose wicket did not come cheaply, he was an excellent leg spinner, and he was a world-class fieldsman. After moving to England, he starred as a spinner and just like

Blaise the Englishmen couldn't read his googly. De Souza was a reliable stock bowler and a hard-hitting lower-order batsman. Like Texeira and Fernandes, De Souza was an automatic choice for Uganda where he often starred with bat and ball. They all made their mark In East Africa and impressed visiting squads.

Jack Britto

Olympian

NEVER SAW Jack Britto (1924-2013) in action. You could say he was before my time but, in Africa, those that knew of him spoke in awe. I had forgotten about him, but he kept popping up while I researched various cricket stories and more recently the Blaise D'Cunha story. I am indebted to his son Desmond for painting the following portrait of his illustrious father. St Pat's High School was a brilliant nursery for budding athletes, especially in Cricket and Hockey. There were four brilliant cricketers in the making: Antao D'Souza, Wally Mathias (both played

Cricket for Pakistan with distinction), Blaise D'Cunha and Jack Britto who graduated with honours in their various sports.

JACK BRITTO was one of a handful of talented athletes of the Karachi Goan Association who reached the top position in their respective sports. His sporting career started in 1936. He showed early promise when playing for his alma mater St. Patrick's High School, where he excelled both at hockey and cricket. He brought fame and glory to his school. Jack always had a smiling face, losing or winning. He also played badminton, table tennis and billiards with an equal amount of enthusiasm. Jack was a fine cricketer, wielding the willow in a style that was a treat to watch, to the delight of his enthusiastic supporters.

He was born on August 16, 1924. Jack represented St Patrick's at the age of 13. He was the first to reach a double century in the Inter-School's Tournament, famously known as the Rubie Shield which was started by his father, Diogo Britto, in 1937. His 232 not out stood, until it was broken by Pakistan Test Cricketer Hanif Mohammed in the same tournament (Inter School Rubie Shield Tournament). Jack's memorable knock had followed an earlier unbeaten 182. Jack was soon Captain of St. Patrick's School. Jack could justly be proud for St Pat's as he held the distinction of winning the Rubie Shield for five years in succession, three years under his captaincy. From 16 to the age of 21, he represented St. Pat's. By now Jack had already been selected to play for the Sind and Karachi Team in the Ranji Trophy. Jack was in the Sind team in the Pentangular between 1940 and 1944. He took the field, with players like Jeomall Naoomal, Gulab Rai Kishenchand, S.K. Girdhari, B. Lanewalla, Jamshed Khoodaddad Irani, MInoochehar J.Mobed, Qamardin, Daud Khan, Abbas Khan Lodhi, Fazal Lakda and several former Sind stalwarts including Ghulam Mohammed, the old Baloch player from Lasbela, who had toured England with the 1932 All India Team. G.S. Ramchand went on to captain India and defeated Australia on the famous turning pitches of India. Another name worth recalling was that of Abdul Aziz Durrani. He worked for the Sind Madressah School. He was also well-known in

Karachi as the Sind Madressah coach. He was the father of Indian Test Cricketer Salim Durrani.

Jack was lucky enough to meet some of the other famous names like the old Maharashtra Ranji Trophy all-rounder and veteran all India cricketer and Pakistan test cricket selector, Jacob Harris, who had high hopes for Jack.

During 1942-1946, Jack played for the 'Rest' in the Karachi Pentangular Cricket Tournament.

In 1946/7, he represented Karachi and Sind in the All-India Tournament (Ranji Trophy) at Bombay. (In 1946, Sind won the tournament).

In the 1949-1950 season, the West Indies included players like Everton Weekes, Clyde Walcott, Allan Rae, George Carew, Robert Christiani, Gerry Gomez, James Cameron, Dennis Atkinson, Prior Jones, John Trim, Wilfred Ferguson, Cliff McWatt, Ken Rickards, Geoff Stollmeyer and the "Black Bradman" George Headley. Frank Worrell was ill.

Jack finally got his call up to play for the Pakistan cricket team against the West Indies team but at the same time, he was chosen for Pakistan to tour Europe in the Hockey World Championships in 1950. After partition, the authorities were forcing him to make a choice, this was heart-breaking for Jack, for he realised that he was good enough to play both hockey and cricket at the top level. Jack chose to tour Europe with the hockey side.

Thus, ended in tragedy, one of the finest careers of a sportsman that could have gone on to international honours, both in cricket and in hockey.

He showed considerable promise in hockey as a young boy. He was a clever tactician with stick wizardry and his ball control was excellent.

Jack started as a centre forward. He soon had a reputation as a good, clean hockey player.

Some even dared to compare him to the famous 1936 Indian Olympic player to Dyan Chand.

In choosing to play hockey, Jack had finally decided to give up his career in cricket. It was a sad day for the game of cricket, but he was soon one of the best centre-halves in the game. The Karachi Goan hockey teams were great crowd pullers at the famous Aga Khan Hockey Tournament held in Bombay. The magic of the Karachi Goan players in the Cabral Shield Tournament in Karachi shone against the top teams from all over India like the Bhopal Wanderers, Calcutta Customs, Kalayam Mills, Khalsa College and Jhansi Heroes. He played in many major provincial tournaments in undivided India:

Jack's hockey skills as a goal-scoring centre-half attracted the attention of the senior members of the squad. It eventually landed him the top spot in the national team and Jack was chosen to play for Pakistan in the 1950 World Championships in Barcelona Spain. He represented Pakistan in the World Championship at Barcelona, Spain and toured Europe. Pakistan were joint winners with Holland.

1951 Toured India representing Pakistan Independents in the Invitation Gold Cup Tournament at Bombay and Delhi Cloth Mills at Delhi. Pakistan were runners up in the former tournament and winners in the latter. Jack was selected for the Pakistan Olympic team for the 15th Olympiad, Helsinki Games in 1952 as a centre-half. He found a place in the side because of his excellent stickwork. He also toured various European cities after the Olympics. (Paris, Lyons, London, Amsterdam, Brussels, Venice, Berlin, Stuttgart, Munich, Hamburg, Duisburg, Zurich, and Rome). He was capped by Pakistan eight times.

In 1953, he toured East Africa (Kenya, Tanganyika and Uganda) with Pakistan Rovers.

In 1956, he trialed for the Pakistan Olympic team to Melbourne.

He captained the Karachi X1 as a centre-half in the national championship at Lahore.

In the late 1950s, he migrated to Malawi. Over the next few decades, he was their star player in hockey, cricket, badminton and virtually any other indoor sport he took a fancy to.

He played Cricket for Mpingwe 'A' Sports Club for many years until 1975. He topped the batting averages for most of the years. He was Malawi's outstanding spin bowler bowling leg breaks, off-breaks, googlies & topspin. His googlies were unplayable. He took five wickets in an innings on many occasions. On one occasion he took seven wickets for two runs. He also captained the side. He was also a brilliant slip fielder taking many catches.

1962 Named 'sportsman of the year' George Summers Memorial Trophy

1966 Awarded Frank Scott Cricket Bat (Highest Batting Average)

1975 Named Cricketer of The Year (Rothmans Trophy)

Jack lived in London from 1976 to 2013 and led a sedentary life. He continued playing social cricket, badminton and tennis. Played badminton in his early eighty's and still won tournaments.

"Although I met Jack only once, it was enough to identify him as someone who could have kept company with the wizard of hockey Dyan Chand. He had the personality of Keith Miller, the genius and patience of Hanif Mohammed and the artistic skill of Sachin Tendulkar," wrote a noted Pakistani writer.

Johnny Lobo

It was my father's brother-in-law S.R. Rodrigues who was the first pioneer from our family who ventured out of Goa and crossed the Indian Ocean on a dhow with the Arab traders to Mombasa in 1895. Later he was instrumental in convincing my father Evaristo Lobo, that he could get him a well-paid Government job in Kenya. My father agreed and came over on a steamer in 1911 and began working. A few years later, my father got very sick and returned to Goa. When he had recovered, we were still in Goa. Typically, a proposal of marriage from my mother's family via Benjamin Mendes from Aldona for their daughter Maria

Mendes. My father married my mother in 1918 and returned to Kenya. My siblings were born shortly after Joseph 1919, Victor 1921, Francis 1923, Eulalia 1925 and Clara 1929. I was the 5th child born on December 27, 1927. We grew up in Ngara in the Government Quarters built by the British rulers for Goan and Indian government staff. My three older brothers were sent to study at St. Stanislaus' Bombay and were active sports players at school, while my sisters and I attended Dr Ribeiro Goan School (DRGS) in Parklands. It was at this school where my love of all sports began.

Each day at our half-hour break, we would race out of the class to grab the cricket bat. We soon realised only the batter stayed at the crease until he was bowled. Soon we started to play actual matches, 11 players on each side. Some of the names I remember are Philip Gracias, Alex and Rui Rodrigues, Willie Paes, Marcus Braganza, Monty D'Sa, Alan D'Cunha and myself. Incredibly our first match lasted three months, but in those three months, we continued to get better.

Our passion for the game continued even after the bell rang to end our day at school. As many of my classmates also lived in my neighbourhood, we would race home and play daily from 4-6 in the evening. The neighbourhood boys included Maurice and Philip Gracias, Bartu and Dennis Noronha, Marcus and Henry Braganza, Alu Mendonca and Silu Fernandes. Building on the newfound confidence, we decided to play our first test match against the Government Indian School (GIS) on matting. It was a remarkable result because we not only won, but I also scored my first century in the game. Boosted by this win we went on to play our next match against the Prince of Wales school and thanks to a fine inning by Monty D'Sa of 50 runs with good support from Alan D'Cunha of 30 runs, we won that game too. Another impressive victory of my own, for DRGS, was when I scored two centuries, against Mombasa Goan School (110) and Allidina Visram School (105).

The Railway Goan Institute (RGI)

My uncle Jack Mendes (my mother's brother), who captained the RGI on weekends would often take me, then just a young boy of 11 years to watch the games. Being the captain of the team and my uncle, if a player did not show up, would ask me to stand in for that player. This opportunity tremendously improved my game as I played with young men who were more experienced in the game than I was.

In the late 1940s, after having finished school, I began playing for RGI and our regular side included Maurice Gracias, Adolf D'Mello, C. Ferrao, Batu Noronha, Piety Fernandes, Henry D'Souza, Willie Paes, Donald Gonsalves, Ruben Rebello, Darrell Carvalho, Sydney Machado, Teddy Gomes and Cecil Fonseca.

Maurice Gracias was a brilliant cricketer who dominated on the RGI side for several years. He was educated at the Government Indian School and was the first Goan to represent the Asians against the Europeans. He retired from cricket two seasons after I joined. While on the team I scored a few centuries most notably against the Aga Khan Club where I scored 130 runs and Nairobi Club where I scored 133 runs.

The Cricket season in Nairobi started in October and ended in March. Every Sunday in those six months, we enjoyed many matches between clubs. The sports secretaries of each club would meet and draw up fixtures for the home and away games.

There were 10 Asian clubs: 1, Suleman Virjee Indian Gymkhana, 2 Patel Club, 3 Sikh Union, 4 Sir Ali Muslim Club, 5 Kathiawar Club, 6 Visa Oswal Club, 7 Sura District Club, 8 Aga Khan Club, 9 RGI, 10 Railway Indian Institute.

There were seven European Clubs. 1 Nairobi Club, 2 European Civil Service Club, 3 Impala Club, 4 Woodley Club, 5 Parklands Club, 6 Wanderers Club, 7 Railway European Club. In the 1950s, we made a trip to Moshi to play against the Tanganyika Twigas, a mostly European side. Blaize DaCunha the great Kenyan spin bowler dominated that game with an inning of 125 runs. The scoreboard read: -

R.G.I. 178 for 5 - 1st Inning declare Twigas 25 follow on 28

In the early 1960s, RGI was invited to participate in the Asian Sports Association Knockout Tournament and had a sensational first match where we beat the Patel Club, then beat the Kathiawar Club in the second match. We went on to meet the Coast Gymkhana side in the quarterfinals at the Sikh Union Club grounds. We batted first and only scored 138 runs, but with great determination, we bowled out the Coast Gymkhana for 125 runs to win the match. Donald Gonsalves bowled well and most of the Coast team were out due to the brilliant catches by the RG I team.

We then went on to face the Muslim Club in the semi-finals. We batted first and only managed 90 runs for 8. Then came Cecil Fonseca our 9the player who scored a sensational 95 runs, hitting four sixes and we were all out for 210 runs. In this match, Zulfikar Ali on the Muslim side was in fine form and bowled well. The Muslim side began batting and, at first, it seemed like they were in trouble 110 runs for 9. Blaze D'Cunha was bowling well, but our captain began to panic and changed him after one over. Then came the Muslim side's Basharat Hassan and Mubarak Ali and led the Muslim Club to victory. A chance at history with a Goan victory was denied, yet again.

It was always the practice of each sports team to elect their captain. However, the rules suddenly changed one year, when the Hockey and Badminton ladies and men's teams took part in the voting process and voted in the new Cricket captain for our team. It was an unprecedented and unacceptable practice which led to a few of us (non-railway workers "associate members" who had no voice in the management of the club practices) splitting off from the RG I side. At this time, Dr Shashi Patel a Railway doctor asked a few of us to join the Railway European Club, which we did for two seasons, as Kenya's independence was looming, players were leaving the country and the clubs were shutting down. We then moved our game to the Wanderers Cricket Club, a beautiful setting at the beginning of the Kiambu Road, where we played for three seasons and they too shut down. The saddest part was to see our RGI. Club House and grounds demolished to make way for a boarding Government school complex.

On my first local leave from work, I was asked to play for the Goan Institute (GI) against the Nazi Moja Club in Mombasa. Playing at the coast with an altitude of 57 feet above sea level with humidity was difficult at first. I only scored 50 runs. My host Armand D'Souza pulled me aside and gave me some profound advice that stayed with me throughout my career, "getting to 50 is the hard part, but once you score 50 you are well set, so just go for a 100". On my next visit to Mombasa, a Saturday game playing again for the GI against Mombasa Club, my partner was Joe Fernandes, I remembered Armand's advice and went for the century.

In the late 1940s, I played for the Nairobi Asian Team touring Zanzibar and Dar-es-Salaam. It was a great game which we won. In the 1950s I was selected to play against the South African Coloured Team which was captained by the famous Basil D'Oliveira in Nakuru at the Rift Valley Sports Club and also played against the Rhodesian Team on the Sikh Union ground. In the 1960s, I played regularly for Asians for season-ending much sought-after match against Europeans.

The Europeans lead 11 to Asians 1. We turned that game on its head and beat the Europeans. The Asians dominated, won one match after the other, equalizing the series with the last match ending in a record win for the Asians scoring 450 runs with Akhil Lakhani's 230 runs not out. and Chandrakant Patel's 220 runs not out.

Kenya Commercial League

In the 1950s, Jasmer Singh a great cricketer and my close friend, together with Maurice Wright, John MacFarlane and myself formed the Kenya Commercial League for teams which included government offices, banks and companies in the private sector. The games would be played off-season, from July to October. The competitive sportsmanship in this league was exceedingly high and most enjoyable and it drew top players from the Asian clubs.

I captained the Ministry of Works (MOW) side and, in our very first season, I scored five centuries in a row, four n.o. and held the record in the league. A game worth mentioning was when Luis D'Souza playing for Gailey & Roberts hit 11 sixes in a match against MOW played on the Patel Club grounds. Other notable great names in cricket in those days included Ramanbhai Patel, Zulfikar Ali, Jawahir Shah, Akhil Lakhani and Chandrakant Patel.

Shortly after my record game in July of that year, the next big upcoming match was Kenya vs Tanzania which would be in August of that year. The selection committee decided to have the scouting selection matches for 17 players at the Patel Club ground. By the time it was my turn to bat, it was about 6 p.m., the sun had begun to set, and the light was diminishing. Throughout my cricket career, my best stroke was on the offside. The bowler was Dr Ranjit Singh, a known fast bowler with a new ball. I defended my wicket but unfortunately got trapped on the pads lbw. I was told later that day, that I could not play off-break bowling, and therefore was not selected to represent Kenya.

Our Wedding in 1959, Nairobi Kenya, with well-wishers forming the bridal arch with cricket bats and soccer balls.

In 1959, I got married to Maura Lobo from Kampala Uganda. We started our family in the early 1960s-1970s with three sons; John, James and Jerry and three daughters; Mary Ann, Melita and Michelle. My cricket career continued after independence and throughout my children's young years into the mid-1970s where I played seasonal games for the Goan Institute (GI) side with players like Sunil Sarkar, Yunis Cockar and Alvito Rego. I finally passed on my cricket bat to my son Jerry and even some of our friend's sons hoping they would take this great game into the future with them.

Having left Kenya in December 1993 and now a citizen of Canada residing in Oakville, Ontario, I still love to watch my children and grandsons pick up the cricket bat and play a match. At the age of 92, my great joy is always when they ask me to join them to bat.

Photograph courtesy of Mrs Anita Abreo taken in 1930 Back row L to R Valu, Adelaide's husband, Celu's husband. Middle row L to R- Olive (Valu's wife), Adelaide's son, Valu's mum holding Celu's daughter, Valu's dad, Adelaide (Valu's aunt), Celu's daughter, Celu (Valu's sister). Front row L to R – Celu's daughter, Patru (Valu's brother), Celu's daughter, Arthur Nazareth (Olive's brother), Celu's daughter, Adelaide's son

VALU!
JOSE MARIE VALENTINO DE ABREU M.B.E.

Valu with his daughter Jennifer on her wedding day

NO history of East African Goans could be written without first mentioning Valu Abreu of Mombasa. He was born in Saligao, Goa on February 14, 1901, and arrived in Mombasa in 1919. His parents were Marcus Antonio Filipe De Abreu and Mafalda Artimizia Dantas. He was the eldest of five but sadly one sibling died in early life. He had two sisters, Anna Celestina (Celu) and Ophelia (Ofu), and a brother, Jose Patrocino Matiniano (Patru), who was born some 18 years after Valu. His father had a butter factory in Amnabad before his return to Goa. As Goa was under Portuguese rule, Valu studied in Portuguese and having completed his primary and secondary education he set sail to East Africa. He arrived in Mombasa in 1919, the same year Patru was born in Goa. This was the beginning of a glorious chapter in his life. Before him, many, many Goans had braved the might of the Indian Ocean in an Omani Arab dhow (later on British steamships) and arrived in the magical island of Zanzibar. The Omani Sultan of Zanzibar welcomed them and offered employment before they moved inland to Kenya. For those early pioneers, including those that worked on the Kenya-Uganda Railways, life was often nothing short of hell. There were strange diseases, wildest animals and some of the terrain that could only have been designed in hell. However, there was also much more that looked like heaven on earth, especially along the Kenyan, Tanzanian coast. And, of course, the pearl of the east, the much written and talked about the island of Zanzibar. The name alone is enchanting! The earliest of pioneers had cut a niche for themselves as some of the pioneering businessmen, later formidable members of the Colonial Civil Service and a community respected (to a degree, as long as it suited the Colonial bosses) by the heads of the civil service. However, so very successful were the Goans that many of them achieved the highest positions and promotion in the civil service to the point that most people said that "without the Goans, the Colonial Civil Service would crumble." One of the great things about belonging to a village in Goa meant that those in a position to recommend someone for a job in East Africa would recommend a family member or a villager from Goa ... so the Saligaocars, who were pretty successful, especially in Kenya, encouraged their fellow villagers to come to Kenya where jobs and accommodation were found pretty quickly ... and the newcomers were settled pretty quickly. It was not a sussegade kind of the life they had been used to, but the money was good and there was enough to send home to Goa. For many, there was the regular long service leave to Goa every four years. A job in Africa meant a new home, new land, or refurbished home, and the respect of your fellow villagers (if you could avoid the evil eye sometimes). So, the early pioneers (within the ranks of the various villagers, or by caste, or by the North-South divide, or simply as Goans) made it as a taken that they would help most Goans when they first arrived in the darkest Africa. Because they maintained their Goa village links in Kenya, promotion of their social needs (the Goan Institutes in Mombasa, Nairobi, Kisumu), their catholic religion, education for the growing number of children (especially in Nairobi, Mombasa, Kisumu) was vital. Valu Abreu embraced the required commitment and challenges. He is easily one of the best known in the service and promotion of the Goan Community in Mombasa. His first job in 1919 was with the Colonial Government in Mombasa. Valu spoke Konkani, Portuguese, English and Hindi, hence he was employed as a Food Controller. Later he moved to the Government Coast Agency, where he served for 40 years. On June 13, 1959, Queen Elizabeth II, awarded Valu the M.B.E. He rose very quickly and with each step up the ladder of success he was able to employ and encourage many Goans into the service. Eventually, he was rewarded with the top job in the Government Coast Agency, Chief Superintendent, and became the first Goan, indeed the first Asian to do so. On July 29, 1951, his father passed away and so his brother Patru and his wife Anita and their three children went to Goa to bring their mother Artemisia to Mombasa and she stayed with them for 13 years. During this time, she developed cancer and Valu managed to get the Portuguese Consulate to agree to pay all expenses for him and his mother. He decided to take his wife at his own expense for support. On June 3, 1929, Valu married Olive Nazareth at the Holy Ghost Cathedral in Mombasa. Olive belonged to the well-known Nazareth family of Moira. Her father was one of the original pioneers and came to Kenya in 1895. Valu and Olive's first daughter was born in Saligao on June 3, 1930. They had 12 other children: nine girls and four boys. Valu became a member of the Mombasa Goan Institute in 1919 and was a member until he died on

13th November 1986. He was president 11 times, a feat rarely achieved in any Goan association. There was always fierce competition for positions on the committee but most of the ferocity was reserved in the competition for president. His dedication to the Goan Institute Mombasa began in 1919 and lasted the rest of his life …unswerving. Valu was instrumental in building a hall with a raised stage that was used for dances and concerts. Valu raised the money for this development through his efforts going house to house collecting donations and debentures. He laid the foundation stone for the hall and was also given the honour of officially opening the new hall on 29th March 1959. This was due to his dedication and personal sacrifices to see the project completed. The event was attended by well over 1000 people. The Institute wanted to install a plaque to commemorate the opening of the new hall but Valu declined graciously In 1959 during the Queen Mother's official visit to Kenya, which included Mombasa, Valu organized an arch to be erected in front of the Goan Institute and bouquet presented to Her Majesty the Queen Mother in front of the Institute by his first grandchild. At the time, members said that this could not happen, however, Valu through the Provincial Commissioner organized for the Queen Mother's motorcade to stopped in front of the Club for the presentation. On the 15th of May 1963, Valu's wife Olive passed on. He had since retired and at the time assumed the role of both Father and Mother. Daddy Valu [as his grandchildren fondly referred to him] cared for his children very well……in those days, husbands did not tend to the home affairs. This was left to the mothers. Mothers were good economists. The fathers looked after the finances etc. He must have had quite a task feeding so many on one salary. It was as if lightning hit and an angel got into daddy with some miraculous powers. He had no one to turn to for help but he did it all wonderfully. He had the help of the older children who rallied to keep the family intact. Each morning he would wake up very early by 5:00 AM to prepare the breakfast for the children so that they would not go to school on an empty stomach. He was very particular about the lunch break, making sure they would also have a good lunch and then proceed back to school.

He took over the role of mother with no hesitation. Valu went walking almost daily to the Vegetable & Meat markets and would come back by bus with two full baskets of foodstuff. The fish market which was located near Fort Jesus was a separate marketing day. He made sure the children continued to eat healthy just like when Olive was living. Valu would even go to Edward St. Rose to buy necessities for the girls until a time they were old enough to shop for themselves. He even made sure the children who were in colleges had pocket money. Valu who was once quite strict while being caring and understanding became very gentle and calm. He would always care for the children and worry when they were not at home. He knew when they came home no matter what time in the night after their shift at work or evening outing. Even after they were married and came home to visit, he would make sure they would have what they enjoyed eating. He loved to give his grandchildren candy. Valu had a houseboy who left employment hardly 6 months after Olive's death and Bekele Ngala started helping Valu in 1964 with the cooking of lunch and dinner for the family and with the other household chores. Bekele Ngala left his previous employment and was employed by Valu in 1965 where he has been in our family for 55 years and currently working at our brother Larian's [Valu's grandson] home. He is a part of our family has worked for Valu, Andrew and now Larian. God gave Valu the strength and courage he needed to look after the children and take charge of the home. When Valu died in 1986, due to his dedication and service rendered to the Institute, the Institute Management requested that the viewing and his leaving be from the club but this was declined by the family as they felt he should leave from his last place of residence. The family, however, accepted that after the church service the funeral procession would stop in front of the Institute. Valu's casket was draped with the Institute colours and a wreath placed on it before proceeding to the Mbaraki Cemetery in Mombasa where was he was laid to rest. Needless to say, Valu also rendered valuable service to the Goan

Community. He not only served as president and chairman on several occasions during an era when members would campaign for the role... very different from the current day and age where no one wants to take up the honorary roles in the Institute but also played an active part in the welfare of the needy members of the community for many years. He had quite a sense of humour and would tell anyone who would listen that his first grandchild was born in 1952 and after that in 1953 Valu and Olive's last child was born. When his friends asked him what happened, his reply was "We were celebrating the Queen's coronation" In 1954 when Valu was travelling by sea to Goa he was asked by the Purser about his family. He mentioned he had twelve children. The Purser was surprised and said "What?" his reply was "it is cheaper by the dozen". In 1959/60 Valu's mother was diagnosed with Cancer and he intended to take her to Bombay for treatment. Being Portuguese nationals, a medical visa was denied by India. Valu contacted the Portuguese Consul, who at the time was in Portugal informing him of the incidence. The reply received was that Valu, his wife and mother were to fly to Portugal, where all expenses to include air tickets, hotel accommodation and medical expenses were borne by the Portuguese Government. In 1961 when Goa was liberated, Valu vowed he would never return to India because they would not grant them a medical visa. Valu Abreu was indeed a very special Goan, an outstanding member of his community and the pride and joy of his family and friends. Below: pictured with his family.

I REMEMBER .... JENNIFER: "Daddy was well respected by all communities for his good deeds irrespective of their race, religion or creed. He never used abusive language and spoke kindly to all. He treated the poor well and when food rationing was in effect pitiful, he made sure they got enough, always trying to follow the Government regulations. He walked everywhere until I bought a used Morris Minor and drove him around. Daddy attended cocktails and dinner parties at the Governor's House. One time after mum's death, he was invited to the Oceanic Hotel for a reception honouring the late President Mzee Jomo Kenyatta and he took me. What an honour to shake the late President's hand and hear him say "habari yako" (a greeting in Swahili meaning how are you? Or what's the news?) He worked for the Government Coast Agency and his hard work, honesty and ethics earned him the position of Coast Agent. Having worked 40 years with such diligence he made his name and earned his MBE Medal (Member of the British Empire). Unfortunately, he was unable to make the trip to the United Kingdom to receive his medal. He was presented with the medal in Mombasa. On retirement, he was presented with four silver goblets and a wooden clock which to date has a place in my home, since Joan left the country for Canada. When Sana (Agnelo) asked daddy for my hand in marriage, dad said, "I was waiting a long time for you to ask me." PETER: His second wife was the GI! Apart from being president for so many years after work and in his spare time, he went door to door asking for donations for the club's building fund. I think all the men who wanted to marry his daughters had to be members of the GI or become members. I have heard my dad say this. He reckoned you had to be of good repute to become a member, and thus suitable to marry one of his daughters. He lost his wife at the age of 49. I think just a month before her 50th birthday. Valu, as he was known, has a living sister-in-law in London. Valu has a total of 22 grandchildren. I am number 21! I have twin girls who are the only descendants born on his birthday, February 14, hence his name Valentine!

The birth of St Teresa's

Left: St Teresa's Church, Eastleigh, as we will always remember, and right, how it all began

St. Teresa's church was established as a mass centre in 1925 by Holy Ghost Fathers who were then residing at St. Peter Clavers Parish, at the bottom of River Road near Mincing Lane market, a poor end of Nairobi.

In 1930 the first structure (church) was established known as Eastleigh mass centre. (Currently Old Hall).

In 1930 the Holy Ghost Fathers in collaboration with Precious Blood

Sisters established the first girls' school.

1936 Lay Missionary Edel Quinn started Legion of Mary. 1947 The current church was constructed.

1953 Two schools were started one for girls under Loreto Sisters and one for boys under Holy Ghost Fathers both under the patronage of St. Teresa.

1955 The current church was officially opened by His Grace Archbishop Kevin McCarthy and was put under the patronage of St. Teresa of Avilla.

The mission at Eastleigh had been started by the Precious Blood Sisters as a training school for girls from St. Peter Claver's (the church built at the poorer end of town specifically for Africans during segregated days). With the outbreak of war in 1939, these girls were transferred to the care of Precious Blood Sisters in Kalimoni and Loreto in Limuru. It was in Eastleigh with the Precious Blood Sisters that Edel Quinn had set up her base and where she died in 1944. With the end of the war, "and since all hope of reopening the Girls' School was gone" (Eastleigh 19. 5. '47), the Provincial and Bishop agreed that the Sisters would be redeployed and the buildings become a separate parish centre with the other four recently delimited city-parishes: St. Austin's, Holy Family, Parklands and St. Peter Claver's, which would continue to develop centres in Pumwani, Shauri Moyo and Makadara(1956). Eastleigh had been a Mass-centre since 1925, but now with the appointment of Frs. Michael Finnegan and Tom Shannon, and later Paddy Hannan, it began several decades of uninterrupted development. In 1947, it also had Mass and catechetical centres at Mathare Valley Mental Hospital and Police Lines, Kayole, Kassarani (where they immediately open a new school), Katani, Kenya Breweries,

Allsop's, Karura, soon adding Njiru Quarries and Ruaraka. During the Mau Mau time, the British Forces bulldoze three villages in Mathare Valley: Mathare, Uraparani, Kariobangi, and evict the population. Most, then, of the Catholic people in Eastleigh are Goan or Seychellois; the Corpus Christi procession is described (27.5.51) as a "large and devout Asian congregation." Yet at Midnight Mass (1952) "many Africans attend despite the police curfew."

The new school for girls, opened in 1953, was allocated to the Loreto Sisters who had been in Kenya from the very beginning, but their more recent development began in 1921 when they reopened the Msongari school for "European children." They had also assumed the direction of Holy Family Parochial School, already started in 1909, "where we have European, Goan and Parsee children all sharing the same class." Even such a mixture contravened colonial apartheid regulations.

ST TERESA'S BOYS SCHOOL – TEACHERS: Back Row:

Fr. Cremins, Yvonne D'Costa, Winnie DeSouza, Theresa DeSouza, Joanita Alvares, Regina Pereira, Edith D'Souza, Fr. Hannan. Front Row: Vivian DeSouza, Lino D'Silva, Peter Thomas, Napoleon De Souza, Basil Denis, Rudolf Fernandes & Michael D'Silva. (Pic St Teresa's website) I remember Napoleon, Peter, Appolonia, Lino and Vivian from my own days at St T's. Vivian had a brother, Lesley, who was also a teacher, but he passed away fairly early.

The founding diocesan and missionary clergy, though of French origin, had been compelled to follow a school-system racially segregating

Arab, Indian, African, European pupils. The early diarist is at first mystified by the word "European." French colonial policy would have equal opportunity for all, regardless of race. Mumford, an English educationalist, wrote in 1935 for London University: "Association of mental capacity with the colour of skin would be placed by France in the same category as judging character by bumps on the head." St. Teresa's Girls Primary and Secondary would, therefore, be classified as Asian, as also the Boys' School which soon followed.

Both schools were built and supported through the continued efforts of the parish community and parents, with some small financial subsidies from the Government. After Independence, of course, segregation was abolished. The imposition of a quota system in the secondary school caused some difficulties, as it meant all qualified primary graduates could not find a place. The same community spirit that supported the schools was evident in a rich devotional and liturgical life centring on the Sunday Mass, Easter ceremonies, with all the historic reforms absorbed happily as proclaimed, the favourite feast-days, confraternities, retreats, home-visitation, the sometime 4,000- strong attendance at Corpus Christi or Lady processions, Annual Novena, "Why can't we have Mass facing the people for the Novena?") people ask. The new church had been blessed by Archbishop McCarthy on October 30, 1955. All funds had been raised locally even in these difficult years; the building site being visited at least once by Mau Mau raiders. It was from here that Fr. Joe Whelan, taking over from Paddy Fullen, visited Mau Mau Detention Centres and Prisons, including Athi River, with Fr. Ted Colleton, and assisted at so many executions. In many years of ministry, only once did a group reject his services. In 1957, we find a regular Sunday Mass at Ruaraka, called after its Goan benefactor F X D'Silva, "Baba Dogo" (Little Father). (D'Silva virtually owned the whole of Ruaraka. He made his fortune in various businesses including selling British forces auctioned supplies, clothing, tents, safari equipment, etc.) With Mr D'Silva's help, a large plot had been obtained and the school expanded. He wanted to see every child in school and was most generous in paying fees.

After the opening of the Junior Seminary in February 1968, on the other side of the Ruaraka River, Fr. John Kennedy informed the Eastleigh Community that he had been appointed to take care of "Baba Dogo" and the new Kariobangi building estate nearby and the other smaller centres to the North and East. His neighbours will be the Maryknoll Fathers in the new Jericho estate parish, bordering on Makadara, which itself neighboured the new Nairobi South parish, where the Dublin Mercies have opened hospital and school. On the far side of the city, the new estates of Woodley and Kibera beyond St. Austin's were allocated to the Guadalupe Fathers.

The new parish in Karen, named after the esteemed Danish settler and writer, had been allocated to the Mill Hill Fathers. The oldest parish on that west side of the city was St. John the Baptist Riruta, partly urban, partly rural. What a contrast between Kevin Carey's thriving 18,000-member parish and Frederick Bugeau's solitary struggle 60 years before that with the indifference of the young and the suspicion of their elders. He had stayed there intermittently for three years. When he is withdrawn, Miss Foxley, veteran Protestant missionary converted to Catholicism, volunteered to stay there and organize a school. She does this till her death in 1923. Riruta is re-occupied again in 1938, when the American Spiritan, John Marx, brings the Teacher Training section of Kabaa there, later transferred to Lioki and thence to Kilima Mbogo!

Br. Josaphat, as usual, had built new buildings and renovated the old, and the modern history of Riruta parish begins. About the same time, colonial urban rules and rates had forced St. Austin's to disband its "Homestead."

For decades they had evaded the law of five families per estate. The coffee-farm was a mere shadow of its past. The coffee must be torn up to make room for growing city suburbs. The proceeds will help resettle displaced homestead families, many of them in Gicharane, a station of Riruta, and finance mission expansion elsewhere. In the 1960s, Fr. Carey will help build up the nearby Precious Blood Convent and hive off Ruku Parish, and in the 70s, Gicharane.

While Fr. Kevin Carey could say that over thirty years he had seen Riruta Parish "grow from a complete backwater to one of the biggest in the Archdiocese," Ruaraka Parish on the opposite side of the city was indeed still a "complete backwater." Nevertheless, unaware of the trauma that might have affected his fellow priests, the newly appointed pastor found a warm welcome in all the six City Council primary schools in the area. Time and space were made available, and soon he found himself drafted into the ecumenical committee working with the Ministry of Education on the pioneering Christian Religious Education syllabus. It was a novel and inspiring experience.

Ethel (Price) Lingard was one of the first to pass her Cambridge School Certificate exam at the St Teresa's Girls School: "There were seven of us. I was the only girl, the others being Steven and Athanasius Lobo, Casimiro Sequeira, Johnny D'Souza, Martin Gunpatrav and Dilip Kumar. My friends were the Almeida girls, Ivy and Clarice, Sarita Menezes, Jean D'Souza, Nina Fernandes. Mother Stanislaus was our teacher.

Mother Gertrude Gallagher was the head of CPS. And music maestro. Mother Teresa Gertrude was the principal of St Teresa's. Mother Stanislaus moved with us (from the Catholic Parochial School attached to the Holy Family Church in the city) to St Teresa's and we also had Mother Thomas More.

Mother Thomas More goes to a church which I frequent. The school that I spent most of my teaching life was the school she attended as a girl. How's that for a coincidence?

Oh, another girl that I still see is Shirley Lobo, her bother was in

Terry's class. She is Jean D'Souza's cousin. I am still in contact with Sarita Menezes, Milena Gracias nee Vaz I have a feeling that St Teresa's church was in existence before the school. We moved into the area in the early fifties, say 1951. School opened in 1953 mid-year.

In the boys' school, Pio Almeida and Michael D'Silva were amongst the first group to have completed the Cambridge School Certificate exam.

IT MAY have been politically correct in 1933 to suggest that the Catholic Church founded a new parish in Eastleigh to meet the religious needs of the devout Catholic Goans, but that would be wrong. Although nowhere as numerous as the Goans, there was a healthy community of Catholic Seychellois, Mauritians and other Indians, especially Tamils from Kerala.

It would not be wrong to say that the Goans were not the backbone of the parish and the community that contributed largely to the growth and expansion of the parish in Eastleigh and elsewhere in Eastern Africa.

There is considerable anecdotal evidence to confirm the above.

Families with young children at the Holy Family Catholic Parochial School had to move to Eastleigh after that school closed its doors. Several decades later I think the Cats of pumping station (Catholic Parochial School) (as that mob from the Goan School turned up their noses and used to call us, we never really understood the implied derision) the school reopened. We, of course, were much cleverer. We called them the Goats of Africa (Goan Overseas Association, whose brainchild the school was). Wow, what an insult that was … calling someone a goat. And a cat, what ignominy! Naturally, there was a fierce rivalry between the two schools. Our opponents were brilliant in almost every sport, so much so that for a long-time sport was somewhat redundant at St Teresa's.

In the early days, a one-armed Kersi Rustomji single-handedly fashioned out a cricket wicket. With the help of Cosmo, the Girls' school's gardener (the politically incorrect term in those days was shamba boy, garden boy), the two regularly cut with a novel scythe, an l-shaped length of iron with the bottom six inches flattened to make the whole look like L, sharpened both sides. One used it as a swinging action cutting in both actions, forward and reverse. But cricket did not last very long, because soon it was an all-girls school. There were no senior boys left and the primary school boys were moved across the road to the boys' school.

There was also an influx of Colonial Government employees and their families from the Government quarters in Ngara.

Nairobi was segregated on racial lines. The Goan community was also segregated … in the occupational sense. The white-collar workers from the Railways and Government were provided housing in Ngara. The catering staff of the Railways lived on the other side of the tracks from Nairobi Railway Station (quite close to the city centre) where they could walk back and forth at odd hours to comply with train schedules.

Many bank and Power and Lighting employees, and non-Government, workers lived in Parklands and the Forest Road area where the whites vacated following a recession in the 1920s.

Dr Rosendo Ribeiro was given a chunk of land in Pangani which he subdivided and made available to his countrymen for a nominal cost. Pangani was higher in the pecking order but below Ngara and Parklands. We are not yet talking about South B, South C and Nairobi West which came much later.

Everyone else who did not fit into the categories above was relegated to Eastleigh. Goans who came from Eastleigh were often looked down upon; even the Dr Ribeiro Goan School had some snobs, often insulting someone as coming from "Eastleigh – Section 3"! Section 3 bordered on the African areas: Racecourse Road, Shauri Moyo,

Kariokor, Starehe.

A friend writes: "Our family went there sometimes for obligatory visits: to fellow villagers from back in Goa. This often led us kids to pray more intensely on coming home. That the Creator would not take our Dad too suddenly. The house would have to be given up and we would have to go and live in Eastleigh! Religion had a high component of self-interest. "Life was what it was: neither bad nor good. Not too many lived in abject misery and if they did, the rest of us as a community did very little to alleviate hardship. Of course, in DRGS, if you were from a brood of 4 or more, the school fees were progressively reduced. At Teresa's, there was a helping hand where it was needed and many survived thanks to such help, as well as that from the St Vincent De Paul Society."

In the Goan clubs and other Goan places of social graces, it was not quite form to discuss the plight of needy in the community. On the contrary, everything possible was done to keep them out ... side ... even out of sight. Many in Eastleigh saved their way to material success. First, they built their homes while making sure St Teresa's did not want for anything. A handful of tailors and carpenters were very successful. The children of Eastleigh went out into the world and did great things. Great contributions to the parish were also made by the Mauritians, Seychellois and the small Parsee community.

GODFREY LOUSADO: Patrick Hannan was the St Teresa's Boys School Principal. He was a strict individual, fond of plays and encouraged the boys to take part in elocution and inter- school plays: *Blind Andy* which won the interschool competition as best play (some actors being Ernest, Vic De Souza, Larry), *Marriage of St Francis* in which I played a small role. *Annie Get Your Gun*. Money raised through plays went to the school extension building fund.

Fr Cremmins was a superb Latin teacher and Vice-principal, others were Lino D'Silva (why did we ever call him Lucha?) History; Regina De Souza – English; Peter Thomas – PT and Maths (I thought he only taught Science, buunsun bunna was his nickname)

St Teresa's Boys' always had good grades at GCE (O Levels), and many students went to join Strathmore College to do their A- Levels. Many Asian kids proceeded to UK, Canada, Australia and others to India like me to pursue University Studies. All emigrated to other pastures post-Independence in Kenya. Most cherish fond memories of their school days at St Teresa's.

WHEN I FIRST WENT to St Teresa's – January 1961 – The Standard 2 class teacher, Mrs Almeida, was on leave and so I was trusted with her class. When she returned, I was a kind of "unofficial supervisor" in the Primary section as there was only one head at the time. I did graduate to some class teaching later. I taught French to the Std. 7 class, but I really have no recollection of what else I did! Apart from being the driver!!

I also remember teaching French to the 3rd form and for this I had to spend time preparing and revising during the holidays!

The Second Vatican Council occurred in 1962 and we used to listen to the reports from the Vatican each lunchtime whilst we were eating our lunch. (In those days, Loreto sisters did not eat in public!)

After two or three years with MTG, I got a new headmistress – Sister Francis De Sales. She was a driver, and so we took it in turns to drive to school.

From the school, one had an uninterrupted view of the Mathare hospital across Mathare valley. Now, this valley has been home to thousands of people and the mental hospital building is no longer in sight.

One Sunday morning, we were called to the school following a break-in. Someone had stolen rolls of uniform cloth which were housed in the office block. We went to Pangani police station and on entering we saw the rolls of cloth in the station. I think that they gave it back to us there and then. They had caught the one who had stolen the cloth.

In the school office, the clerk was Mrs Blanche Nazareth. She was a very efficient and pleasant lady. She used to take me into the city for my driving lessons in the afternoons.

Teachers on the staff were usually quite young and were all very friendly. The older ones were Mrs De Sa, Miss Maisie Nazareth, Mrs Mary Fernandes, Mrs Caroline Alpin and Mrs Delphine Noronha. The "youngsters" were Miss Jeannette, Miss Clemmie, Miss Olga, Miss Florrie, Mrs Marie, Mrs Almeida, Miss Ivy (who married Silu Fernandes who played hockey for Kenya). I remember going to a local park with MTG to see him play in an international match. Miss Elma

We had great dealings with the Boys' school which was presided over by Fr Hannon CSSP and Fr Cremmins CSSP. On St Teresa' Feast in October, we had the day off and both staffs went on an outing which was very popular. 'The Brown Trout' in the Rift Valley was a place which we enjoyed.

The pupils were usually very biddable and had respect for their teachers. Some of the teachers had their own children or sisters in the school. The Paes family, Verona, Maureen and Lilian were sisters of Miss Jeannette. Mrs Noronha had June, Sonya, Fernanda and Colin (we had boys up to Standard three and when we had "housetrained them, they went across the road!!). Mrs Almeida had Francesca, Amelia and Gerard in the school. Mrs Alpin had Teresa and Gail.

Some of the other pupils whom I remember were Rosalind and Maria De Silva, Rosalia D'Mello, Yvette D'Souza, Maria Margaret Fernandes, Fanny and Driscoll D'Costa, Jeanne Nazareth, el al.

In 1972 when I was home on leave from Kenya, I attended the wedding of Fanny D'Costa and the church was full of ex Nairobi Goans. As I had been out to a hospital in London, to visit a former pupil (Irene

Barros) and it was Saturday afternoon, Rosalind D'Silva and I arrived late. In fact, we had just time to get into the back row of the church when the happy couple came down the aisle! We were in time for the reception where many stories were exchanged.

In past years, I have been to two or three reunions of pupils from the Girls' and Boys' schools. These have been very well attended as the Goans like to keep up their club systems.

I was transferred to the Catholic Parochial School in January 1966 and then was involved in the building of the new school which was a building crying out to be refurbished.

In 2004 I attended nephew's wedding in Idaho and then went over to North Carolina to visit my sister and her family. Because of meeting Rosalia, I was invited to visit Toronto and had a wonderful week with her. One day I met up with about 40 past pupils and teachers at a park in the city. They were all excited to talk about school days and we had a lovely afternoon.

During my time there I met up with Elma D'Souza and her husband and was taken to visit Niagara Falls. Elma came down the corridor looking as young and youthful as she had done so many years ago.

Whilst I was in Toronto, I was able to visit Loretto Abbey, the home of the Loretto Sisters of the Canadian Province.

Since I returned from Kenya, I have met up with Ethel Price, now known as Gill, who taught music to the girls in St Teresa's. She is very involved in the local Parish where she plays the organ and trains the choir.

I think that that concludes my memories as after the Catholic Parochial I taught in Eldoret, one year in St Teresa's, Valley Road and Loreto Msongari. I returned to England in 1995 when my mother had a stroke and I was able to visit her before she died in 1995.

Bless you, Sister Thomas More

Anthony B. Almeida

Born to design

ANTHONY B. ALMEIDA, the internationally known architect, who passed away in 2019 at the age of 98 in Dar es Salaam, Tanzania, was one of those rare Goans who chose to live and serve the African country of his birth. However, you could not take the Goan out of him completely. He was also close to Tanganyika's (later Tanzania) first President, Julius Nyerere, himself one of the most outstanding leaders of an African country and one who stepped down from high office and into quiet retirement until his death. Tony, as he was known amongst his friends and family, designed Nyerere's first home.

Tony was born in 1921 in Dar es Salaam to parents who had emigrated to Tanganyika from Goa. He was quite proud of the fact that he went to the J J School of Architecture in Mumbai (1941- 1948). He often said that his architectural studies could be said to have been greatly enhanced by the fact that they took place in a land uniquely endowed with a rich heritage of ancient architecture. He was impressed that the college also placed a great score on the study of this fine heritage.

Another element that also impressed was the group of foreign lecturers who taught at the college. The lecturers also enriched the library with publications and books on architecture from their home countries. Through this, Tony was able to keep abreast the modern trends in architecture from around the world. Through the library, Tony came to learn much about some of the giants of the architecture of the time: Frank Lloyd Wright, Le Corbusier, Erich Mendelsohn, Alvar Santo and Oscar Niemeyer. Their influences instilled in Tony a conscientious search for modern solutions.

Tony worked for a little while in India and was soon elected an associate member of the Royal Institute of Architects of London.

He returned to Dar es Salaam in 1950 and quickly began designing commercial and residential buildings for the Asian community. His Indian influence was easy to spot, mainly by the soft/hard colours his creations were painted (colours that visible in abundance around India and especially during the festival of Holi). "The introduction of Art Deco in the trading quarters of the African cities is of predominantly Indian origin. It characterises itself through pastel coloured concrete, and plastered masonry façades applied too often quite uncomplicated and simple buildings. Most of these buildings have a combined commercial and residential use. In East Africa, these are called the *duka,* shops kept by the Indian trader, the *dukawalla,* who lives in the apartment above his shop. This typology and style remained popular throughout the 1930s to the late 1950s," was how it was recorded in print many years later.

The first few years were a bit of a struggle but then the colonial government, in 1953, asked Tony to design various police stations/posts around the country. In 1954, the Goan community invited Tony to design a primary school (St Xavier's). While some colonial architects turn up their noses at the finished project, Tony would always remember it as the one that made him in Tanzania. When independence came in 1961, Tony was in the right place at the right time. It was not long before, Tanzania was bereft of any white colonial or Asian architects and he was soon designing large office blocks, a library, hospital and lots and lots of new projects. One that is close to his heart is "new" home of the Goan Institute Dar es Salaam he designed for the Goan community. In its infancy, it was quite posh and revolutionary. Folks loved the place.

Amongst other architects that advocated an African' critical regionalism' in their work and writings are Anthony Almeida (born in 1921) in Tanzania, Jean François Zevaco in Morocco, Norman Eaton in South Africa and Demas Nwoko in Nigeria. Engineering Modernity in African Architecture.

The introduction of Art Deco in the trading quarters of the African cities is of predominantly Indian origin. It characterizes itself through pastel coloured concrete and plastered masonry façades applied too often quite straightforward and simple buildings. Most of these buildings have a combined commercial and residential use. In East Africa, these are called the duka, shops kept by the Indian trader, the dukawalla (shopkeeper), who lives in the apartment above his shop. This typology and style remained popular throughout the 1930s to the late 1950s.

VIVIAN A. D'SOUZA: (In Goans_*Tanzanite*) Relatively short in stature and slight in build, but a Giant of a personality. This is our late departed beloved Tony Almeida. He was friendly but unassuming. Of course, my memory goes back to the time I last saw him, over 50 years ago in Dar es Salaam. He was an architectural genius. Our Dar es Salaam Institute is one among many brilliant designs that came from his drawing boards. Our club was founded and known as the Goan Institute until the name was changed in 1963 to Dar es Salaam Institute, in keeping with the times Tony's concept of the building, was like a giant "G" when seen from a bird's eye view. The G enveloped the 'i' which was the open-air sunken dance floor...

The land for our Dar es Salaam Institute was acquired after the First World War, from the Custodian of Enemy Property. This great piece of property was strategically located and convenient to the Goans who all lived in town. The original Goan Institute was like a giant red roof tiled bungalow, with the Hall being the centrepiece of the building, with a large playground on the side where we played football and hockey etc. With a burgeoning membership, the club became too small to serve the membership. Hence a new building was planned. And who else to design the building then our very own member and illustrious architect Tony Almeida.

Tony faced many design challenges. To pay for our new building, half of the playing field was sold to an Oil company to establish a Petrol station. Part of the building (below the Hall) gave way to commercial space, which provided a stream of revenue to pay the building loan. So Tony was, left with constricted space, to construct a facility that would meet the need of our Goans. And the result is evident for all to see. It is a lasting legacy to this great architect.

As long as the building stands, it will be a lasting memorial to him. I do not recall a plaque within the DI acknowledging who the architect was. Tony, probably in his unassuming manner, would have objected. But now that he is no longer with us, I think, a plaque placed in a strategic location within the building should be installed in lasting memory of this great guy.

Tony, may you Rest in Eternal Peace, in the arms of the Lord! *Kwaheri Mzee! Tuta onana (in Swahili, Farewell old man (sign of respect, elder), will meet again.)*

Hemingway and Wife Are Reported Safe After Two Plane Crashes in East Africa

By THE ASSOCIATED PRESS

MONDAY, JANUARY 25, 1954

A New York Times clipping from the Mel D'Souza collection

In 1954, while in Africa, Hemingway was almost killed in two successive plane crashes. He chartered a sightseeing flight over the Belgian Congo as a Christmas present to Mary. On their way to photograph Murchison Falls from the air, the plane struck an abandoned utility pole and "crash-landed in heavy brush."

Hemingway's injuries included a head wound, while Mary broke two ribs. The next day, attempting to reach medical care in Entebbe, they boarded a second plane that exploded at take-off, with Hemingway suffering burns and another concussion, this one serious enough to cause leaking of cerebral fluid.

They eventually arrived in Entebbe to find reporters covering the story of Hemingway's death. He briefed the reporters and spent the next few weeks recuperating and reading his erroneous obituaries. Despite his injuries, Hemingway accompanied Patrick and his wife on a planned fishing expedition in February, but pain caused him to be difficult to get along with. When a bush fire broke out, he was again injured, sustaining second degree burns on his legs, front torso, lips, left hand and right forearm. Months later in Venice, Mary reported to friends the full extent of Hemingway's injuries: two cracked discs, a kidney and liver rupture, a dislocated shoulder and a broken skull. The accidents may have precipitated the physical deterioration that was to follow.

After the plane crashes, Hemingway, who had been "a thinly controlled alcoholic throughout much of his life, drank more heavily than usual to combat the pain of his injuries."

HEMINGWAY: The commander of the ship Edwiges Abreo, was an Asiatic and had long hairs growing out of both ears. For some reason, possibly tribal, which we always respect, he had never cut these hairs and they had attained a length which was, if not enviable, certainly extraordinary. One might even say that they bristled like a hedge and gave him, possibly, his only true distinction. They grew not only from inside his ears but also from the edges of the lobes. He had demanded as a fee for carrying us, Shs. 100/ a head. Since Mr. McAdam had paid for the charter and considered rescued characters could ride on a ship free at his invitation, he protested this charge. Being conversant with maritime law and knowing that the master of the ship was well within his rights even though an exaggerated amount of hair protruded from his ears, I paid this charge and Mr. McAdam made formal protest in writing. I explained to Mr. McAdam over a bottle of Tusker that you always paid these charges and then recovered them when you were in the right. This was subsequently proved true by the receipt of a cheque for Shs. 300/ from the East Africa Railways and Harbours, an eminently just institution which employed the skipper with the slight overgrowth of hair in and on his ears.

RAILWAY CHEF COOKS FOR ROYALTY

1959 P I M Fernandes was pictured as the Chef de Cuisine Royale on the cover of the February 1959 issue of the East Africa Railways and Harbours magazine.

'Pim' Fernandes, who spent most of his 20 years working in a swaying railway coach kitchen at temperatures often around 120 degrees, deserved the royal title. Not only was he a master chef for the railway, he also provided numerous meals for various members of the British Royal Family.

In 1952 he was called to oversee the kitchen at the Royal Lodge in Sagana when Princess Elizabeth and her husband Prince Philip came to Kenya. The Princess and her husband used to pop into his kitchen four or five times a week to weigh their newly caught trout. He used to help them and listen as they chatted about 'wonderful Kenya.'

When the Royal Party were on an overnight at Treetops, they heard the sad news of the King's death in England. Pim remembers with wonder and pride how, despite her deep sorrow at the death of her father, the new Queen came back to Sagana to shake hands with her cook, thank him and say farewell.

During his career with the EAR&H, Pim also served up wonderful meals for other members of the Royal Family: The Duke and Duchess of Gloucester on the special train from Nairobi to Naivasha; Princess Margaret in Dar es Salaam; and the Queen Mother at Government House, Nairobi.

After retiring from the railways, Pim could regale his wife and nine children with stories of how he had cooked for Queen Elizabeth when she was still a Princess.

Pim Fernandes was a really royal cook.

Pim Fernandes, who cooked for royalty, had a 20 year career for EAR&H preparing meals in hot, swaying railway coaches.

The Prince and the pomphret

By Mel D'Souza

(from conversations with Martin, son of Sebastião Rodrigues).

Mel D'Souza is a retired Canadian Goan living in Brampton, Ontario. He is a self-taught cartoonist and illustrator and enjoys writing about 'characters' that he has met over the years. He is the author of FEASTS, FENI & FIRECRACKERS, a book he has written and illustrated about growing up as a schoolboy in the village of Saligao, Goa, (1947 – 1952) when Goa was an overseas territory of Portugal.

During the era when Britannia ruled the waves, Goan cooks were always in demand in India, the jewel of the then mighty British Empire, and in Britain's colonies in East Africa. Like their clerical counterparts in the offices of the Colonial Civil Service, they were competent, reliable, and, above all, adaptable.

Having been raised in a strict Catholic environment in rural Goa, then a Portuguese territory, they acquired respect for higher authority and, from their frugal mothers, learnt to appreciate good food and the way it was cooked with loving care.

It is no wonder, then, that Goan cooks found employment readily in hotels, railway diners, passenger ships, the merchant navy, and even the Royal Navy. Goan cooks adapted well to European cuisine, and many rose to the position of chef. Among this exclusive group were a few who gained renown for their exceptional culinary skills and the introduction of Goan specialties to the fare. One such chef was Sebastião (Sebastian) Benedicto Rodrigues.

Sebastian was born in the village of Moira around 1900 and grew up in a poor family. His father was a "tarvoti", a ship steward, who worked on a British passenger ship, like many a Goan breadwinner of that era. The wife was left at home in Goa to bring up the children.

Sebastian went to the village parochial school and in his spare time was a "gorvan rakno" – a cow herder.

At the young age of 14, a relative took him to Delhi and got him a job as assistant to the cook in a hotel. Sebastian worked diligently and was soon promoted to 'cook'.

In 1925, as a young man with an established profession, Sebastian was offered a job as cook to Col. J. B. St. John, the Resident Governor of Quetta (in Pakistan today). The Resident Governor was the Agent of the Governor-General in Delhi. Sebastian worked in Quetta for three years.

In Karachi at that time, there was a well-known Goan tailor, Trinidade by name, who catered to the rich and famous British elite. He had two attractive and single daughters. One day, a friend suggested that

Sebastian should settle down and start a family and asked if he would consider a proposal from one of Trinidade's daughters. As a humble cook, Sebastian didn't think he stood much of a chance but agreed that the matchmaker put his name on the list anyway. Much to his surprise, he received a formal proposal from one of the daughters which he readily accepted. Thus, Sebastian married Luizinha, and they were blessed with two boys."

When Col. St. John was promoted to Premier of Jaipur, Sebastian moved his family to Jaipur where they lived for about eighteen years. In 1939, Martin was sent as a boarder to St. Anselm's European High School in Ajmer, 30 miles from Jaipur.

In 1945, Col. St. John returned to England, but before leaving introduced Sebastian to the Hon. C.L. Corfield, Agent of the Governor-General in Punjab State, stationed in Lahore.

Sebastian worked for Corfield in Lahore, and when the latter came to Delhi as advisor to the British Government of India under Lord Wavel, he brought Sebastian along with him.

Shortly before India gained its independence in 1947, Corfield moved to South Africa, and Sebastian and his family returned to Goa.

When India gained full independence in 1947, Sebastian returned to Delhi. Foreign countries were beginning to open up new embassies in the capital, and he soon got a job as cook to Capt. William Settle, the US Naval Attache. Barely six months in the job, Sebastian was offered the position of chef to the Belgian Embassy on the recommendation of Mr Corfield who was a friend of the new ambassador, Prince Eugene de Ligne of the House of Beloeil. Sebastian accepted the offer and moved to the Belgian Embassy.

After a month on the job, Prince Eugene held a diplomatic reception at the Embassy, for which Sebastian was given sole charge. Prince Eugene was so impressed with the manner in which the reception was executed, that he showed his appreciation by having a photograph taken of Sebastian with himself, Pandit Nehru and other dignitaries. Regrettably, the photograph was lent to a relative and eventually lost.

Sebastian worked at the Belgian Embassy in Delhi for about four years – a period that was the highlight of his career.

One memorable episode took place during the Belgian Trade Exhibition in Bombay when Prince Eugene hosted a gala banquet at the Taj Mahal Hotel for the diplomatic community and other dignitaries. Sebastian was put in charge of all the arrangements. This is when Sebastian chose to debut 'pomphrets' on the menu.

Now, "pomphret" is a flatfish (*pampus Chinesis*) with a smooth silvery skin that Goans would usually fry in a pan, but over a layer of straw that gave it a unique and distinctive flavour of a fried/smoked fish.

Prince Eugene was so impressed that he asked Sebastian to demonstrate how the fish was prepared. During the demonstration, the secret of Sebastian's perfection was revealed when he flipped the fish in the pan with his bare hands, obviously to remove any strands of straw that could burn and mar the pomphret's silvery skin.

Upon returning to Delhi, the Taj Mahal Hotel requested Prince Eugene to send Sebastian to Bombay to teach their cooks how to cook pomphrets. But Sebastian, who didn't like the attitude of the European manager (at the banquet during the Belgian Exhibition), turned down the invitation.

Back in Delhi, Prince Eugene would not have any chef cook for him other than Sebastian. And one of his favourite dishes was fried pomphret.

One day, the Prince asked Sebastian about his wife's cooking, and Sebastian replied that Luizinha was good at cooking only Goan food. The Prince asked if he could try some of her cooking, and Luizinha obliged; she cooked Goan curries, without chillies, and these became a hit with Princess Yolande, (Prince Eugene's daughter), and her friend, Indira Gandhi. Luizinha also introduced the two ladies to one of Goa's traditional pancakes, 'alebele' (ah-leh- beh-leh); Indira Gandhi loved these so much that she sent her cook to the Belgian Embassy to learn how to cook them.

At the end of his term as Ambassador, Prince Eugene returned to Brussels and took Sebastian along with him. In addition to his full-time job as chef, Sebastian would drive along with Prince Eugene to the racetrack on weekends (free admission as a member of the Royal entourage), and while the Prince sat in the Royal box, Sebastian watched the races from the public enclosure. At the end of the afternoon's races, he would walk back to the Royal box where he got into the car with Prince Eugene to return to the palace. Sebastian had the best of European life going for him, but like every true Goan, he lacked the company of fellow Goans. After only six months in Brussels, he called it a day and returned to Delhi.

Unfortunately, Sebastian didn't get to enjoy retirement for very long; he died in Delhi in 1951.

Making Music

Pictured with Walter(centre) are Godfrey Rodrigues (brother of hockey Olympian Danny Rodrigues) Rosario Rosa (photographer), Peter Coutinho, and Hilary Carasco.

Walter Fernandes

29 May 2020: Bambolim, Goa. ALBERTO RODRIGUES.

Born May 1925. Ex Nairobi. It is with great sadness that we announce the death of Alberto Rodrigues following a short illness some days after celebrating his 95th birthday. In 1955 Alberto took over management of the famous Sequeira's Bar opposite Jeevanjee Gardens in Nairobi from his father and ran the business until it closed in the late 1970s. He was a passionate amateur musician and enjoyed playing the violin and singing. He was well known in Nairobi musical circles and among music lovers in Goa following his retirement there in later years. He will be sadly missed by his surviving brother Scipiao and his many nieces and nephews and their families who held him in great affection. Due to lockdown restrictions, a small funeral service took place in Alto Porvorim on 2nd June when he was laid to rest with his beloved wife Iva who passed away in October 2018. *Goan Voice UK*

By Walter Fernandes

I WAS born in Nairobi, Kenya in 1941. My first love in music was the drums but fate took another hand as I will explain. When I was around six years of age, I was struck by the then relatively unknown disease, polio. I was paralysed in the leg whilst my sister Thelma was affected in the left hand. I was surprised one day when my dad surprised me with a drum set. Being still unable to use one leg, dad would rent the drum set to a Goan band for 50 shillings. Unfortunately, after a few rentals, one drum came back home with a large hole. That did it; he promptly sold it. I was very, very fortunate to recover from polio.

I attended Dr Ribeiro Goan School. One Saturday, my dad returned from an auction with a violin that he purchased for 12 shillings and 50 cents. My musical career kicked off the next Monday when dad arranged for me to be tutored by A.R. D'Costa who was the choirmaster at St. Francis Church.

Sometime in 1957, Dr Ribeiro Goan School Ex-Students awarded me a bursary together with Diana D'Souza, Rudolf Gonsalves and Leandro Saldana to study music at the East African Conservatoire of Music. There I was coached by Nat Kofsky and then Anthony Alvares, a brilliant violinist.

Another award for the young Walter Fernandes

Following that, I won at the Kenya Festival of Music the best violinist under the age of 16. I was very proud to be presented with the trophy by the Governor-General Sir Evelyn Baring.

Dad would make me practice 5 hours a day come whatever, so by the age of 18 was pretty good. Having completed school in 1957, I played as a second violist with The Nairobi Orchestra and in the orchestra at various musical plays brought up by City Players.

I had the pleasure to get to know prominent Goan Musicians well known to the Nairobi musical circles. They were Anthony Alvares, Anthony Noronha (better known as Oboe), Albert Rodrigues (Viola), Luis Pires (Violinist) Guilherme Pires (Bass).

On July 20, 1966, a farewell recital was organized for Anthony (Oboe) Noronha at the residence of J. M. Nazareth Q.C. Oboe had sacrificed so much of his time promoting music within the Goan community. For years, he conducted the junior orchestra. At this farewell recital, nearly every known Goan musician took part. Oboe soon left for the UK, where he, unfortunately, passed away.

In 1984, I was running my own video business. On this particular day a woman, unknown to me, walked into my office, asked me if I was Walter, then asked me if I would like to take part in a movie that was going to be shot in Nairobi. I said yes, after which she asked me if I could arrange for a Goan drummer and pianist. I chose Clifford D`Souza, an excellent pianist and Ronny Coutinho, drummer. It turned out to be Out *of Africa* with Merle Streep and Robert Redford. This movie won 9 academy awards.

Isabella Wise nee de Souza: Sadly, Albert Rodrigues, the violinist mentioned passed away in Goa on March 29, 2020. RIP>

Unknown: Isabella, Albert was a great violinist. Very often Albert with Anthony Alvares, Pires (second violin), Albert (viola). I forget the fourth, would play quartets. Sorry to hear of Albert's passing. Cyprian Fernandes: This was the golden age of classical Goan music in Kenya.

Unknown: Going through my files I found a copy of "A FAREWELL CONCERT TO OBOE". The concert took place at the home of JM Nazareth QC on July 20, 1968 and included sopranos Helen de Souza and Euphemia Fernandes. Brought tears to my eyes. Oboe taught me chess.

The day terrorists attacked our home

By Sultan Somjee

I was seven-year-old when the terrorists attacked our home. We lived in an isolated house in Eastleigh on the outskirts of Nairobi. It was a stone house surrounded by a twelve-foot-high bamboo fence that my grandfather had built to keep away hyenas from the forested Mathare River valley about ten kilometres away. Behind the house was a thirty feet high thorn fence of the St Teresa's Catholic mission and then, there were no other buildings or trees around.

Around mid-1951, we began hearing about an insurgency brewing in Kenya. The elders talked about it on their evening walks. In the same breath, they talked about India's recently ended a hundred yearlong freedom movement and the violence it entailed. Sometimes, I accompanied my grandfather on his walks with his peers because his vision was failing, and he had difficulties seeing in the evening. A year later, in 1952, the governor declared the state of emergency. It was then that we learnt that the gang that had attacked our house was called the Mau Mau, a freedom movement against British colonialism in Kenya. I feared as much as I hated the Mau Mau. To me, they were the terrorists, who had looted our home and terrified us.

It was around two am in the dead of night when I heard the door break like there was an explosion. The crash that seemed to come out of pitch darkness shocked me out of my sleep. It was so intense that even today more than half a century later, I cringe every time when I hear a door slammed. A rock jumped twice on the floor and landed near my bed. Splinters of wood weighed down on my mosquito net like a haul of shells and shrimps in the fisherman's net. We lived in one room. We were a family of five, my parents, my elder brother and my four-year-old sister. The revolutionaries entered immediately. It all happened at once: the bang, the rock, wood splinters flying about the room, and then the phantom faces, their bewildered eyes and sweaty faces set in black wiry dreadlocks. I felt their looks pressing me down. Like ants, they spread around the room with clubs and machetes.

One stood over my mother with a club and another over my father with a machete. A smell like that of caged jungle animals at the zoo filled the room. Later, it was reported on the radio that a contingent of the Mau Mas lived in the caves of the Mathare Valley and that the residents of Eastleigh were asked to immediately report any suspicious character to the police. The guerrillas who roamed from late evenings to dawn were in two groups: forest guerrillas who mostly attacked white plantation owners, and urban guerrillas who attacked residences in the towns. We were, most probably, attacked by the urban guerrillas.

At that moment of the horror of the attack on our house, all I saw was the terrorists' bloody eyes scuttling about the room, impatient and jumpy like a flock of trapped birds. When one of them looked at me, I felt stabbed. I saw my father dragged across the room and tied to a chair. They gagged my parents with dirty socks left for washing in a bucket. My brother and I sat back-to-back on one bed, terrified. Our backs were wet, absorbing each other's sweat. I continued looking down, pressing my chin to my chest and calling on God to help, while all the time, I felt bloodshot eyes tearing into me.

They started emptying clothes and whatever there was from the cupboards. From under the heap of clothes that they had made on the floor, my sister's doll cried musically, which fascinated one of them. He stood there momentarily and then picked up the pink plastic English doll and began turning it over, listening to the melodic note from its perforated back. Hearing the sound of her doll crying, my little sister woke up suddenly, bright-eyed in wonder, smiling and talking excitedly as four-year-olds do, chattering to herself, and walking around her cot holding the bars of the metal frame. Then she stopped and watched, her eyes widened, inquisitively, puzzled at what was happening. "My dhingly doll!" she wailed in Swahili. "I want my dhingly doll." She began crying and looking around for Mother.

The General, as I heard them calling their leader, turned around and looked at my sister. His bloodshot eyes stilled on her. I froze. He was over six feet tall. He stood there like a giant by the cot. He had his palms on his hips, arms akimbo. Then his red eyes softened like a father's eyes put to the child appealing for a favour.

"Don't take the little girl's ka-rendi, and anything else that belongs to this child," he instructed his men. When finally, the Mau Mau left after what seemed like a night of plunder and terror, they had taken everything in the house that they could carry. My clothes, shoes and even my Mechano set was gone. But there was a pile of dresses, toys and shoes left behind on the floor. The revolutionaries had left behind everything that belonged to my little sister.

Years went by. The horrific propaganda against the Mau Mau lessened, and the story of the attack on our home faded into a distant nightmare. Kenya became independent in 1963. We celebrated liberation from colonial rule and end of racism only to pave a way for nationalism and brutal dictatorships that followed. I completed my high school, joined the university, went overseas to do post-graduate studies and returned in the early seventies to join the University of Nairobi as a research fellow in material culture. I was interested in Africa's indigenous cultures and its history from 'the people's point of view'. I had started leaning towards socialism and joined the rural theatre that was an outfit of the underground against the despot Jomo Kenyatta.

I worked with the communities of peasants, farm and factory workers in an area that was known as the hub of the Mau Mau. I came across former Mau Mau fighters and almost everyone had a relative in the anti-colonial organization. Ironically, the first play, *Ngaahika Ndeenda* (I will marry when I want), that we put up was about the Mau. The experience had an impact on me for I began to think differently about the Mau. They were no longer the wild terrorists who had looted and traumatized me and my family but revolutionaries fighting for liberation from colonialism. They became heroes in my young man's mind. I read everything I could lay my hands on about the Mau. I even drew them from photographs. The frightful images of their eyes in my mind changed to those of heroic warriors with idealism shining on them faces that spoke of sacrifice for freedom and human dignity. Today, as I turned 75, my mind sometimes immerses in reflections from the past that come and go like waves of an ocean washing so vast a shore of my lifetime. There are self-thoughts on the good deeds and bad deeds I have done. Some fill me with pride about my achievements, and some with sadness about my deceits and failures.

Some are full of fear and even hate that sometimes I speak out loudly to myself in abuses hurled at someone or something. Self- talk, I have come to accept, comes with aging in some people. Sometimes, a dream from my childhood returns in a scream. The sound of the door crashing down on me has stayed with me. The image of the bloodshot eyes of the Mau revisits me. Sigmund Freud would call them childhood memories in my sub-conscious and construct a theory around it to write an essay on my personality. However, when awake and with a conscious mind, when I talk about the night when the Mau attacked our house in Eastleigh in Nairobi when I was seven years old, I speak about the compassion of the leader they called the General. How he looked at my four- year-old sister and kindness filled his bloodshot eyes even as he held the deadly machete in one hand.

I speak about this incident as a reflection on humanity that I have come to know we all have in us. That even the fiercest looking people from other countries, other cultures, and other religions that we see or hear about on the media as enemies carry compassion in their hearts. One day, I wish to write a story for children called 'When the terrorists attacked our home'.

Olaf Kenneth Ribeiro an extraordinary man

Olaf Kenneth Ribeiro was born in Nairobi Kenya, the son of Dr Manuel & Angel Ribeiro de Santana. His siblings include the late Dr Gerry Ribeiro – Cancer researcher at the Christie Holt Radium Hospital in Manchester, UK, the late Hubert de Santana – writer and poet, Toronto, Canada and sister Teresa Quadros presently living in Paradise Valley, Arizona. His grandfather Dr Rosendo Ribeiro was the first medical doctors in Kenya arriving on a Dhow in 1900. He made his medical rounds on a zebra. The only person to have ever tamed a zebra!

I went to the Doctor Ribeiro Goan School in Nairobi and later transferred to the Technical High School to finish my secondary education. I then went to Britain to finish my pre-college curriculum. Then received a scholarship from the Kenya Government to attend Egerton Agricultural College, Njoro, Kenya where I also managed the 1500-acre farm splitting the animal husbandry duties with a colleague while I managed the agronomy aspects of the farm.

After graduation, I worked at the Grasslands Research Station in Kitale. I then received an AID scholarship to attend West Virginia University to study Plant Pathology and returned to the Plant Breeding Station, Njoro the after obtaining my master's degree. After a year of working at this location decided to go back to the US to obtain my PhD degree in Plant Pathology. I was then hired by the University of California Riverside to work on a particular disease of Citrus and Avocado. I became a world authority on this pathogen –Phytophthora. This pathogen originally caused the potato blight in Ireland in the 1850s. Because of the importance of this pathogen to agriculture worldwide, wrote two textbooks on this pathogen.

I got involved with plants through the influence of my mother who was an avid gardener and taught me much about growing plants. However, I was always curious about trees and how they managed to go so big and survive so many years. I so realized that just about everybody I met loved trees and the calming effect they had on people. However, everyone took them for granted. It was much later that I realized no one knew how to diagnose tree problem – or how to treat diseased trees. I decided that with my background in plant pathology I should develop techniques to save trees. This has been successful resulting in my being asked to give seminars across the US and in Britain and Hungary.

Meanwhile, I realized that saving trees also clashed with developers who wanted to remove trees for their developments. This resulted in many contentious exchanges with developers and the city. In a couple of cases resulting in taking the city to court to save trees! Also arranged for demonstrations to save trees! My campaign to save trees continues. After some 20 years of campaigning, finally got the city to pass a tree ordinance to protect important and historic trees.

Also, I give tree walks to show people the importance of trees. Last year with the help of a computer specialist, tagged the trees downtown with an IT address that people could scan and get information on their cell phone about that particular tree.

History's Heroes Feb 2019 Speech for Olaf

I am so honoured to be here tonight to honour a very special islander. Dr Ribeiro has been active in our community in meaningful ways that restore and protect our island's most vital natural resources. In my opinion, Dr Ribeiro is a genuine example of Bainbridge Island's 'old guard.' These engaged citizens, like Olaf, stand watch as sentinels for our quality of life, and as advocates for systems-thinking which is the gateway towards ecological health for all.

Dr Ribeiro was born in East Kenya and had an international career in plant pathology before he arrived on our island in August of 1981. His life-long passion as a plant pathologist and horticulturist are highly valued among islanders, and our city government as well. Dr Ribeiro has been able to use his vast experience as a scientist, steward and educator to inform and rescue many heritage trees on our island.

We oft regard Dr Ribeiro as Bainbridge Island's real-life Lorax. In this wildly popular Dr Seuss children's story, the passionate creature called The Lorax "speaks for the trees." In all the years many of us have had the honour to know Dr. Ribeiro, or as we call him, Olaf, he certainly embodies the spirit of giving voice to the voiceless, much like the whiskered creature that rises from the stump to question and halt an act of deforestation.

Here on Bainbridge Island, we don't have any native Truffula trees, but we do have trees — and lots of them! Environmental, educational and cultural organizations such as Island Wood, the Bainbridge Island Historical Museum, and Sustainable Bainbridge have for several years collaborated with Dr Ribeiro on many community events. You might be familiar with Olaf's wildly popular Historic Tree Walks of Downtown Winslow, and I gather – a tree walks to Crystal Springs soon too. Olaf was instrumental in organizing our island's first-ever Earth Month Bainbridge Island, now an annual event, that serves as an umbrella for much non- profit organization's programs about Arbor Day and Earth Day.

Our island needs advocates and a citizenry that is informed and engaged in the protection of our natural resources. Dr Ribeiro walks his own talk every day. Dr Ribeiro is certainly one of History's Heroes. I'm also proud he is my mentor and my friend.

His expertise, generosity of spirit and humour inspire us every day.

Christina Doherty

Kenya lost a warrior, Goans a champion

THE VILLAGE of Saligao, Goa, has lost one of its illustrious sons. Kenya has lost a warrior and the dwindling pioneer Goan community has lost a champion in many ways. CYPRIAN FERNANDES pays tribute Dr Manuel (Manu) D'Cruz with the help of a few friends. He was one of the few Asians to be decorated with the award Order of the Warrior by the then Kenyan President Daniel arap Moi. This just was one of many other awards and recognitions showered on him.

Manu was an ultra-dedicated Ear Nose and Throat specialist and consultant surgeon. He travelled the length and breadth of Kenya as a medical philanthropist to thousands of Kenyans who otherwise would have gone without. Most of these services were free of charge.

I think, at one time, Manu was the only ENT specialist and surgeon in Kenya and almost every Goan knew him. If not as a doctor, they knew him as a champion of all things Goan. He was the founder of the Goan Cultural Society. He played a significant role in the Kenya Goan Sports Association and the powerful Kenya Hockey Union. Above his social love was the Nairobi Goan Gymkhana. He was president/chairman on many, many occasions. If there was a committee position to be filled and no one to fill, Manu usually put his hand up. He played a little badminton and loved his glass of Tusker beer. He attended virtually social and sports occasions at the club.

Outside the club, he was an outdoors fanatic. He loved camping, fishing and celebrating the millions of stars on show in the Kenya bush. He put his surgical skills to fair use when it came to skinning that night's dinner.

Others join in paying tributes to the late Dr Manu: JERRY LOBO (Moira): We all have very fond memories of Dr Manu. I still recall a trip to Mombasa in early 1980. I went with Dr Manu and Dr Clara in his white Volvo 244 "KQT 243". He was a very skilled and fast driver, I must say. We left early and were in Mombasa for lunch.

During this trip and while we were at the Mombasa Institute, I felt a sore throat coming along and told my mum about it. She suggested I speak to Doc and I did. He looked at me and said: "Come with me". I thought he was going to his car to get me some medication. Instead, we headed for the MI bar and he ordered me a nice shot of Brandy which did the trick. The best place to find him on any Saturday was the Nairobi Goan Gymkhana from 12.30 pm sharp. One Saturday I got there a little early. Like clockwork, Dr Manu arrived and ordered a cold Tusker beer and some hot samosas! We enjoyed our meeting and he insisted it was his "shout" instead of the other way round – that was Doc Manu. At Dr Clara was waiting for her husband to come home to lunch.

JOHNNY AND MAURA LOBO (Moira): We have been friends for a long time. One afternoon in our earlier years, we saw Mrs D'Cruz carrying Manu in her arms, running towards our house and screaming to my mother that her little boy was dying. My mother opened the door and Mrs D'Cruz told her Manu had stuffed an acorn seed in his nose, stopped breathing and turned blue. My mother, who was crocheting at the time, had the presence of mind to use the crochet needle and with a steady hand dislodged the seed and Manu began breathing again. Manu told us while growing up, he heard that story many times from his parents, and it was one of the reasons he was inspired to become an ENT.

When Manu practised as an ENT Consultant, our memories of him were of a loving, compassionate gentleman. He was fond of our six children. Whenever I took them for a check-up, he would come out and say, 'My girl, what's the problem and which one of them is it this time?' He was always so kind with his words and deeds and looked after us all with such care. We have very fond memories of our dear friend Manu.

Dr Manu founded the Goan Cultural Society in Nairobi, Kenya and contributed to the success of uniting the Goan community under the umbrella of cultural and social gatherings. These included the Annual Mando and Theatrical Festivals promoting and showcasing our Goan and Portuguese heritage through music, song and dance. He also presented them with an annual trophy in the shape of copper *gummot* (a traditional Goan clay pot with a leather tied firmly at the opening and another at the bottom. It is often referred to as the national instrument of Goa.)

MERVYN MACIEL: My recollections of Manu go back to my childhood as we were neighbours in Nairobi. It was to the D'Cruz household that we were taken to when my mother died. I met Manu briefly when we were both schooled at St Paul's in Belgaum. He later left for Bandra and we lost touch. We were to meet again when he returned after completing his medical studies in Edinburgh.

Manu was a great help to my late brother, Wilfred. We were to meet again during his regular trips to London when visiting Lillian. Manu and I are of the same age and I are already missing him.

CYPRIAN FERNANDES: When I first met Manu D'Cruz not many Goans knew what a medical consultant was in those early days. Neither did I. I would pop into his office in Vedic House on my way to the Court House, City Hall for coffee with the lawyers or a snack at one of the nearby outlets. We had long hours of talks about the Kenya Hockey Union and his passion for improvement. He had a vast imagination and lofty ideas. Once, he even though the game could go professional, like English soccer already had. But, in Kenya and one murram ground at City Park? And his answer was: You never know. Time will tell.

We rekindled our friendship when he was on a brief visit to Sydney. I was president of the local Goan association, and he seemed to spend every moment encouraging me to greater deeds in the service of the local Goan community.

Doc was that kind of a guy, just one of kind, the very good kind, and the world is surely the poorer for his passing.

Braz "Matatabooks" Menezes (Saligao): Manu was senior to me by about ten years. I knew him growing up as his father was very active in the Goan Gymkhana. He left for boarding school in Goa or Bangalore in about 1948 and didn't return to Nairobi for nearly 25 years. After that, we met each other regularly at the club. He was always very involved in the club's activities, on every committee, and was never short of ideas for moving the club forward. I enjoyed the early days as we all had time on our hands, and until his dear Clara came along, his evenings were free.

He was the first to respond when my mother collapsed and died on the GG's dance floor on December 26, 1967.

Dr Manuel Joseph D'Cruz, son of Priscila and Lawrence D'Cruz was born in Nairobi, Kenya in 1928. He had three sisters: Lina, Lydia and Lillian. He started school at the Dr Ribeiro Goan School but he and his sisters left for Belgaum near Goa when his mother passed away when they were all pretty young.

Dr Manu attended high school at St Paul's high school in Belgaum and secondary school at St Stanislaus High School in Bandra, Bombay. He did his junior Bachelor of Science, in St Xavier's College Bombay, and was enrolled to study medicines in B.J. Medical College, Ahmedabad, Gujarat University.

As a true Goan, he taught his friends to let their hair down, especially during his medical degree days. He had a song in his heart too, Ole Man River in a minor baritone voice.

He did his post-graduate degrees in the UK: DLO, RCP&S om ENT in London from the Royal College of Physicians and Surgeons, and his FRCS in Otolaryngology. He returned to Kenya and had been in consultative practice since 1962. In 1972 he married Dr Clara D'Cruz. Nationally and internationally, Dr Manu held numerous professional appointments (especially as a consultant) and served on just as many committees. He was renowned.

During his long illness, he often told friends he "was in his transit lounge. His call for boarding on the stairway to heaven came in November 2019.

Harold George D'Souza

This celebration of a great buddy has been long overdue. I have been slow getting off the mark for one unforgivable reason or another. His fans have been quite vociferous: write the story! At last, here it is.

IT IS one of life's greatest gifts when you meet someone who is a very special human being: genuinely popular with everyone he has met, naturally honest, unassuming and humility personified. You would think anyone with the happy baggage of all those accolades might be overloaded with a tendency to trip here or there, but not HAROLD GEORGE D'SOUZA.

He was blessed with great parents. George D'Souza was a great club man and a public speaker in demand at the club, at weddings, christenings and other social events. He was also an avid sportsman and instilled this love of sports in both his sons: Harold George and the late Peter George, who left this earth doing what he loved most in his leisure hours, fishing.

I think his greatest gift has been the God-given ability to look any challenge, any mishap, anything that life has thrown his way, including several challenges of limb and illness dead-straight in the eye and soldier on regardless of whatever might be.

Perhaps his greatest blessing has always been the four women in his life: wife Hazel and daughters Hayley, Gail, Hylette. These joys of life were increased ten-fold and more with sons-in-law David Walker, the late Sean MacKay and Greg Evans and, of course, the greatest delights of all, the grandchildren: Aaron and Shanyce Walker, Lachlan Mackay, Ethan, Blake, Noah and Willow Evans. Harold is not one to show-off or big-note himself, even when talking about his grandchildren, he does it with quiet elegance, almost understating the praise but it is written over his beaming face. Tony and Rebecca D'Souza, the late Tony Coutinho and Lucinda, my late wife Rufina and I have spent many summers as guests of Mal and Margaret Ferris at their mountain lodges at Eaglereach in the wine country not far from Sydney. Once when we had a whisper of wind in our hair, we used to meet on most Saturday nights for dinner, a few jokes, and happy banter and grateful that we were able to do so.

Harold has an infectious smile, a sharp defence of his beliefs and his considered points of view, a hearty laugh and consideration for others above all. He is also a fish curry and rice addict, prawn curry most welcome or any traditional Goan dishes. He is just a jolly good bloke.

Of course, Harold and Hazel were also big supporters of the Goan Overseas Association since its inception in Sydney during the early 1970s. They still are, to a large degree.

But that is not the reason for this humble celebration of a man we all admire. More than anything else, Harold has always been a dedicated sportsman. He grew up in Kisumu and Mombasa and most of the capital cities, the provincial headquarters and where a few Goan got together their lives would be dominated by the Goan Institute whose members had an almost religious dedication to sports, social events, concerts, and this and that. But it was sports that dominated club life both in individual events and team sports. This love of sport was nurtured by success at district and province-wide competition. Perhaps the greatest rivalries were reserved for inter-club sports visits. Club sport was more than just playing the game, there was always all the social aspects of growing up, boy meets girl and vice versa.

Goans mainly from Mombasa and Nairobi produced half players at each of the Olympics since 1956.

There was plenty to play for and, if you did not make it at representative level, there were plenty of rewards at club level.

Harold and some of his siblings were born in Kisumu, the charming pioneering town on the shores of the mighty and legendary Lake Victoria. Like everywhere elsewhere there was a sizeable Goan community, there was the Goan Institute mainly sport, social and cultural events. When he was eight years old, his parent decided to send him to St Paul's High School in Belgaum, a few hours' drive from villages in Goa. He spent a year in Parra, Goa after he fell ill.

Soon after he arrived in Mombasa, he was playing those games little boys play including seven tiles (I wonder how many of you remember this, hop, hop, hop etc game) and, of course, cricket and hockey. He was soon captain of the Mombasa Goan School cricket and hockey teams. He played centre-forward in hockey and was an opening bat in cricket. He says, he was a shy a little boy. Hard to believe, with those large laughing eyes!

At school, he also excelled in 100m, 200m, long jump, high jump, shot putt, triple jump, javelin, discuss. Harold won the junior Victor Ludorum and Albert Castanha won the senior Victor Ludorum.

It was long before he had smoothly slipped into the senior club sides in both sports. He picked up the cricket captaincy fairly early in club career and visited the neighbouring coastal towns in Tanzania and, of course, Zanzibar.

He also visited Nairobi many times to play in the M R De Souza Gold Cup which was the pre-eminent knock-out hockey tournament in East Africa. His Mombasa teammates included some of the legends of the Mombasa game: Alban Fernandes (who played cricket and hockey for Tanganyika), Peter George D'Souza, Patrick Martins, Albert Castanha, Walter Castanha, Reynolds Pereira, Franklin Pereira, Michael Pereira, Edwin Fernandes, Silvano and Leslie Pinto, Procop Fernandes and his son Michael.

The legend, Sana (Agnelo De Souza) coached many a team Harold played in.

This was especially true of Baobao team which was founded by Sana.

Most hockey players also played cricket. Eventually, Harold was poached for the Coast Gymkhana team, where he enjoyed a lot of success. Even more, success came when he swapped his bat for the cricket umpire's hat. A rare honour came his way when he was asked to umpire the MCC v Coast XI. The English team was led by a young former South African, Tony Greig, who went to lead England and later spent most of his life as a top cricket commentator.

Naturally, Harold was also a gifted track athlete, specialising in the 100m and 200m dash and trained and ran against the like of Seraphino Antao, Albert Castanha (one of his best friends), Joe Faria and Alcino Rodrigues.

As I said, Harold was a sports nut and good at all of them: hockey, cricket, soccer, tennis, badminton, table tennis, and snooker. Harold was the father of sport in the Goan Overseas Association in Sydney, NSW. He began with organising sports at the various picnic days the association hosted and eventually raised two teams to play indoor and outdoor cricket, a hockey team and indoor soccer team to take on Melbourne in two reciprocal visits. He also introduced and nurtured a healthy men's and women's darts teams as meeting the needs for table tennis fans at the annual- club sports days. MALCOLM MONTEIRO: When I first arrived to go to University in Sydney in the early 1980s, my parents put me in touch with a few Goan icons from Kenya. One of those was Harold George, who would have known my parents through the various Goan clubs and sports connections from the old days.

Harold had been living in Sydney for some time and was the Sports Secretary and Hockey Captain of the GOA NSW. Harold invited me to play and train with the club on Sundays. He gave me the chance to play at centre-half position for several years under his captaincy. I remember catching the public transport from the University to the northern suburb of Hornsby, where Harold would pick me up and drive me to training. We always enjoyed a beer after training, which was the highlight of my Sunday. The GOA Sydney/Melbourne matches were incredibly competitive, and the blue-ribbon event of the sports visit long weekend. It pits Goan family against Goan family and all the boys played seriously as if it was for 'sheep stations.

Harold was a great captain who was humble, calm and exemplified sportsmanship. The team played well together under him. I will always remember Harold, as a great sportsman who put a lot of effort into developing and mentoring young players. He is also a committed family man and I enjoyed spending time with his family during our sports visits.

With the assistance of Tony Fernandes, he organized several full-programmed athletics meetings. As much as he achieved in encouraging adults to play sports, he was more delighted to see so many youngsters taking up the games of their choice. In Sydney, Harold was the eternal cricket wicketkeeper and captain and Alban Rattos the two formed a formidable bond. Alban was one of my favourite batsmen and I got to see him just a few times, but he was all class and polish. He was GOA Sportsman of the Year one season and his daughter Hylette was Sportswoman of the Year the same year.

He scored his first century playing for the Grace Brothers team. These days he is happy to enjoy his sport from the armchair and the TV screen. Njoy, you more than most have earned the right to relax after having given so much of your life to sport and encouraging so many youngsters to take up the sport of their choice. As they read this, I am sure they will be raising a glass or two in celebration of their friend: Harold George.

Harold seated extreme right

Harold and Hazel

Ray Batchelor

The Sultan of sport

"Defeat is not declared when you fall down. Defeat is declared when you refuse to get up".

Was training on the sweet sands of Mombasa beaches the secret of their success?

Raymond Harold Walter Batchelor, (24-06-1924 – 5-02- 2006) better known as Ray, is known the world over as the coach who partnered the British Goan legend Seraphino

Antao to the 1962 Perth Commonwealth Games sprint double for Kenya one year before independence from Great Britain. Antao was born in

Chandor, Goa, and brought to Mombasa by his parents. In 1954, Antao was a promising soccer player, broke an ankle and thought he would never play again. A friend took him to an athletics meeting in Mombasa. Later he met Ray and the rest, as they say, is history.

Ray was born in 1924 in East London's Canning Town. For centuries Canning Town has remained one of the most deprived areas in the UK, with long-time residents suffering poor health, low education and poverty. Canning Town appears to come directly out of a Charles Dickens novel, depicting the dark, grey, dimly lit pathos of the poor London town of his era. It is no surprise then that with dedication and hard work, young Ray set about changing his life. At the age of 17, he volunteered to serve in World II. He joined No. 6 and later No. 12 Commandos. His group were among the first to parachute under night cover in German-occupied France to blow up bridges and prepare strategic areas for D-Day. He was said to be "brave" and never one who did things "by half measures".

After being Africanised Kenya, he went to Malawi in 1967 as Director of Sport and Coaching for five years. He built up an incredible football side which had many successes against other powerhouses like Ghana, Zambia, Uganda and other African countries. He was also heavily involved in Malawi athletics and boxing and prepared teams for both the Olympics and Commonwealth Games.

Later he moved to Zimbabwe where he successfully coached Mangula to several soccer trophies and was awarded "Rhodesian Football Coach of the Year."

In 1982 he moved to Witwatersrand University in South Africa until he retired at the age of 70. He enjoyed a lot of success with the Wit's Club. As usual, he was highly successful in various aspects of sports life at the University and much admired. Again, as always, his enthusiasm was infectious. Later he moved Cape Town and worked at the famous Newlands Cricket Club in administration. His daughter Claire says: "Sport was his life. He was one of a kind! He was one of the kindest, hardest working and loving fathers. We miss him tremendously and will always be so grateful for our wonderful, special father. As always, we wish we could turn the clock backwards."

In Kenya, Ray held many of jobs including Community Sports and Welfare Officer, Provincial Sports Officer, Athletics and National Football coach (1960-66) National Schools soccer coach (1962-67), PE teacher and games tutor in St Thomas Aquinas Nairobi, Alliance Boys' High School, Njoro Agricultural College. He also did a lot of work with the Kenya squads in hockey, athletics and boxing especially for the Commonwealth and Empire Games and the Olympics. Ray held high positions in the various national sports organisations. He was the founder of the National Soccer League, Secretary of the Coast Sports and Boxing associations, secretary or chairman of other sports association throughout the country. His CV would fill a mini book. He qualified as a Football Association coach at the famed Loughborough College in the British Midlands. As he did in Kenya, Ray played a massive role in the emergent sporting life of Malawi. The rugged Ray was in the very first place a sports-crazy guy. He loved to play soccer, cricket, run around the track and dedicated to physical education (muscle building). He once said: "While cricket does not appear very much in my CV, I have enjoyed the game thoroughly as player and coach. I played the second XI with Essex County who sent me to the Alf Glover Coaching School in London. In Kenya, I played provincial cricket and gained caps against Pakistan, India, Commonwealth Cavaliers, MCC and other teams. I coached quite a bit until a knee injury forced me to hang up the bat."

He coached and played for the mighty Liverpool soccer team in Mombasa. Here was a white man playing and coaching young black guys, Arabs, Swahilis (a mixture of African and Arab by breeding) and Goans, at a time when the Kenyan colony was slowly loosening the grip on its version of apartheid, "separate development." The Ray I knew could not have given a stuff about the colour of anyone's skin; he was more concerned that if you were there to train, then your commitment had to be total.

Ray coached Liverpool to championship wins of the Kenya Football Association cup several times. Their derby encounters with the local Feisal Club are now mostly forgotten. Hence, Ray was the Sultan of Coast sport. Anybody who could coach a team to a soccer championship win had to be a king or a sultan. After he had moved on from the Coast, he would go on to coach the Kenya national soccer side for several years.

Ray had started his soccer career while growing in England. He was a junior in the great West Ham United before playing in the English Southern League. West Ham has been a part of the English Premier League, on and off for many decades.

Ray fell face-first into some big soccer storms with the Kenya national team. One was not of his making but the negative stuck. I was there in 1965, at Jamhuri Park Showground where Kenya was playing the Ghana All-Stars as the Republic Day drawcard attended by the President of Kenya, Jomo Kenyatta, and a vast array of local and international dignitaries. At half time the score was 6-1. Kenyatta walked out and never went to another football match in his life. The final score was 13-2. To be fair to Ray, he had taken over the role of coach just before the start of the match. Peter Oronge, who had been in charge, had a mental meltdown and abandoned the team.

The Kenya team was: Joseph Were, Tom Sabuni, Jonathan Niva, Anthony Mukabwa, Moses Wabwai, Joseph Okeyo, John Rabuongi, Nicodemus Arudhi, William Chege Ouma, James Asibwa and Moses Ambani.

Kenyan writer Roy Gachuhi wrote of that day. "Ray Batchelor was a determined man. He believed in all things being possible. He was one of those White people who believed in the African cause and had thrown his lot with black Kenyans full- bloodedly. He always wore a cheerful smile – but it was conspicuous by its absence today. He was red in the face. And yet, there was still friendly game two against the Black Stars in a harrowing two days to come."

Ray Batchelor told me: "Many people told me I was mad to take charge of the team at such short notice. Maybe I am mad but, I am a coach and, when Kenya needs me, I will do my best. But I am not a magician, nor can I perform miracles." For a long time, he had a lot of difficulty in coming to terms with the 13-2 thrashing. He knew there was another defeat coming his way. He was having nightmares in daylight. I could not see anything to shout about on the horizon. Kenya was thrashed, comprehensively beaten, annihilated and if there is ever a sure bet, this was the one to put your house on. I wrote that day: "Kenya face the almost frightening prospect of taking on the Black Stars again at Nairobi's Jamhuri Park Stadium. Another crushing defeat is the only reasonable forecast after the events of Saturday." According to Batchelor, "The Black Stars gave us an abject lesson in hard, accurate shooting. This is a lesson our forwards must learn before tomorrow evening." Anyway, he found a way and the result in the second match was a respectable 3-3.

Athletes who represented the Coast at the Kenya National championships with the legendary British middle- and long-distance runner Sir Chris Chataway: Rear from left: Albert Castanha (sprinter), Hugh Winder

(Shot Put), Chris Chataway, Alfred Vianna (Discus and Shot), Joe Faria (sprinter), Francis Soares, Seraphino Antao (sprinter, hurdler, long jumper). Front row:

Jaswinder Singh (Olympic hockey, middle distance), Alcino Rodrigues (440 yards, 8 80 yards), Austin D'Souza .... (??), Norbert De Souza.

In the early days with Seraphino, Ray had his work cut out. Seraphino "could sometimes be a handful" (very strong-willed about what he thought was best) but once he began to see the results he was getting out of working with Ray, they took the baby steps on the long hard road to history with somewhat complete dedication. Multi-sports winner: sprinter, hockey star, netball, badminton: Laura Ramos says "Under Coach Ray Batchelor's guidance, I homed in my sprinting skills, improved starts by watching Albert Castanha, Seraphino Antao and the other male sprinters. Later he taught me how to use starting blocks to get fast starts. As a coach, he set examples of respect for other competitors, not resting on your laurels, using your inborn energy and talents to be a winner. I never heard him put down any athlete and boosted anyone who showed any disappointment in being second-best. I have used all this advice my entire life in all I do.

"I looked up to him as My Hero and a Godsend. I have never forgotten him as I hold him."

Alcino Rodrigues, Albert Castanha, Seraphino Antao

Laura was part of the Coast athletics clubs called the Achilles Club started by Ray its membership comprised of the best Goan athletes around the Coast and on the national scene: Albert Castanha, Joe Faria, Seraphino Antao, Pascoal Antao, Alcino Rodrigues, Jack Fernandes, Laura Ramos, Phila Fernandes, Juanita Noronha, Meldrita Viegas, Alfred Vienna, Bruno D'Souza. And several others whose names I do not have. Most of those named above are all winners at one time or another in their events. Most of them were sprinters. Alcino Rodrigues was a promising quarter and half-miler.

ALCINO RODRIGUES: "Ray Batchelor was singularly instrumental in the sporting careers of many in Kenya and especially in Mombasa. Fortunately, I was one of the few blessed to be the product of his great contribution to Kenya Sports. In 1956, given the choice between Soccer & Track, Ray felt I would be better off in Track. Hence my specialty in the 400 which, through hard work, Ray's guidance and dedication to the sport, I earned the Coast and Kenya colours in the event. In 1968, I carried these skills into the Canadian Masters Track &

Field for several decades, with great success, retiring from the sports at 80 a few years ago.

"Ray arrived in Mombasa as a Soccer and Athletics Coach in the 1950s. Although he initially worked on soccer players' physical fitness, it was in Athletics that he made the most impact in Mombasa and Kenya despite many challenges from other coaches in the country including claims for the success of many coast athletes and soccer players.

"In Mombasa, Ray was fortunate to embrace several unpolished diamonds as his trainees, which he singularly and painstakingly polished and shined making some, in Track & Field, the envy of Africa and the world.

"To me, Ray was more than a Track coach. He was a true role model, a confidante and a hero. Someone to look up to. Ray was also a disciplinarian. He minced no words and would always say the way it was, whether you liked it or not. In my life, of four scores, I have come across very few of his like. One of his greatest saying to me was: "Defeat is not declared when you fall. Defeat is declared when you refuse to get up". What a confidence builder. I have carried this advice all my life, both in my personal, corporate and professional life, and have passed it on to our only child Dominic. I am now drilling it into our four grandchildren who are already exhibiting signs of sporting prowess, albeit in soccer and swimming.

"At a time when the non-whites, especially the Africans, were viewed differently in Kenya, Ray genuinely and sincerely showed that he was one of us and was often pilloried by his Mombasa Club mates for leaning too much towards the non-whites. Amidst all this, Ray also exuded his true humane side by always making time to listen to our concerns and was ever ready to help, including financially. Ray was not your normal "Kaburu" (Swahili slang for white man) we knew in Kenya but a unique individual. So were his wife and his two children. To me Ray was special, and I am sure he was also to many of his trainees.

Although I never had the opportunity to tell him personally, I would like his children to know that their "father" has left an indelible mark on the lives of many."

The day the Antao-Batchelor partnership ended, my sports editor at the time (in fact the many who gave me my first job as a sports reporter, Tom Clarke, wrote: "Take a good look at this picture (featured on the first page). It is symbolic of the greatest partnership the Kenya sports world has ever known ... Seraphino Antao and Ray Batchelor, the man who transformed the lean Goan from a good footballer into one of the world's top sprinters. "The partnership has ended." Seraphino returned to his Mombasa home. Ray, the long-time Coast Sport Officer was transferred to the Rift Valley. It was not long before he left for southern Africa beginning with a stint coaching in Malawi.

CRESCENTI FERNANDES

Cresenti Florence Daniel Fernandes passed away peacefully on July 31, 2020, in the UK, in his 85th year, with family at his side. He was the loving and devoted husband of Thelma, dedicated father of Caroline (Richard), and sons: late Valentino, Douglas (Idoia) and Christopher. He was also the cherished grandfather of Nerea, Monica and Alex. He is predeceased by his siblings Elias, Rita Gracias, Theo, Moses, Lucy and Joe and survived by brother Thomas.

Cresent was born in Nairobi in 1935, to parents Bella and Martin.

Despite a difficult start in life, his father passing away when he was 2 and 1/2 years old, and thanks mainly to his older siblings, Cresent managed to succeed with distinction in his professional and personal life. Part of his success was his partnership with Thelma who he married at Holy Family Cathedral in Nairobi in 1962.

He started his professional career as a life insurance adviser with Old Mutual Insurance Company in Kenya in 1951, where he stayed until 1976, regularly achieving top producer status of new business. His success continued with American Life Insurance Company (ALICO), also in Kenya. On coming to England in 1983, Cresent joined ALICO's Agency 237 in Wembley, the following year. His consistently high production of quality business resulted in a Life Membership of the Executive Club, as well as Conventions in Portugal, Amsterdam, Rio de Janeiro, Madrid, Monte Carlo, Vienna, Tenerife, Paris and on a cruise around the Caribbean. He became a member of the "Million Dollar Round Table". When asked why he was successful, he said a great deal of his new business came from satisfying the needs of existing clients.

In the early 1990s, he established himself as an Independent Financial Adviser. His professional advice, which extended to those beyond the Goan community, enabled many people to purchase their first homes and establish their financial security. His exceptional persistency ratio indicated just how much confidence his clients had in his advice and the products he offered them.

In his personal life, Cresent was a keen sportsman and a very sociable man – this combination led to his active participation in the life of the Railway Goan Institute (RGI) and the Goan Institute (Gi) in Nairobi. He was President of the GI in 1971-72 and Chairman in 1977-78. He led the Gi's 75th-anniversary celebrations committee in 1980 at the Kenyatta Conference Centre. During his term as President, he raised sponsorship for the renovations to the bar and kitchenette area and the building of two squash courts, which was a new sports facility for the club.

In his youth, he took part in all sports, his two favourite ones being field athletics and hockey. He was a founder member of the Spartan Athletic Team, the forerunner of all the track and field clubs in Kenya and excelled at shot put. In field hockey, his team won the Gold Cup tournament (A photograph of this hangs in the Gi today). He was Sportsman of The Year in 1974. He was also on the Kenyan Billiards Society committee and brought well-known players of the day to Kenya to compete. When not on the sports fields, he enjoyed playing cards, Trouk and Rummy.

After retiring from active team sports, Cresent became the General Secretary of the Kenya Goan Sports Association, a body representing all Goan sporting clubs in Kenya. They were entrusted by the donor, to organise the prestigious M. R. de Souza 'Gold Cup' Field Hockey tournament in Nairobi, which attracted many of the top field hockey teams in East Africa. His organising skills raised the profile of this tournament, which became internationally recognised as a premier annual event in Kenya's sporting calendar and contributed vastly to the improvement and interest in the sport.

He broadened community horizons, by seizing opportunities to introduce famous personalities to them, such as Valerian Cardinal Gracias of Mumbai, Miss Universe, Reita Faria, Billards/Snooker champions Michael Ferreira and Wilson Jones, US Roving Olympic Ambassador & Olympic Medal Athlete Mal Whitfield.

As a pillar of the Goan community, he was selected by the British High Commission to represent the Goans in Nairobi, where he assisted many people with their passport applications for emigrating to the UK.

In 2004, with the collaboration of Ayres Fernandes, Dorothy DaCosta, Norma Menezes Rahim, Eunice Barros and Tony Joe, Cresent organised the first ex-Catholic Parochial and St Teresa's student reunion. This event grew in popularity with the 2017 event attended by ex-students from overseas.

He was popular, affable, down-to-earth, but a larger-than-life personality. He will be remembered for his generosity of heart and his willingness to help anyone in need. Due to him having the rarest blood type, he donated blood regularly to the local hospital, which would also contact him in an emergency. This underlined his selfless personality. He was a big man with a big heart and the epitome of a socialite – anything for a party – from organising a small get-together at the Regency Club in Queensbury, extended family picnics, dinner parties, larger events at home to parties at the office, where partners and their children were also invited. He was in his element organising events, but more importantly, loved seeing people enjoying themselves. He would always say, 'Have one for the road' before you left an occasion.

Photo: E⁴ Fernandes Family Collection
Winners M.R. D'Souza Gold Cup 19??
Standing L to R: Raul Montiero, Dunstan Rodrigues, Osborne D'Souza, Ivo Colaco, Oliphant D'Souza, Oscar D'Souza, David Carasco   Sitting L to R: Ossie D'Souza, Edgar Fernandes, Renato Monteiro, Anthony Vaz, Egbert Fernandes   On the Floor L to R: Remy ?, Cresent Fernandes

Cresent Fernandes will live on in the hearts of his close and extended family and in the hearts of folks who knew him and in the hearts of those who have come to know him after his passing. Comparatively few men or women are so blessed.

THESE ARE tough times for the Vanishing Tribe of East Africa (Goans, now in their 70s, 80s, and 90+). With the passing of each one us, the Grim Reaper appears to march ever closer. Nonetheless, we remain true to our faith and our trust in the Maker is renewed with each prayer. However, with the passing of the icons of the community, we feel the loss on any even greater personal basis. It is our loss as much as it is for the family and extended family. The loss of Crescent Fernandes causes such grief and a sense of loss that is reserved for the best amongst us, for royalty and great brains and achievers in the world. Crescent was no royalty, no earth-shattering achiever but he was nonetheless our own, personal hero. He was always larger than life (and I don't mean his size). He was one of us, the one we most admired.

The phrase "the world is poorer for his passing" was never truer than with Crescent's departure from this earth. He will always be remembered for the great work he did in supporting the community, both in the UK and in Kenya.

He was always there when you needed help. This was especially true of anyone in sports. He made sure they were never wanted for anything.

He went to the Catholic Parochial School in Nairobi. The school and the Holy Family Church (later cathedral and now the Basilica) were built by Goan Catholics with help from the Catholic Church. The Goans were later joined by Mauritian and Seychellois Catholics. He never forgot it for a moment.

He was a great supporter of St Teresa's Eastleigh. He grew up with a large, wonderful family not too far away from the church and schools. His folks were amongst the earliest migrants to this quarter which grew into a Little Goa.

He was our hockey player. He was not an international but, in our eyes, he was even though he never played for Kenya. He was the organiser and brought players together (the Caltex team, for example). He was a dedicated club member both at the Nairobi Goan Institute and the Railway Goan Institute. He enjoyed a game of cards (when he was not playing sports).

He was an insurance agent and a financial adviser, and we were happy to put our faith in him and even happier to collect the money when the insurance or investment matured. I know of many, many people who remain indebted to Crescent for encouraging them to invest in an insurance policy which came in handy especially when migrating to the UK, US and Canada when forced to leave Kenya.

But perhaps more than anything else, he was blessed with a great memory and he was the unofficial keeper of much of the Goan history, especially Kenyan Goan history. Any time my memory made me struggle, I could always turn to Crescent, especially on my Facebook page and while writing my various books. What I could not recall, names, places, events, Crescent would, as a matter of course.

We are all shattered, a little broken, somewhat wounded, even a little betrayed by the inevitable and as we apply the balm of prayer to soothe our aching hearts and our pained hearts, let us take comfort that he is in a better place. He booked that place the day he was born. A good man to the last and we shall all weep for him and missing more with every drop.

His departure leaves a huge gap in the memory of Kenya stakes. Now it is left to a few like Tony Reg D'Souza, Felix Nazareth, John Noronha, Oscar D'Souza, Braz Menezes, Mervyn Maciel, Amand Rodrigues and a few others who may have dropped off my brain's memory card.

Crescent was a treasure trove of memories and always made a contribution to the hundreds of posts on my Facebook page. Here is the last one, just a few days before his passing: "I knew Blaise very well in Nairobi. He played cricket for East Africa against Pakistan as a googly bowler, Table Tennis for Kenya and the RGI and he was a high jumper in athletics. He worked for the National and Grindlays Bank in Nairobi." CRF.

With a good buddy Cajie de Menezes

Steve "The Joker" Fernandes

DECEMBER 23 2018: It is an understatement to say that my friend Steve, who passed away a couple of days ago in London, loved life ... he did, he did, loved a joke (around the world are many victims of his light-hearted pranks), loved baking his favourite marble cakes, loved Ladbrokes (the UK betting shops), loved the chicken at Nando's (when he was critically ill in hospital, the first thing he asked for was, yes, Nando's chicken), loved sports especially hockey. I think I made him one of the revolving captains of the Hornets team in Nairobi. He enjoyed card games. Who will forget the marathons Gilbert Fernandes, the late

Tony "Fats" Pereira and the Indian teaching mafia used to hold during Easter time or other long weekends, especially at the magnificent farmhouse managed by that fine, fine man, Angelo Costa Bir. Of course, with the cards were an ample supply of alcohol and a variety of curries or barbecued game meat which had been shot by Angelo earlier in the week.

He loved to teach and, in Nairobi, as headmaster, he took a middle of the road school and turned it into one of the most popular, best-performing schools in the country. He was an incisive and innovative educator who was always abreast of all new ideas happening overseas. He adopted these to Kenyan conditions, much to the delight of students and parents alike, something that is often difficult to achieve universally. When they moved to the UK, he was even more invigorated and enjoyed it all. Steve honed his teaching skills at the Nairobi Teacher Training College in Ngara, Nairobi. Most Goan boys went to this college to graduate as primary schoolteachers as did the girls at the Highridge Teacher Training College.

He was, of course, a living patron saint, no, no, no, a high priest of a bunch of guys, most of them teachers who went by the panhandle of The Jokers. Just a bunch of singles who loved fun, music, song, dance, the movies, hockey, the clubs, Tropicana restaurant in Nairobi on Saturday morning, picnics, visits to the Kenyan coastal town of Malindi for all-night rave parties, camping trips they included Gilbert Fernandes (Toronto), the late Tony "Fats" Pereira, Tony Reg D'Souza (Sydney), Rudolph Fernandes (Toronto), the late Tony "Coco" Cardozo, Pio Almeida (Brazil), Yours Truly, Ben and Julie, Albert D'Souza and lots of other guys. Even though I am biased on this score their dimly lit parties were the events you did not want to miss because they were usually the talk of the town the next Monday.

Growing up with these guys (actually, for the life of me, I cannot remember how I came to join these guys) was quite blissful. It was an era when if you did not have any money, it did not matter because one of your good mates would look after you. My best friends for life were Steve and Gilbert Fernandes.

The past few years, the three of us spoke to each other regularly. I visited the UK and Canada a couple of times. WhatsApp and the pretty good telephone deals meant that I connect with them quite regularly. I was speaking to him the day the car he was driving was in a motor car accident. He sounded a bit down and seemed to lack in energy but, he kept his chin up and said everything was all right ... three days later I called him again and, this time, he told me "Skip, when I spoke to you the other day, I was in a car accident. I am OK, but the airbag exploded, and I suffered a few wounds." A few days later, he was in hospital. He called me from his sickbed. We chatted, and joked, quite confident that he would be home soon. Many weeks passed, many operations later, he wanted to speak to me but, UK time was never Sydney time. We never spoke again, and he never recovered.

Steve and I were dating our respective girlfriends at around the same time. Both Marjorie and Rufina used to come and visit Steve when he was very poorly after a motor car accident. I was staying with him at the time. Marjorie nursed him through his nightmare. From that moment on, their love was forever. He used to enjoy showing off his "beauty queen" bride. When we used to speak late into the night, Sydney time, he used to give me a running commentary on his grandchildren. Like most grandfathers, he was blown away by them ... each of them was very special to him. He would pretend to grumble, but he used to love babysitting and, of course, playing silly games and pranks. Jennifer and Paul's children, Dylan, his eldest grandchild who he had many fun adventures with and Nikita who Steve called "the Boss". Steve also adored Cliff and Meera's children - Aaron and Leah who loved singing 'the naughty little flea' song with him. He just worshipped them, just as much as he loved his children, Melvyn his eldest son and rock, Jennifer his beloved daughter and Clifford his cheeky youngest son.

He will be missed by his brothers Thomas (Nairobi, Kenya) Sylvester (Silu) Toronto, Raul (UK) (RIP, Raul has since joined Steve) and by their wives, his cousins, his nephews and nieces, and all his friends around the world. Steve lost his younger brother Leslie much earlier. His brother Raul passed away a while after Steve did.

Suddenly, there is a little less fun and laughter in the air. Steve is not around anymore.

Steve, Pio Almeida, Neville Pinheiro, Tony Reg D'Souza, Coco Anthony Cardozo

The Longest Honeymoon

By the late Elsie Maciel

After the wedding, I left with my newlywed husband Mervyn on the evening of our wedding day. We left our guests still celebrating.

I had dreamed about getting married on the roadside of the Great Rift Valley escarpment in the beautiful little chapel the Italian prisoners of war had built to mark the end of their work on the building of the Nakuru-Nairobi highway. But my parents wanted the wedding to be in their newly built home in Kitale. So, we had a wonderful wedding day at my family's Kitale home. At dawn, one of the Italian war prisoners came carrying in his hand a shallow basket of real orange blossoms. What bride could not hold her breath at such a sight? Trust an Italian to bring that romantic touch. Our honeymoon in the wilds began as we left Kitale by the sleek weekend train, joining the romantic Uganda-to- Mombasa Mail at Eldoret, and then on to Nairobi for a short stay. The dinner on the train was a perfect wedding celebration. The next day we boarded the Nanyuki-bound train from Nairobi. Two friends picked us up at Nyeri and we drove on to Isiolo via Nanyuki. At Isiolo, our friends had organised a royal reception, which allowed us to meet many of the townsfolk.

At sunset the next day, we boarded a heavily- loaded truck in Isiolo for the onward road journey to Marsabit. We drove through part of the night before pitching camp at Laisamis, amidst roaring campfires. I sat on a log absorbing the atmosphere and looking out for a roaring lion. As we settled down, I saw, through the haze, a hysterical Rendille woman holding a child and making a dash for Mervyn. In what appeared like a begging posture, she pleaded for a lift to Marsabit to take her sick child to hospital. She turned to me and said, *'Watoto wengi,'* wishing me many children in Swahili.

I watched Mervyn as chiefs and leading tribesmen arrived to greet him and shake his hand warmly as though he'd been away for a long time. He handled the situation with authority and good grace.

I looked towards the sick child, about 11 years old, and as I shook his hand, I felt his fevered skin. I offered the Rendille mum half an aspirin tablet, which she promptly gave her child. I thought no more of it.

The sky filled up with more and more stars I had never really noticed stars as I had never camped out in the open before. The breath-taking scene made me feel I could touch the sky! Ever since, the night sky, rare shooting stars and stardust remained my grace before bedtime.

They set up two camp beds for us, and with my hand in the hand of my hero, I fell asleep, safe and secure. We entered Marsabit early the next morning in an unusual almost magical cold mist. A group of delighted women waited around a U-bend to surprise us with presents of sheep and lambs, the best of their flock. I was lost for words and did not know how to cope with such kindness and generosity. By the time we arrived in the government boma, we had six animals, with more people waiting along the route to surprise and greet us.

We ate breakfast with our neighbours, yet another celebration spread! Our host and hostess, who had also recently married, knew the feeling. After breakfast - came the most spectacular moment. Mervyn walked me down the garden path, his eyes beaming with pride and laughter, to the door of our home. We made a fairy-tale entrance. From the moment I saw on the lovely stone cottage with its tin roof, I couldn't stop making plans for it.

By the afternoon, the township Chief and Elders had a tea party for us. The women turned out in bright-coloured clothes of satin and silk and the men wore their traditional attire. They welcomed us warmly to the festive occasion. Beautifully dyed, hand-woven circular and square straw mats, almost in geometric design, decked the walls of the reception room. Our hosts sang, danced and ululated after which we drank very sweet, hot and strong spicy tea and soft drinks. The Chief's wife presented me with 12 large walnut-sized amber beads. One afternoon soon after we arrived in Marsabit, there was a knock at the door. I opened it to find the most magnificent Dubas (Tribal Policeman), in his special white uniform, gleaming in the bright sunlight with his post-office red turban, the ammunition in his bandolier all polished, his rifle strapped on to his left shoulder, and in his right arm a great big bunch of fireball lilies, which matched his turban. I stood spellbound and speechless. What could I say that would thank him enough? He seemed to sense how I felt. He laughed, handed me the flowers and bade me farewell. There shall never be such a gift of flowers for me again!

A couple of weeks into our stay at Marsabit our cook, Sheunda, came to announce a visitor. Reluctant to leave my sewing of new curtains, I stood up slowly and followed him. I found at the kitchen door the very same Rendille mum who had appeared at our honeymoon campsite. Beside her stood her now fit and healthy- looking son. Having tracked me down, she had come to thank me for the *dawa* (half an aspirin), which she said had made her little boy well again. She bowed low in an obvious gesture of gratitude, wishing me once again many children. I offered her a mug of tea. The whole experience left me so humble I wanted to hide! And so, continued our unforgettable honeymoon in the wilds, an experience I shall treasure for the rest of my life. Over the next few days there would be many Elsie and Mervyn had been married to 68 years: Elsie Antonette Collaco and Mervyn Maciel tied the knot on August 16, 1952, at the Church of the Immaculate Conception in Kitale, Kenya with Fr John officiating.

End of a Bachelor Era (excerpt from Bwana Karani)

As each day passed, I soon became aware that my days of bachelorhood were not to last very much longer. My fiancee and I had planned a wedding in August (1952) — there was much to be done in the way of organising the whole affair. We were hampered in the planning by the absence of telephones at Marsabit. Most of our arrangements had to be dobe via the mail and with the mail being infrequent, things did get hectic at times. The local post office must have made a small fortune from the many telegrams we often had to send!

I spent Christmas of 1951 with my fiancee in Kitale, and on Boxing Day that year, we got engaged. A very simple occasion at home where only the immediate family and the Parish Priest, Fr. John Hawes, were present. The announcement must have taken everyone by surprise as nothing had been planned. We were thinking about plans for the wedding, but the engagement itself was a spur of the moment decision. The following week, our engagement notice appeared in the local Press and many messages of congratulations started pouring in from relatives and friends alike. We had also informed my brothers abroad of the forthcoming event. Within a few months of my returning to Marsabit, the Notice of Marriage was out in Kitale (my fiancee's hometown), and the DC's office there had sent a copy to the DC Marsabit so that it could be similarly displayed locally. Our friends were quick to offer congratulations. I felt really great — it was a proud moment in my life, even though some remarked that we were too young to be thinking of marriage. Young we may have been, but we certainly knew we were in love and were equally aware of the great responsibilities that lay ahead of us. The only preparation I had so far made, was to save up a whole case of Scotch whisky from the monthly ration of one bottle that my friends and I received. I was grateful to all those who had sacrificed their quotas so that I could build up this stock. Scotch was hard to come by in those days, and since my fiancee's parents would be doing all the catering for the wedding at home, I felt that this small contribution would not come amiss.

Fully satisfied that the arrangements for our wedding were proceeding very smoothly, I returned to Marsabit after my short leave in the certain knowledge that there was now not long to wait before the Big Day or Siku Kuu (holiday as they say in Ki-Swahili). On many an evening, there would be 'extra' celebrations at Marsabit. Some of my friends who knew I would be losing my bachelor 'freedom' felt that the last few days of this carefree era should be suitably remembered. I must admit that the six months between returning from my casual leave and leaving to get married, flew by. I was back at Kitale once more a few days before the wedding, and together my fiancee and I were able to attend to the last-minute details.

My future in-laws had recently moved into their brand-new house — an architect-designed bungalow with four spacious bedrooms, a modern lounge-cum-dining-room, with an equally modern bathroom, toilet and kitchen. The whole house had been tastefully decorated and adequately furnished; as this was to be the first family wedding to bc held in the new home, no expense had been spared to make the place look like a mini 'palace'. The builders had also worked round the clock to ensure that the house was completed in good time for the family to move in well before the Big Day.

My fiancee was very popular in the Kitale area and the district generally, and the wedding presents that were beginning to arrive from all manner of people, brought home to me the great regard and affection these people had for her. There were gifts from the simple folk and the well-to-do alike, among the latter was one from the then Secretary to the Duke of Manchester (Mr N. O. C. Marsh — an imposing figure of a man). Many local farmers who knew her well when she worked at the KFA (Kenya Farmers Association) had also sent in their gifts and good wishes, and we were greatly touched by the generosity of so many. Even those who could not make it to the wedding, and those who weren't even invited (we had to restrict numbers because of the available space), had sent tokens of affection. Most of the arrangements for the wedding were well advanced by now — the bride's trousseau was complete, so were my suits, the bridesmaids' outfits, etc. The parish priest of the small Catholic Church had asked us over a few days before the big occasion — for a general face-to-face talk on the all-important religious significance of our marriage, and the great responsibilities we were soon to undertake. Being a close friend of the family, talking plainly to us both came so naturally to Fr. John Hawes. My younger brother Wilfred, who I would dearly have liked to have been my best man, was away in England pursuing his studies, so I had to choose my next favourite relative instead. Here, I must admit, I broke away from tradition and asked my married cousin, Jock Sequeira (an Education Officer in Mombasa) — to do the honours. Normally the person chosen is, I believe, a bachelor. Jock arrived a day before and was the only member of my immediate family at the wedding; sadly, due to family commitments, Beryl was unable to accompany him. Most of my other relatives were too far away to make the trip — a paternal uncle (Luis) in Mombasa, others in Zanzibar, Mocambique, Uganda, and my two brothers in Bombay and England respectively. Still, I knew they would all be with us in spirit.

My Els

Elsie was the perfect spouse - very loving and caring, thinking always of others rather than herself. Healthwise, she's not been lucky both in Kenya and here; had several operations here and spent many days in hospital following many operations; despite all this, she was at her happiest when entertaining visitors and enjoyed spending a lot of time with the children and after grandchildren.

In addition to her culinary skills, she was a seamstress (made the wedding gowns for both our daughters, just days after she's returned home after a major operation. Also made the 3-tier wedding cake; made her dress for the wedding and even a Pageboy outfit for our grandson.

She has knitted endless jumpers for me and the whole family and friends. She even made a 2-piece suit for me.

In addition to all this, she was a great cake maker and made cakes for family birthdays and also for people's anniversaries or weddings. Her pickles were much sought after especially by the Curry Club of Britain - her Bombay duck and Tendlim pickles were a /Goan favourite.

She excelled at pottery and her work was exhibited here in Sutton and also at some other Craft Fairs.

There is so much I could write about her. A great samosa maker. Friends and family still rave about her unique samosas and pickles. She adored her grandchildren and encouraged them to take an interest in arts and craft. She was also a great gardener and later a great help in the allotment we worked at for nearly 15 years.

She was not a party person, nor overtly religious but her faith meant a lot to her.

Elsie Antonette (Collaco) Maciel 1934-2020

Tears of a daughter

By Heather-Gail D'Souza

My parents were inseparable. They had the same hobby - travel. That was their game. In the earlier years, they each travelled on business trips alone, and more recently, my Mum (**May 7, 1945 – August 29, 2019**) was more an executive assistant to my Dad on his marketing trips abroad.

As a young girl growing up, I watched my Mum from the corner of my eye with her designer shoes and handbags, her perfectly groomed nails, and her constant array of new outfits.

Hoping I would secretly turn out like her. What I didn't realise at the time was that I was learning to be like her.

Mum worked for Kenya Airways and, as a result, I was in the privileged position of being able to travel the world from the day I was born. Through these experiences, my mother gifted me her passion for travel and I eagerly embraced it with both hands.

In the early days when Dad was starting up the family business, Mum would regularly whisk me away to London, Bombay, Australia, the US – just the two of us. Mum took me to Goa one time to her village Tivim and Mapuca once showing me off telling everyone I was her daughter and telling everyone she was Lily and Micks' daughter. It was so exciting. While we were away, she would teach me about how to live, how to shop for the home, and we always brought back beautiful products for us all to enjoy. She would tell me, 'Travel is the best teacher'.

Although she was a director of Visit Africa Ltd, she never interfered with the business, preferring to stand by me and encourage me as I built my confidence in the world of safari tourism operations. I confided a lot in her, with my petty problems at times. She always listened and offered me her sage advice and unwavering support. When

I moved to the UK to study, Mum spent ten good years between the UK and Nairobi, sharing her time with Dad and me. She worked part-time while visiting me and always got better jobs than me, always with parking included. I was so impressed by this! Here again, she would make sure I had everything I needed – buying me the goodies I deprived myself of, such as salmon.

She took me to university, handed me a 50-pound note and said: "You have a bank account, you know how to use it." This was one of my scariest moments in life after the rollercoaster ride as a child in Disney Land. My friends and even the hostel warden thought my Mum was a student at university when she came to stay as she always looked her best and young. It was Mum who encouraged me to do my master's abroad, which I thank her for. I thank her for making me, me!

I was raised loving dogs and people. My parents' network of friends reaches all corners of the world. I can't count how many of their classmates and friends have reached out to me during this past week. More recently, Mum became somewhat of a *Facebook* and *Whatsapp* expert, which allowed her to stay in touch with her friends and family.

Mum was a good cook she loved the finer things in life, yet she was so unassuming. She was elegant in her own way. Setting the table with the finest and cooking us Cordon Bleu meals. She would cater for 30 people at a time single-handed. She loved to entertain around a beautifully set table.

After Dad's passing Mum, cried every day, and I regularly reassured her that she would be OK. I am not sure she believed me; that she could see her way without my Dad. She gave up, and I wish she could have been that strong woman I knew when I was born. I always remember thinking she lost her Dad at 18, and how lucky I was to have my parents, not knowing I would lose them both in the same year.

I have very few words this time around. I have some very dear friends supporting me. I would not have been able to stand here today if it was not for my Godfather Olly his wife Mel, my nutter friends, my Dad's brother Simon, his sister Pam and their families, My Mum's first cousins, and, of course, my strongest supporter Clive, who my parents loved and trusted always.

RIP Mum, I know you are happy with dad fly now fly. Please watch over me always. I hope your love never died and you continue to love as you did – for yours was one love story that we will not forget. I will miss our chats. I love you.

My Dad and I

1943--2019 I started working with my Dad 10 years ago when I returned to Kenya after studying and working abroad. I have had a front-row seat to observe and learn the ropes of running and managing a successful company from 'The Master'. My Dad was a humble and ethical man who stressed the importance of being diligent, transparent and trustworthy. It earned not only the respect of the business community but also of his employees, many who have kept faithful vigil at his hospital bed for the past few weeks. My Dad was a very loving family man who showered my Mum and me with abundance. He enjoyed his leisure time at home in the company of my Mum and his dogs and cat. He had a passion for good food: prawns, cheese, pate and most of all, chocolates.

He also loved the finer things in life and ensured that he had the latest aftershave lotions and well-tailored Italian slacks. From a young age, he developed a love of automobiles and was so very proud of his fleet of 23 top-of-the-line Toyota Highlander vehicles and personally oversaw their maintenance and roadworthiness. His attention to detail was inspiring.

Although he was born and bred in Kenya, Dad never forgot his Goan heritage. He kept up with Goan politics and made sure he introduced me to every person from Anjuna, his village in Goa! He also spent a fair amount of his free time keeping tabs on his school's Alumni Association and supporting their endeavours whenever possible.

I am very grateful to my Dad for having made me what I am. From small beginnings, assisted with Mum's career and expertise in the travel business, he has left us with a viable business. Almost a year ago, recognising the need to pass the torch, Dad appointed me to the position of Managing Director at Visit Africa Limited. I will be so proud to carry on my darling Dad's legacy, but I have to admit, it will be somewhat bittersweet because I will forever miss working side by side with him.

Edna + Renato

IT WAS a match made in Heaven when Renato Monteiro married Edna Fernandes on October 14, 1963. They were both dedicated hockey players and loved the game! Edna's two brothers, Edgar and Egbert were Olympians and younger sister Ellen played for Kenya. The four Monteiro brothers were lifelong 'one club' Goan Institute stalwarts, who continued playing for the club through the 1950s and 1960s. Their fierce loyalty to the club came about because their father C.J de C Monteiro (Caetano) was instrumental in building a new home for the Goan Institute, Nairobi.

4 January 1936 – 2 November 2019

Renato was born in Nairobi, Kenya. He went to Dr Ribeiro Goan school. He represented the school in many sports at the highest level and played hockey in the first XI for the Goan Institute (G.I.) when that team was at the top of its form! He captained the G.I. team for many years and was the only player to be part of the Gold Cup-winning teams in both 1952 and 1961. He also was a key member of the Kenya Goans

Hockey team that was highly successful in Kenya hockey in the 1950s, winning every trophy in one season.

He loved the social club life in Kenya; this continued throughout his life with some great stories from his days in both Nairobi and Canberra to be told at another time. His working life began as a sales representative for Ahmed Brothers, a stylish gentlemen's outfitters in the centre of Nairobi. He later trained as a butcher and worked in the family business in Hurlingham where his father (Caetano) owned the Caltex Service Station and meat supply business Booths Butchery.

In challenging economic times, many Goans would receive free meat from Booths! He loved customer service and would end his professional career in Kenya in sales firstly for City Brewery and then Coca-Cola where he spent the last 15 years with many great friends. These included his good mate soccer legend Joe Kadenge and IOC representative Charles Mukora. Renato was well-loved by many in Kenya because he was passionate about multi-racial friendships. This was before the 1963 independence of Kenya when this was frowned upon by the existing British Government.

Renato had many friends from different communities around the country who were attracted to his charismatic personality and incredibly loyal friendship. These bonds remained strong with many friends across the world and who remain steadfast throughout his life. Always generous in spirit, Renato helped many Goans resettle after the Asian expulsion from Uganda by Idi Amin in 1972, and again in 1974 when Malawi expelled its Goan population. He opened his home in Hurlingham,

Nairobi, to many Goan refugees, enabling them to transition through Nairobi before they settled in either Canada or the UK. These Goan families still remember the help their parents received in this transition at the most difficult time.

Rento moved to Australia in 1982 with his wife Edna and two sons Malcolm and Julian. His vibrant zest for life and love of family has continued through his sons and grandchildren.

16 June 1939 to 6 May 2020

EDNA was born in the Kenyan town of Kisumu in 1939 on the shores of Lake Victoria, where her father Vincent, had been posted by the British civil service. After several secondments in regional towns around Kenya, the young family of four children finally arrived in the capital, Nairobi, in 1953 where Edna attended Dr Ribeiro Goan School.

Edna was very social and, like her brothers and later her younger sister, had a natural ability to excel at sports. In her final year, Edna was rewarded by the school, she won the Victrix Ludorum for all-round athletic excellence. With her life-long best friend, Sr. Trifa De Sousa, she focused her sporting capability mainly on athletics and hockey, working and training during the week and travelling to championships and tournaments on the weekends.

Her first hockey team, the Collegians, was the best women's hockey team in East Africa. The team members remain close to this day.

After marrying Renato Monteiro in 1963, Edna worked in administration for Sassini Coffee Estates. She strived to balance the demands of career, family and an active social life. During this time, Edna played hockey for the Goan Institute where she captained the team and mentored many of the younger players. She also got a lot of satisfaction from being on the Ladies Committee which did so much to organise community events. She enjoyed cooking with the other ladies. They called these sessions "Board Meetings" because they would bring their cutting boards and talk about the week's activities. Edna developed a passion for cooking and won several cooking and recipe competitions in Nairobi. In Canberra, Edna subsequently spent a lot of time doing community work with her local Church and charity organisations. She loved gardening and joined the *Friends of the Botanical Gardens'* where she volunteered for decades. She was known for her practicality and ability to just get on and do whatever was required. This trait is fondly remembered by her immediate family whenever they called on her.

Edna will be remembered for her true colours. She was a strong woman with a big smile, a genuine personality, and an ability to maintain loyal friendships across many decades and generations. Edna was the matriarch who guided her family to a new country and taught us always to look forward and not be afraid of what lies beyond. Her strength as a strong woman continues to live through her granddaughter, goddaughter and nieces who loved the special time spent with her.

Pictured: the late Vincent and Mary Fernandes with their hockey stars: (late) Edna, Edgar, (late) Egbert and Ellen

The Goan Clubs and Goan culture

The following is not a criticism. I have respect for Goans of all walks of life in East Africa. I count many, many from all walks of life as my very dear of friends. Here is how I saw things firsthand, from stories I heard as a child and some of the written material I was able to get hold of during my young years. I ate with my hands at home, mostly if it was rice and curry. My friends used cutlery. But outside of the house, I used cutlery except if it was fish head ambot tik (Konkani for salty, hot). Not a problem.

Goan Clubs in East Africa did not always foster Goan culture or the Konkani language. They couldn't. There was a directive from the colonial Minister for Education that all Asians, especially the parents, should stop speaking to their children in their vernacular languages and dialects. The reason? Translating these vernaculars into English was producing a horror kind of pidgin, the butt of jokes and satire (some of which still stands to this day) and it was all quite ridiculous. The Asian children and their parents ignored this (some students lied about it in school) and the ridicule continued.

Goans had no such problem. The sons and daughters of civil servants, doctors, engineers, nurses and other professions all spoke English at home because most parents understood the need for their children to speak proper English, even that hoity-toity version called Queen's English.

There were others, sons and daughters of tailors, carpenters, shoemakers and like, who continued to speak to their parents in Konkani because Mum and Dad could not speak English. However, as the years went by that too diminished, yet these children had no problem reading and writing excellent English.

Talking about Queen's English, a friend of ours flew over the UK en route to somewhere or the other and came back speaking pukka HM's English. That could be an urban myth, but I know the name of the guy involved.

I remember with considerable affection that my late wife Rufina held a conversation with my mother mixing English, Swahili and Konkani. Somehow, they managed to understand each other. One or two of my siblings, the youngest, spoke very little Konkani. There quite a few Goans who spoke very bad, broken English and they made themselves understood with an insertion of some Konkani into their conversations. Sadly, they were the butt of jokes and hilarity. Some folks took to English as a matter of class as did the Goans in Goa with Portuguese, I was told.

Most of the teachers in Goan schools and parish schools spoke pretty good English. Even those with a decisive Subcontinental twang made themselves understood pretty well. Some sadly were mercilessly the butt of jokes: one of our science teachers, a delightful bloke actually, was called "*Boonnsen bearner*" something to that effect.

For those households where everyone spoke English, parents spoke to each other in Konkani when sought wanted a little privacy from the children or when they were talking about the children. When these same children migrated to overseas and wanted to make secret talk, they spoke in Swahili. From a 1962 production of Tor Zait Con here are the players: Flavia Andrade, Olive Tavares, Brigitte Dias, Lily Collaco, Bertha Zuzarte, Daisy D'Costa, Carmen Fernandes, Ruth Fernandes, Alzira Zuzarte Vaz, Max Fernandes, Charlie Vaz, Jack Fernandes, M. Rod, Zig-Zag D'Mello, S.V. Barros, J.P. Leitao, Juliao Noronha, L.

Santimano, Bonnie D'Souza, Joe Fernandes, Wolfgang Collaco, Tolley Baretto, Jose Fernandes, Cajie Fernandes.

The diaspora Goan, especially their children, have built a new life in a new world and that does not include East Africa or Goa or Goans for that matter.

Many of the educated Goans also tried to mimic the colonial British. As part of their work, they may have come to develop a taste for English food, even it is only finger food that they like most. There were Goan chefs on the Railways, some most important hotels, many of the exclusive whites-only clubs and they would have introduced their friends to the English finger food had parties they held at their own homes. Some even did part-time catering for engagements, birthdays and the like. But it was not long before Goan women were mastering these skills and teaching them to their daughters and the cooks they employed. Friday night was always fish curry and rice, so was Lent. Some homes always began their meals with a bowl of soup and ended with a suitable dessert.

While the Goan cuisine was dominant in most homes, others chose to serve marinated roast beef or pork with roast potatoes in jacket, vegetables and chutney for the main course. This was not the norm but the exception. For most Goans, however, it was just curry and rice and a vegetable dish if you were lucky. If you wanted a dessert, you whipped up avocado, sprinkled sugar and thought you were heaven. If avocados were not in season than its dark brown sugar or jaggery sprinkled on a chapati) or thick Whitehouse bread) and rolled up, or banana fritters for dessert or there was plenty of fruit not too far away, even if it was other peoples.

In our teen years, we began venturing into Indian restaurants and later into the "white" restaurants like the New Stanley Hotel's Thorn tree and a whole new world opened up to us. It was the same time Kentucky Fried Chicken and its derivatives and of course fish and chips were always available. I got to love the rare roast beef (still do more than 65 years later) sandwich at Brunner's or Queens Hotel which also served the best potato chips and unadulterated Heinze tomato sauce (most other places it was watered down).

Oh, by the way, there was always the best authentic food available at the Goan Tailor's Society at the weekend, special feast days (such as December 3) or on days when loud, noisy, boisterous trouk (Konkani, card game) tournaments were held. Not much English, though.

Oh, there was a bit of culture at the Goan clubs at Christmas, Easter and New Year's ... traditional dances and community singing.

As far as cooking classes, I think the best most people came up with was Elsie Maciel's Cookbook, nothing wrong with that. At the RGI, there was something else: Salim's Seekh Kebabs and Ismailia Hotel made the best lamb samosas and potato bhajia. Anyway, by the time the 1960s came along, turned-up noses, class consciousness, prejudice, airs and graces, and all of that human rubbish had disappeared. Much of it has been erased by nature of need long before that. People stopped treating their fellow Goans as some folks in the UK treat the folk from Swindon and Wembley with their Goan Wild West ways. They too will learn in time.

Bye Sis

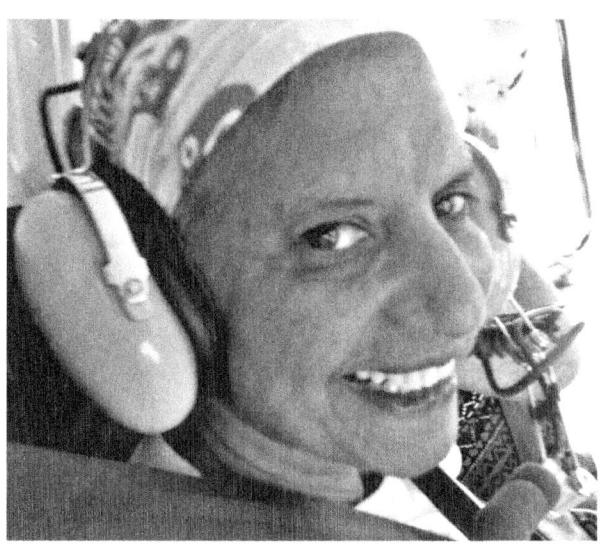

In the dark light of the Midnight Hour when all is calm and silent... just 30 minutes after Australia Day had ended and a new day began, you quietly went away on January 27, 2018, in Westmead Hospital in Sydney where you had battled to survive for a month. We will always be grateful that you did not suffer on your journey to Heaven.

And we all died a little with you.

From that saddest of days, October 26, 2017, when you were diagnosed with Pancreatic Cancer, you never once lost heart over the next 14 months. You never lost your unforgettable smile or your supreme confidence that you "would beat this thing" and you were "never going to let anything stop you from living your life to the fullest." And that is what you did. I sat with you through all those months of chemotherapy. You never missed a weekday or a Sunday in church. Your faith was always eternal.

You reveled in your life, "You don't need too much money, Skip," you told me often. Financially, you were the most successful in our family.

Within a few weeks of setting a date for the first chemo session and, with time on your hands, you asked me to come on a safari to Australia's Northern Territory, Uluru, Alice Springs, Darwin, Kakadu National Park. A two-week holiday for things that needed to be said, and, always of course plenty to laugh about and there was always one more thing you wanted to tell me (or I wanted to tell you) about the wonderful time we spent together.

Of course, once the chemo started, you came to stay with me. I felt truly blessed for the time I would spend with you and memories we would make. Those long chats in between glancing at the TV screens, cooking your favourite dishes or just letting you get on with whatever took your fancy. You were never a patient, always your bubbly (sometimes very strict about this or that, putting your foot down and say simply: No. That is not good enough.) self, your funny, funny little jokes about this or that or nothing in particular.

Also, particularly special for me was the time you spent with Mum. She lived with you in the UK and migrated with you to Australia. With your sister Regina Flora, you were always together and shared some fantastic memories, especially with mum being the funniest and sometimes with a temper that resembled the hottest dried red chillies. However, take Mum to the local bookies or the slots at the local clubs and she was your friend for life!

All of your life, you have been close to your siblings. Our hearts broke when we lost Hippol very early in his life and Peter a few years ago. Both played a big role in your life and gave lots of encouragement on your path to young womanhood. Your brother Johnny was always just a phone call away and you called every day, sometimes three and four times, especially recently. Your sister Regina Flora, the baby of the family, has been the one person who has been by your side for always, especially after Mum left us and you were on your own. The three of you seemed to be together all the time. It was an unforgettable time in your life.

The thing that astounded me about you over the past 14 months was that you did not show the slightest hint of being a cancer patient. You did everything, went everywhere and enjoyed whatever you wanted to. You used to even regularly visit your other "home" Blacktown Hospital where you worked, and they would all be smiling (and a little curious) to see you looking so well.

One of your friends there described you as "the light that shone on everyone, especially with that beautiful, caring smile".

Like the rest of your siblings, you were a self-made person. You were smallest in height (not much taller than Mum), huge in heart, you let nothing get in the way of your success in every aspect of your life. Each new job taught you a new lesson in life ... remember the guy in North Sydney who would not let you have a new pencil until the old one had reached less than an inch (2.5 cm) you hated that first but you quickly learnt the lesson of prudence, thrift and economy. Or the boss who told you: Do it yourself and that was your life motto from that moment on ... she will be smiling when she reads this.

There are many, many people in and around the world whose hearts you touched but especially at Blacktown Hospital in the anaesthetics department. The place has not been the same without, according to several of your colleagues. You were never afraid. You did things, went to places, found new adventures, everything on your own. You encouraged everyone you met to "do it on your own, don't be afraid."

You certainly inspired your goddaughter Mary-Ann:

"Aunty Bridget is my Godmother. She was always happy and full of fun to be with. I spent time with her on her trips to visit us in San Francisco and on our many family vacations in Sydney. We always had a great time together. She was always keen to watch me grow up from a little girl to a young lady and had a lot of advice for me.

"Aunty Bridget had always told me that I should learn to be independent, to not rely on anyone to help take care of me and to be able to stand on my own two feet. She seemed like she felt very strongly about this and that it was essential to her that I too become independent, strong-willed, and strong-minded.

"Her message was heard loud and clear, as that's exactly what I've become. She has always been an inspiration to me, whether it be through her travels around the world on her own, even getting married when she saw fit, and how she lives her life, eating healthy and exercising. Nothing ever seemed too adventurous or too courageous for her.

"When I made my trips to Eastern Europe and then Greece, I had her in my mind when I thought I shouldn't travel on my own, that it would be too difficult, that I would feel lonely, or get lost, or something bad would happen and I wouldn't be able to fend for myself. I felt if she could manage it and have fun, and then I could manage it as well. I understand that God has his plan for each one of us. She has been one of the most resilient women that I know.

"I will always have a special place in my heart for my dear Aunty Bridget."

You were always a networker (even when the word had not been invented,) especially in Nairobi. You knew exactly who to talk to or whom to turn to for help on behalf of anyone who asked your help. In Sydney, too, your address book was full of names of specialists, doctors, surgeons, nursing staff ... and none of them ever said "no" if you ever needed their help ... well, maybe just one. You had a smile for everyone, anyone, anywhere, anytime.

Over the past 17 years, you devoted yourself to your husband Gary Wilson. You showed him things that opened up his life, especially the travel.

When the time came, you knew it was time to say "goodbye". You had been confident that the "pain in the stomach" would go away and asked if you could come and stay with me to recuperate. And I said, "of course". You said: "You know I love your cooking." (Later when you could not open your eyes or talk too much and I promised you fish curry and rice, a broad smile would light up your face.)

Then some 16 days ago, you looked at me and quietly said: "Skip, I think I am going to die." Both of us with breaking hearts, trembling bodies, quietly looked at the road ahead. You said: "No regrets, Skip. I have loved my life, my family, my friends, and the things I have achieved. I will never give up the fight ... but I know now the Lord may call me sooner ... and I will be with Mum, Dad, Hippol and Peter." We both knew this was "Goodbye", but we could not get ourselves to say the word, it was enough that we just thought it in silence. It was the hardest time. Thank you for being so generous about your feelings towards me. And the next day, you took the first steps on that journey as your body began the slow, slow process of shutting down. But every day, Gary, Flora, Priscilla (niece), Johnny, Matilda and I were with you day and night ... we tried to cheer you up, joked, Priscilla played videos of your favourite music especially *Jambo Bwana* and *Abba*, and that office video you made ... you dancing away to an Abba number ... or that scintillating speech you made at a party thrown by Johns family at their home in Strathfield (you were instrumental in hiring Dr Bryne John, and she never forgot that you stood up for her) and lots of other nostalgia. We would get a tiny smile, a twitch, a shake or a nod of the head ... in your comatose state you heard everything and everyone ... we were grateful for small mercies.

And that day when Johnny arrived from San Francisco. You could not say much, but your face and your smile lit up like a big, big full moon, the Nairobi kind. We were afraid he would be too late; you knew better and waited for him. There were no tears at our farewell, just a celebration of gratitude for the good memories and promise to face the future as we have always done with courage and a prayer. "But," you said, "I will keep on fighting."

There are many who will shed a tear at your passing ...none more so than the many, many people you helped in Western Sydney. You collect clothes, shoes ...anything that was useful to the needy and you would share it around. You were always thrifty, but it when it came to the needy, you were very generous. In the end, it was not the Pancreatic Cancer that killed you, but complications developed from that "pain in the stomach" which led to the eventual shutting down of the kidneys. Our greatest fear was that you would be in pain and suffer an agonising end to your life. You never gave up. The doctors made you comfortable and said the end was imminent ... 31 days ago. You lived your life your way. You grabbed every single moment in the day and made it your own, inspite of the cancer. You were no less a battler in your last days ... you astonished your doctors, the specialists, nurses and other medical staff who were amazed how managed to cling on to life for so long ... you only left us when you were ready to say goodbye

The last time I got any response from you was on January 17: I was kidding with you and reminding of the days when you and your friends looked so stylish in those bell bottoms, or flared pants, finished off with pastel-coloured blouses, your picnics, visits to the movies, etc in Nairobi. And a tear rolled down your left eye. When you could not speak with your tongue, you spoke with your eyes and your limited gestures. That image of that final tear will live with me forever. Treasured. Always.

Vicky Antao Lory

The Antao family from Eastleigh were among the best of our family friends. We had many of those growing up. My brother Hippol's middle name is Floriano (Vicky's dad's name) and his Godfather was Gonzac Antao, Vicky's eldest brother. We lost touch, all you were always on my mind and in my prayers. Rest in Heavenly Peace Vicky.

Victoria "Vicky" P. (Antao) Lory, 72, of Montpelier, VT became a beloved ancestor on May 5, 2020. Her warmth touched many hearts, and she will be missed.

Victoria was born in Nairobi, Kenya to Jose Floriano and Luiza Maria Antao. After graduating from St. Teresa's Girls' School, Victoria worked at Catholic Relief Services (CRS) regional office in Nairobi. At age 21, she accepted a position at CRS headquarters located in the Empire State Building in New York City.

She embraced all the city had to offer, attending musicals, concerts and visiting museums. She travelled around New York State, visiting the Finger Lakes Region and Niagara Falls, enjoying their unique beauty. She came to appreciate the seasons of the Northeast, especially fall foliage and the snow.

She met and married James Lory in New York. They worked on humanitarian disaster relief projects in Bangladesh, Sri Lanka, India and Liberia. They moved back to the United States and lived in East Hardwick, VT where they raised their two daughters. Later the family moved to central Vermont, where Victoria became a homeowner and resided for the remainder of her life.

She loved the Vermont landscape and its biodiversity. For nearly 25 years, Victoria had a career with the State of Vermont as a Legal Secretary for the Department of Forests, Parks and Recreation, the Vermont Fish and Wildlife Department, and the Environmental Board/Natural Resources Board, under the Agency of Natural Resources, where she proudly worked on ACT 250.

Victoria had a strong faith that helped her through life's challenges, and for over 30 years was a parishioner at St. Augustine's Catholic Church in Montpelier.

She was a proud US Citizen and supported family members who immigrated to the United States. A world traveller, she spent time in over a dozen countries on four continents. She knew four languages: Konkani, Swahili, French and English. Early in life, her family took annual trips from Nairobi to Mombasa along the Indian Ocean. The wildlife of eastern Africa inspired her to care about conservation. She worked tirelessly to give similar experiences to her children and expose them to the wonders of travelling, respecting the environment, and helping others.

Victoria's humble kindness, consideration for marginalised people, and fearless way of leading her life was an inspiration. She was a force to be reckoned with when she witnessed or experienced injustice. She took a particular interest in the history of Black America and Native America and cared deeply about human rights. She was proud of her children for their dedication to social justice.

Hard-working and known for her self-sufficient and independent nature, Victoria had a creative DIY approach to life. She baked and decorated birthday cakes, stayed up all night to sew dresses and costumes for her daughters' special occasions, and took on home fixit projects. She was generous-hearted, smart, and regal, like her namesake.

Victoria led an active life, working out at the gym, taking walks, hiking, biking, and going on outings with her best friend, Martha. In her downtime she liked listening to the radio, reading, following the news, learning about world cultures, watching travel shows, and watching late-night talk shows.

Advanced progression of Alzheimer's and dementia led her to be under the care of her daughters for the last part of her life. Victoria enjoyed the company and comfort of their animals. She continued to love family gatherings, nature watching, car rides walk and helped to cook meals, and tend the garden.

Victoria was predeceased by her parents; her newborn son, Francis; and her elder brother, Gonzaga. She is survived by her daughter, Sandra Lory and son-in-law, Zach Tonnissen of Orange, VT; daughter, Yvonne Lory of Barre, VT; sister, Veronica of London, England; brother, Sebastian of Hove, England; brother, Thomas of Maryland; former husband Jim of Barre, VT; and numerous in-laws, cousins, nieces, nephews, grand-nephews and other loved ones who were special to her.

Her family and friends will cherish the memory of her remarkable life, and of their time together. The last few months of life were spent at Woodridge Nursing Home. Victoria's family would like to thank the staff of Maple Grove, especially for their care after her stroke during the pandemic.

An icon at the centre of attention

By Norman Da Costa

Silu, Sindhi, Hilary: a gallery of great icons

There was an aura around him when he took his place at the centre of the field. Surjeet Singh Panesar - also known as Sindhi or Junior - was always the centre of attention not only because of the position he occupied on the field. Everything he did, smacked of elegance. He mastered the art of pinpoint passing, timely tackling and deft dribbling. But what elevated him to a higher level as one of the finest centre-halves in the world was his vision. Gifted by this unique ability, this classy player could open up holes in the opposing defences for his teammates. This great centre-half for Kenya and Sikh Union passed away in Nairobi at the age of 81 after a brief illness on Nov. 6, 2019. He leaves behind his wife Deepi and a family spread across England, Canada and the United States.

His death has left many fans and his international teammates speechless. This doesn't come as a surprise as Sindhi endeared himself to his teammates and supporters alike always put his team ahead of individual accolades

"Sindhi, as we used to call him, was in his day one of the best centre-halves in the world," said ex-international teammate Edgar Fernandes who lives in Melbourne. "His death leaves me speechless, but he will be remembered and admired for not only for his exceptional ability in hockey, but his outstanding personality."

Edgar was Sindhi's Olympic teammate and also played at the club level against him for several years for Nairobi Goan Institute against the Sikh Union. Edgar was one of Kenya's three greatest wizards of the dribble in the game along with Hilary Fernandes and Sindhi.

Surjeet was one of three players to represent Kenya at four Olympics with the late left-winger Alu Mendonca and full-back Avtar Singh who were both selected for a world X1 during Kenya's heydays. Surjeet was born in Nairobi and received his early hockey training in India at the Maharaja Patiala Public School and Patiala University where he was trained by the legendary Harbail Singh, who coached India to Olympic gold in Helsinki in 1952 and Melbourne in 1956. On returning to Nairobi, he joined Sikh Union, the most dominant club team in East Africa, with whom he hoisted the M.R. de Souza Gold Cup, the Blue Riband of hockey tournaments in Africa, a record 13 occasions. While he made his mark as a centre half the versatile Surjeet started his international career as a centre forward and ended it as a full back.

He won his first international cap on May 29, 1960, against

Uganda upfront as the centre half position was filled by the great Surjeet Singh Deol. To differentiate between the two Surjeets, Deol was called Senior and Sindhi was universally referred to as Junior. Junior made an immediate impact in his international debut with two goals in Kenya's 4-0 triumph and eventually moved to centre half when Senior retired following the East African Championships in Zanzibar in 1962. The versatile Sindhi, who also filled in as a fullback, earned more than 100 caps and was an integral member of the national team ever since 1960 when he was picked for the Olympics in Rome where Kenya finished eighth. He was a member of Kenya's greatest teams in the 1960s and '70s including Tokyo four years later where the country finished sixth. A couple of right bounces and Kenya could have ended on the Olympic podium in Tokyo, but it was never to be. Kenya was eighth in Mexico in 1968 and 13th in Munich in 1972 where Sindhi played in his last international after a record 31 Olympic matches.

Fellow internationals Silu Fernandes and Hilary Fernandes, who both now reside in Toronto, heaped praise on their teammate.

"My friend and teammate Surjeet dazzled the opposition with his style internationally, at home and abroad and at the Olympics," said Silu Fernandes, who played for the Railway Goan Institute and was vice-captain of the national team. "He will surely rank as among the best in the world." And Hilary Fernandes, who played against Surjeet for Kenya Police and the Railway Goan Institute and later as his teammate on Sikh Union, added, "Surjeet was a natural and gifted hockey player.

"I enjoyed playing alongside him on one of the finest club teams ever for almost five of my glorious hockey playing years." Amar Singh, another Sikh Union and Kenya teammate, who lives in Calgary, considered Surjeet one of the greats of Kenya hockey. "He was one of Sikh Union's most outstanding players and I will always remember that when I captained the club, he was always punctual."

Full-back Raphael Fernandes played with Surjeet in his later years.

"He was my mentor and he always referred to me as his son. I learned a lot from Surjeet and always tried to portray him," said Fernandes who also resides in Toronto.

Apart from being an exceptional player, Sindhi also made a fashion statement for being stylishly dressed and always perfectly groomed.

One of Surjeet's closest friends was teammate and full back Avtar Singh, who I was fortunate to make contact with two days ago, while he is vacationing in India. "Right from the start of our careers we were close family friends," said Avtar. "There was great understanding among us, on the field and off the field, we had a fantastic time and you know about it."

Avtar, who lives in Nairobi, added he and Surjeet engaged in a competition when it came to taking penalty hits. "If I missed, he would take the next one. I will miss a great guy."

Uganda's international centre forward Malkit Singh came face to face with Surjeet on several occasions at the club level and internationally. The dashing centre forward for Kampala Sikh Union played against Surjeet from 1964 to 1972 in the Gold Cup and in the East African championships. "Sindhi was a legend; he invented the scoop shot which became his signature play. I always remember him as the defensive backbone of the Kenya & Nairobi Sikh Union teams," added Malkit who lives in England. "He was naturally talented, intelligent and a very good game reader of the game. He loved to dress well, had an immaculate beard and turban, loved cooking and enjoyed his whisky."

Sindhi was a field hockey icon and I had the unique opportunity of playing against him for the RGI and also reporting on who in my opinion was one of the greatest centre-halves of his era that included some extraordinary Indians and Pakistanis. Off the field, he was a dapper individual with a sense of good clothing and an immaculate beard and turban. I recently met Surjeet in Nairobi in 2018 when I and my wife

Delphine were invited to Sikh Union by him, Avtar, Del Mudher and Ramesh Bhalla. They presented me with an autographed brochure of the club at the newly built Mahan Hall of Fame that houses photographs of all of the club's capped players. Of course, no visit would be possible without Sindhi cooking his world-famous chicken *koroga* dish. We then visited this talented architect's house he designed on the outskirts of Nairobi. We were invited to this fabulous house along with Willie Lobo, a former soccer goalkeeper with Kisumu Hotstars and photographer Anil Vidyarthi, my colleague for several years with the Daily Nation.

His garden was a picture of colour and included a fishpond, a waterfall and a huge barbeque area tended by his wife Deepi. Farewell, my friend. My other regret about the passing away of an icon was that I will never receive the *koroga* (a dish involving those around stirring the pot) recipe he had promised me.

John J. de Souza

Just special

A couple of friends: Juliet Rebello and John
By Norman da Costa and Merwin de Souza

John de Souza was an indefatigable soul who, like Martin Luther King, harboured a dream. He was a Goan icon. He was a man of many talents. He was passionate about everything to do with the community – the Goan archives, his alma mater Dr Ribeiro Goan School and the local clubs. He was a historian and had the pulse of the Goan community at his fingertips. Ask him a question and you would get the answer within 24 hours. Always willing to help on the condition he was kept in the background. He shunned being in the limelight.

John had his finger in every pie and many wondered where he got the energy to keep on motoring day in and out after making that long trek to work from his home in Brampton to the Pickering Nuclear Plant a distance of some 70 k/ms each way. He would get home, freshen up and then give a few ladies a ride to bingos or any function that evening. That was John, always willing to lend a hand.

His younger brother Romeo discovered John had passed away overnight on March 20 after a few phone calls went unanswered. The family usually met on March 19 to celebrate St. Joseph's Day – the patron saint of Dr Ribeiro's – and also to remember the day their father had died. This man with an encyclopedic mind saw his journey end at the age of 79 way too early since he had so many irons in the fire that needed urgent attention - primarily getting the different Goan organizations in Toronto together under one umbrella. He was rebuffed on several occasions, but John wasn't one to throw in the towel. He trudged on but his body obviously couldn't pull him over the line. He will be remembered fondly for being the driving force behind several initiatives including the formation of the 55 Plus Goan Association, an organization in the west end of the Greater Toronto Association with a membership of 840.

The 55 Plus was formed when the West End Seniors could no longer accept any new members. He was also the heart and soul of the Active Goans Club at Mississauga's Square One. John, of course will always be remembered for single-handedly running the popular Goan Voice Canada website that featured local clubs and more importantly death notices. After several years John was forced to bring down the shutters on his favourite venture much to the chagrin of the community at large after Romeo had asked him if he had a succession plan. For the first time, John admitted defeat, but he still had so much on his plate to keep him going. With help from Goans across Canada he promoted the Konkani Rosary in video and was a founding member of the Friends of Goan Welfare Society along with Jerry Lobo, Teresa Mandricks and me to raise funds for needy Goans in Kenya. We intend to close the account in the coming weeks with a final donation in memory of John. John and I had a long relationship. We worked closely on three Dr Ribeiro Goan School Ex-Students, Canada, functions. John also kept in close contact with Merwin de Souza, another ex-student, who lives in Florida and, like John, spends countless hours keeping the popular Goan School website alive. John and I also worked on the Railway Goan Institute 100th anniversary celebration committee held in Mississauga on September 20, 2009, and as co-editors put out a comprehensive 46- page glossy brochure. Of course, this piece wouldn't be complete without a word from Merwin.

"John was a history buff, particularly our Goan history," wrote Merwin. "He had an obsession for details most of us would miss. Recently he was obsessed with the old G.I. Duke St. building which was one of the few stone structures built-in 1905 or so. "Why stone? Do you know how much-corrugated iron roofing cost at the time... temporary permits?" He'd question. Like I knew the answer?! He was fascinated by a seminal 1955 Golden Jubilee G.I. brochure my dad published which to this day is often quoted in lieu of any other community records. Interestingly, among his many roles, he also assumed the responsibility of community historian placing on record, in the many brochures he produced, the journey of our generation. John would often say "If we don't know where we came from and the mistakes we made, how do we know where we are going and avoid re-inventing the wheel each time." A hint of his engineering background and continual improvement process would come out. "Never know why we don't do post-mortems on community events, figure out what worked, what didn't, what we can improve on the next time and pass the info on to new committees instead of reinventing the wheel . . . the only way we can make progress as a community."

His concern for the community was widespread, from archiving a record of our contributions on this planet to raising the question should we as a community be concerned that our men and women of the cloth are being well looked after in their retirement.

Lately, it was becoming apparent John felt the time was running out and I could sense he was getting frustrated. The community has just lost its most valuable resource." Like Martin Luther King, John's dream of unity in the Goan community remains just that . . . a dream. Farewell, buddy, I will miss our weekly chats and I wish all those boxes filled to the brim containing prized newspaper cuttings will find a new home.

Jack Simonian

John Levon (Jack) Simonian who was the East African motorcycling, East African Safari driver, motor rally and track champion and who represented Kenya at hockey at three Olympic Games passed away in Sydney, Australia on December 23, 2019. He was aged 84. Jack, who lived in the UK since 1978, had gone to Sydney, Australia earlier this month and celebrated his 84th Birthday. Replying to his friend, George Brink's greetings of Happy Birthday, Jack wrote "Yes, thoroughly spoilt by family and friends from all over. California, Canada, Kenya, England, Australia, New Zealand, Sardinia and last but not least South Africa!! Great day and being taken out to dinner this evening!! Life is Always

Great!!

However, WE are all leaves on a tree, some fall off and others stay on for a while!! Wish All of you a very Merry Christmas and a Happy New Year with all Blessings, Health, Happiness and Prosperity. I do miss all your company, but memories will have to suffice. Such is The Precious Life that we are gifted!! Anyway, enough of all that!! Totsiens for now."

Jack was born on December 1, 1935 in Wad Madani, Sudan. His parents had emigrated from Armenia to Egypt and then to Sudan. In 1948 the family settled in Kenya. After his primary school education in Sudan, he studied at St Mary's School in Nairobi, Kenya. He was a good tennis player at St Mary's and played hockey and tennis for his school team. After schooling, he joined East African Airways as an apprentice Aircraft Engineer. Jack enlisted in the Kenya Regiment on September 30, 1955 (National Service) and he then underwent basic training at the Kenya Regiment Training Centre at Lanet near Nakuru from October 3 to December 10, 1955. He was awarded the Africa General Service Medal in 1956. He played hockey for the regiment.

After completing two years of National Service, he re-joined East African Airways and qualified as an Aeronautics Engineer. He took up motorcycle racing, grass track motorcycle races being his first love. He played hockey for East African Airways. He joined Parklands Sports Club in Nairobi and played hockey in the Kenya European Sports Hockey Association League. He was a member of Parklands Sports Club that won the Craig Cup in 1960 against Nakuru Athletic Club. He represented Parklands at hockey, tennis and snooker.

He fondly recalled that one Saturday afternoon in 1959, the Chairman of his Club, Ron Cooper, who was vice President of Nairobi Hockey Association at the time, asked him what he was doing that afternoon. He invited him to play in goal for Nairobi X1 in a match that afternoon in a couple of hours. That day was August 1, 1959, against the visiting Indian Hockey Team. The Nairobi X1, which was captained by

Chris Wevill of Impala Sports Club, included Kirpal Singh Bhardwaj, Krishan Aggarwal, Silu Fernandes, Edgar Fernandes, Surjeet Singh Panesar (Jr), and Egbert Fernandes. All went on to represent Kenya at Rome 1960 Olympic Games. The Indian team in that match also included seven players who went on to represent India at Rome Olympics. It was hockey's good fortune that Jack did not have a motorcycle-racing event that afternoon. That match started his international exposure in hockey and he never looked back. But he kept his motorsport going on at the same time, which was a remarkable feat. He progressed to Motor Rallying and track racing which ran side by side with his hockey feats.

Only two Europeans were considered for the Olympics in Kenya when the trials for the squad started. One was Jack Simonian of Parklands, and the other was Impala's Chris Wevill. Jack was the only European selected for the Kenya squad for Rome 1960 Olympic Games. By this time, he was already Kenya's top racing motorcyclist. He made his international debut in hockey against Italy on September 1, 1960 in Rome, a match which Kenya won 7 – 0. From that moment he became a regular member of Kenya squad. He toured Rhodesia with the Kenya team in August 1961 and played against South Africa and Rhodesia at the international Hockey Festival in Bulawayo. In 1962, he joined Sikh Union Nairobi, a club with a rich history of hockey. He told me, during one of our many chats over the years, that Tari (Avtar Singh Sohal) and Sindh (Surjeet Singh Panesar (Jr)) were a big influence on him joining Sikh Union. He added: "We have a lot in common. My best friends are Sikhs."

He played for Sikh Union for more than a decade. The club won every tournament it took part in. He was a member of the Sikh Union team that won the M R D'Souza Gold Cup seven times. The Gold Cup was the Blue Riband of East African Hockey and played in Nairobi during the Easter weekend. With winning the Gold Cup went the title of unofficial East African Champions. At the same time during Easter, another sporting event – The East African Safari Rally used to take place and Jack had to juggle the two sports. There are many stories of Jack managing to play in both these sports during the Easter weekend.

Jack went on to play his second Olympic Games in Tokyo with Kenya finishing sixth, her best position at the Olympic Games. He also toured Europe in 1966 with the Kenya team and played in the 12 Nations Hamburg Tournament. Three months later, Kenya had a tour of Zambia, but Jack was unable to go due to work commitments. There was concern about too much time being taken from work, having only recently returned from a six- week tour. It so happened that Kenya's selected goalkeeper, Ahmed Hassan Sharman, got injured in the first test match and Jack was flown to Zambia in a private plane to play in the two remaining Test matches

Jack went on Kenya's tour of Pakistan for the Pre-Olympic Tournament in Lahore in January 1968 and following a successful East African Championship in Kampala in August 1968 and India's tour of Kenya, Jack was selected for his third Olympic Games: Mexico 1968. In Mexico despite losing their captain and full-back Avtar Singh Sohal through injury after only two matches, Kenya needed only to draw in their last pool match against Pakistan to proceed to the semi-finals. They lost 1 – 2 and had to play Australia in a pool playoff match which they lost 2 – 3. Kenya finished 8th. Jack was named the "best goalkeeper at Mexico Olympic Games".

Following a lengthy break from international hockey, during which he set up his own business, a Caltex petrol station, he drove in the RAC Rally in the UK and the East African Safari Rallies, Jack was recalled for the match against West Germany in Nairobi on March 18, 1972. The Kenyan Management wanted a commitment for a three-week training at the high-altitude Athletics Training Camp in Kiganjo along with other fitness camps before selection for the Munich Olympic Games. Jack was not prepared to take so much time away from business and thus ended Jack's international hockey playing career.

Jack was a true sportsman, so much so that he would often stop during the race or car rally to help a fellow competitor, sometimes in the process allowing a rival to win. In the 1969 Kenya Motorcycle Championships, for example, a good friend and foe Mike Kirkland and Jack were lined up on the grid for the final and deciding race. Kirkland noticed that chain on his bike had a problem. Kirkland knew he would not be able to start and would have to forfeit the race. He pulled off the track to allow the race to start. Jack pulled out as well and started working on Kirkland's bike and that helped Kirkland to go on and win the race and his only Kenyan bike championship.

Jack excelled with both two-wheelers and cars, both on and off the track. He was a World Rally Championship driver for Lancia, Alfa and Nissan teams. His mechanical genius to develop and improve the durability of machines was legend. He spent many years developing cars for the East African Safari Rally (later he Kenya Safari Rally). If you had a mechanical problem with any vehicle, Jack would fix with parts or modify it so never happened again. He was equally brilliant in the kitchen, Punjabi curries being his favourite dishes.

Jack emigrated to the UK in 1978. It did not matter where he lived, he was popular everywhere. After all, he was cooking the best curries and folks were flocking to his home! – *Dilgit Bahra and Jeremy Sirley.*

Jack Simon, left on the ground, with the mighty Sikh Union team

From Left: Melody Melodists Dance Band, from right to left: A. R. D'Costa, J. F. Lobo, Abel Menezes, Alec Pereira, Luis D'Lima, Ralph D'Souza (trumpet unidentified).

The talented Mr D'Costa

Antonio Remedios D'Costa was the son of Mr and Mrs Bernard D'Costa. He was born and grew up in Per Seraulim/Colva, Salcete, Goa. As a young man, he came to Kenya with his goals set on making a future in Nairobi. He married Clara Gracias, daughter of Mr and Mrs J. F. L. Gracias, MBE. Mr Gracias was a prominent member of the Goan community. He worked for the East African Railways & Harbours (E.A.R.& H.) in Nairobi, Kenya, and was a founding member of the Railway Goan Institute, Nairobi.

D'Costa and Clara had a happy life together for 57 years. They had four children, Bernadette, Matilda, Joseph and Mariella. Clara was his most vital source of inspiration and motivation in all that he set out to do. D'Costa, in turn, supported Clara in her dressmaking as she was trained seamstress. He loved cooking and came up with his recipes. He enjoyed decorating Christmas cakes with designs their children gave him. Woodwork was another one of D'Costa's hobbies. He made desks for the pre-school that Clara had for 25 years.

Before he married Clara, D'Costa had already begun a career in accounting with the E.A.R.& H. He worked in the Pensions Department where he climbed the ladder through dedication to his work. In the 1960s, the E.A.R.&H. launched its Kenyanisation program and D'Costa was assigned to train the incoming Kenyans in the Pensions Department.

However, it was not long before the E.A.R. & H invited him back and he worked in the Administration Department until 1976. D'Costa took an interest in the future of the long-serving employees who were retiring or would retire soon. He wrote to the Crown Agents in the United Kingdom on behalf of the expatriate employees regarding their pension status on retirement. He was invited by the Crown Agents to visit London to make a presentation on behalf of the E.A.R.& H. Administration. The London meeting was moved to Nairobi. He made a compelling and convincing presentation which was accepted by the Crown Agents. He was an inspiration to those employees when they left the service. With him, they knew they were in good hands.

He played a vital role in the various employee associations attached to the E.A.R.&H., namely, the Pensioners Association, the Widows & Orphans Fund, the Railway Asian Union, and the Railway Indian Institute.

As a member of the Railway Goan Institute, he served as vice president and on the Institute's management committee.

D'Costa offered his services to assist with the running of the Dr Ribeiro Goan School in Nairobi and was elected a member of the governing body, the Goan Overseas Association. It is of interest to note that Clara was among the first students to attend the School. In later years, three of their children attended the School. With that in mind, D'Costa took on an added responsibility to serve on the School Board of the Parents Association. He volunteered to train the Brass Band.

D'Costa as a noted violinist, having learned to play the violin at a very young age. He also taught himself to play the saxophone and joined the "Merry Melodists Dance Band" under the direction of J. F. Lobo. Later he joined the "Moonlight Serenaders" led by Xavier Noronha. These bands played at the Railway Goan Institute for the dances and other social events, and most often for weddings and other private occasions. Clara loved dancing.

D'Costa's love for music prompted him to conduct a group of

talented musicians and singers to perform on the "Konkanim Program" broadcast on the Voice of Kenya Radio Station. He was associated with a group of friends who were string instrument musicians. Among them were Anthony Alvares, Anthony (Oboe) Noronha, Campos Ribeiro, Joe Gonsalves, John Gracias, and the Pires brothers, to name a few. D'Costa also played the accordion and the clarinet. He also tutored young Goans in playing the violin. He taught his daughters to sing, play the piano and clarinet, and his son the keyboard and drums. He wrote music, composing songs, and translating to Konkanim, English songs that he loved to sing.

D'Costa took a prominent role at the St. Francis Xavier's Church, Parklands, Nairobi. For over 36 years, he conducted the Church choir which he appropriately named "St. Cecelia's Choir" in honour of the Patron Saint of Musicians. The choir, under D'Costa's direction, took part in a program broadcast on the Voice of Kenya. In his role as a choirmaster, D'Costa learned to play the church organ. He served on the Parish Council and various committees for events hosted by the Church. In recognition of his services to the Church, D'Costa was honoured by Pope Paul VI with the "Benemerenti Award and Medal".

In keeping with the Goan tradition, D'Costa was a member of the Colva Union in Nairobi. The highlight of the Colva Union was the annual celebration of the Feast of Menino Jesus. He was always on hand to help the Nairobi Goan Tailors Society and its members.

In 1976, the D'Costas and their youngest daughter, Mariella, emigrated to San Francisco, California, U.S.A. Their son, Joseph and his wife, Antoinette joined them in 1977. In 1984, they were joined by their younger daughter, Matilda, her husband Johnny and their three children. Their eldest daughter, Bernadette, had emigrated to Sydney, Australia in 1974. She came to visit the family for about two months every year, a trip that included a cruise with the family. D'Costa continued his career in accounting with the County of Alameda, Bay

Area Community Services. He took a course in the U.S. tax laws and the intricate preparation of taxes and manually completed all the complicated tax forms. Clara worked for 15 years as an administrative assistant at The International Institute of the East Bay. D'Costa kept up with his musical talent and joined the choir at St. Lawrence O'Toole Catholic Church, Oakland and became a valued choir member. He became a member of the San Francisco Goan Institute and served on the Managing Council and as an Auditor.

D'Costa, passed away on November 22, 1997, on the Feast of St. Cecelia. Clara passed away on November 9, 2019.

Mrs D'Costa was a very good dancer judging by her admirers

Armand Rodrigues

Armand Rodrigues/Tony Fernandes/Roque Barreto/Aloysius Vaz/ Tony D'Souza. Missing: Willy Monteiro.

Fifty years as a vibrant social and sporting club is a significant milestone in the life of the G.O.A. (Toronto). The Golden Jubilee is on April 23, 2020. **COVID-19** put paid to the lavish celebrations that were planned for the months leading to an anniversary celebration worthy of the occasion for December 2020. Celebrations are being planned for 2021, Covid or other catastrophe's permitting.) A historical perspective of this iconic club follows.

Whether in the humble "khudds" (village clubs) of Bombay or sophisticated institutes and gymkhanas elsewhere, the Goan has always been a gregarious creature with an inborn need for camaraderie. This characteristic has endowed him/her with the propensity to form clubs for social, sporting and literary purposes wherever they go, after coming to terms with the necessities of life -- food, clothing and shelter.

Back-pedalling now, before 1970 there were only a few amorphous Goan groups in Toronto, and their interests were either religious, social and sporting, but only marginally, as they were loosely knit and accountable to no one. In the broader sports arena, field hockey was the common factor that brought several Goans together, though they played for different teams. At house parties or gatherings, folks paid lip service to the need to form a proper Goan club to foster a sense of belonging, with no evidence of any initiative to start one.

In 1969, it occurred to most of the Goan hockey players that if they played together as a team, they could easily be the best in Ontario, Canada. Roque Barreto was the driving force behind this initiative, with Aloysius Vaz and Willy Monteiro as his lieutenants. To this end, a preliminary and exploratory meeting of all known players and well-wishers was called in December. It could be because of winter, lack of proper transportation, or simply inertia, that attendance was dismal, and the meeting proved a failure. Undaunted by the setback, and winter notwithstanding, another meeting was called in January 1970. Of the thirty people notified, only six roughed it out. They were Roque Barreto, Aloysius Vaz, Willy Monteiro, Tony Fernandes, Anthony D'Souza (Jnr) and Armand Rodrigues.

Decisive action was taken to (a) form an interim committee,

(b) enter a Goan team for the forthcoming Canadian Field Hockey tournament, and (c) explore the allied issue of a coherent body under whose banner to play.

Spearheaded by the six, word of mouth brought 24 people together for a general meeting, on April 5, 1970. The idea of a club under whose auspices a consolidated Goan hockey team could play was unanimously endorsed and morphed into the Goan Overseas Association (Toronto) on April 23, 1970. The rest is history. Before long, membership started escalating rapidly and the club gained momentum in the realm of sports and socials. It was a force to reckon with when it came to field hockey, cricket and soccer. Tennis and badminton had a fair list of adherents. When the Uganda Goan refugees swelled our ranks in 1972, they came with enviable credentials and gave our teams a welcome fillip. The club garnered trophies in many an open tournament. Egged on by its success, it floated the Norbert Menezes Memorial Gold Cup field hockey tournament for a number of years. This tournament became pre-eminent on the continent and attracted teams from as far away as India, England, the Caribbean and the States. And the ladies were not forgotten. They competed for the Savio & Joyce Barros trophy. Many members also donated floating trophies for other tournaments at parochial level.

Dances were always a sell-out to the extent the Lions' Club in Etobicoke could cope with a capacity crowd. The dinners were beyond comparison and the band was the best our means would allow. The camaraderie was exceptional. As would be expected, members formed the Goan Theatrical Group and kept lagging cultural traits and language skills alive with regular offerings of Konkani plays ("tiatr") and lively songs. Annual Track & Field meets brought sister-clubs together in healthy competition.

The hugely successful International Goan Convention in 1988 (under the aegis of the club) was the brainchild of Zulema D'Souza, our first female President. It put the club firmly on the map and remains unmatched to date. The International Goan Youth Convention held in Goa in 1990, was a spin-off from the Toronto Convention. Embracing all facets of Goan life, "Viva Goa" festivities serve to showcase the community to all and sundry. And, not forgotten are the disadvantaged people in our community. The Goan Charitable Organization – a registered charity—comes to their aid.

In the early heady days, the vibrancy of the club was palpable. It was the largest Goan club on the continent, and the most active. Credit for managing the club and catering admirably to members' needs, goes to the hardworking men and women who over the years have given selflessly of their time and energy in fostering the aims of the club.

That was then and this is now. Over the years, like clubs everywhere, the membership that peaked some years back has started to ebb somewhat. Population growth has not translated into a corresponding increase in membership. Societal factors such as fragmentation, diminishing community allegiance, inter- marriages and insularity, in our second generation Goans, are changing our physiognomy, and our clubs are gradually lapsing into a terminal mode. Seniors' clubs, spawned by the motherhouse, have picked up the slack and have been doing a commendable job, at both ends of the city of Toronto.

When all is said and done, it must be noted that a younger set with nostalgic traits, has taken over the G.O.A. (Toronto), from the old guard, for some years now. Selwyn Collaco has been the President for the last few years now and has used his managerial and business acumen to keep the club abreast of developments in this digital age. He has done more than any other president of the club, to bring Goans from different camps to the G.O.A. (T) tent. He is ably assisted by like-minded committee members. And Greta Dias keeps tending to the social needs of retirees, with unprecedented zeal. These volunteers keep the flame alive and pulsate to the rhythms of the times.

To celebrate the Jubilee, an elegant bash, with sit-down dinner and appropriate libation, and the accompaniment of two bands is slated for August 1, 2020.

A hearty toast to the club is in order!

DOWN BY THE SEASIDE

Our family home in Goa was about half a kilometre from the ocean. We could hear the howling winds and the waves crashing ashore incessantly. WW II was at its peak, but Goa was a neutral port in this "Province" of Portugal. Shipping was at a standstill and foreign goods were not coming in and, so, we had no toys to play with when we were young. We made crude toys and devised our fun and games. Four to six of us youngsters would get together to play. A favourite pastime was going to the beach and visiting the cashew trees on the way. All of us had home-made catapults and a supply of pebbles in our pockets. On our way, we passed several vegetable plots in the midst of fields. Any errant pigs or crows raiding the sweet-potatoes, watermelons, gourds or beans, made for good target practice. Off and on we were able to down a white egret or two and take them home for a nice soup or chilli-fry.

A dip in the ocean was a lot of fun. We would go in up to our necks, wait for the huge rollers (waves) well above our heads, to start bearing down on us and, at the last moment, leap as high as we could to catch a thrilling ride back to the shore. We did this over and over again until we were pooped.

Quite often there were fishermen laboriously pulling in their nets by hand. They waited for the incoming tide and with the Konkanim version of "heave-ho" had to get their timing right. Their primitive boat had already been dragged ashore on top of logs used as rollers. The upper part of their nets had circular floats made from branches of softwood trees; the lower part grazed along the sandy bottom. The inverted "U" configuration had them haul their nets ashore manually, from both sides... For us boys, it was an adventure chasing escaping fish behind the nets. We had small baskets (called "kondools") woven from coconut palm fronds, in one hand, and grabbed the struggling and slippery escaping fish with the other, tossing them into our "kondool". It was a smorgasbord of fish: mackerels, sardines, pomfrets, kingfish, baby sharks, lobsters, were plentiful in season. We were careful to avoid stingrays, catfish and crabs, which carried a painful sting or a pinch with sharp pincers. If we collected a lot, the fishermen expected us to give back some of" their" fish. Fish were not the only things that slipped away. One day a friend's "khasti" (trunks) joined the escaping fish! When we had collected enough of fish or became tired, we took our "loot" to where a younger brother was minding our clothes. He could not join us in the "catching" game as he was not tall enough to be in the water. He was tasked with the job of collecting twigs and dried palm fronds for a fire. It was a real treat roasting some of the fish over an open fire. No seasoning was required as the fish came from a salty ocean. The aroma worked up an appetite in all of us. The remaining fish were taken home for a tasty fish curry or *"rechada"* (fish stuffed with spicy condiments) or fish-fry.

Then there were times when we became beachcombers. There was no telling what the ocean would disgorge on to the shore. Assorted shells and debris from passing ships and dhows littered the shore for miles. With the receding tides some of the residue was taken back by the sea, never to be seen again. Arab dhows did a lot of trade along the coast. For safety reasons, they stayed within sight of land, but away from the treacherous waves, as their craft were fragile. But, from time to time, disaster would strike. A rogue wave would cause the dhow to succumb, disintegrate and send any floating commodities to stretches of the shoreline. Heavy items hit bottom. The hapless crew that survived the disaster swam ashore with only the clothes on their backs, with all their hopes of profit "drowned". Insurance for the dhow or its cargo was unheard of in those days. The Christian villagers would help them with food that their Muslim faith allowed, and shelter. (Incidentally, Arabs were skilled sailors and navigated by following the stars. However, the dangers lurking on the high seas defied interpretation)

If bagged goods like rice, flour, lentils, copra, washed ashore, they had already been rendered unfit for human consumption by the briny waters. But canned and bottles stuff was still useable. On one occasion we, boys, came upon 5lb. cans of Dalda Vanaspati (rarified butter) on the beach. "Finders keepers" was the order of the day. We each lugged a heavy can home and considered it a godsend. On another occasion, bicycles were flung ashore after a stormy night. Finders could not believe their luck. There were fights when two people grabbed a bike at the same time, from either end. The one nearest to the saddle was allowed to claim it. Another time some fishermen thought they had a really good catch when their nets were unusually heavy. They had "caught" sewing machines sitting on the ocean bed! After scraping off the rust, the machines were in good working order. As tailoring was outside their line of work, they sold them to the villagers, for a neat profit. Ripped sails were put to good use by the fishermen, in their flimsy shacks by the sea. Lumber from the wooden sides of the dhows, and their frames, floated to shore and did not go waste.

No doubt, the coastal villagers will have many an interesting tale to tell of what may have come ashore. Not surprisingly, it is highly unlikely that they would say a word about money in tin trunks salvaged.

THE JACKFRUIT

Next to the mango, the jackfruit may be one of the more exotic fruits in Goa. In weight, it is only second to the giant coco- de-mer of Seychelles, for a tree-borne fruit. It originated in the forests of South India, but, over the centuries, it has migrated to all of South-East Asia, where it appeals to the tastebuds of all and sundry. In Latin the jackfruit is called *Artocarpus heterophyllus*, in Konkani *ponos or borkoi*, in Swahili *finisi*, in Portuguese *jaca*, in Thailand *khanum*, in the Philippines' *nangka*.

In Goa, the fruit may be soft and mushy or firm and crunchy. The flesh of the soft type can be used to produce a type of alcohol after a fermentation process. It can also be used in curries, jams and chutneys. Rolled flat, the soft pulp is dried between layers of banyan tree leaves and becomes a tasty snack. Other than yellow, the firm variety also comes with a distinct orangey colour. Both types may also contain a little nectar. The firm variety is the kind sold in cans.

The fruit is unique in the sense that it grows on the trunk of the tree. The tree can live up to a hundred years. The outer casing of the fruit is like a prickly rasp. It turns greenish-yellow when ripe and ready for harvesting. At this stage, the smell becomes somewhat revolting but is a far cry from that of its cousin the Durian fruit. The latter is the bane of hotels and aircraft everywhere. When sliced open, one finds conical yellow pods like bulbs, clinging to the inside of a jackfruit. Trying to extricate pod results in having to do battle with a sticky, messy, white latex that oozes from everywhere and encrusts one's fingers and knives, with a vengeance. Cooking oil has to be used to free the fingers and clean the knives. The silver lining to the latex is that it can be used on branches to snare singing birds that alight above a bird feeder or sprinkled seed. The birds make good pets.

Jackfruit seeds can be saved to be roasted, boiled or ground into flour. Even the leathery leaves of the tree serve a special purpose in Goa. They are shaped into a cone held in place by dried broomsticks from palm tree leaves. A mix of desiccated coconut and jaggery is then encased in rice flour and placed in the cone. Steaming completes the cooking process. These cones are served, as per tradition, after friends and neighbours join in singing the litany of the saints. If a ripened jackfruit happens to fall to the ground, it becomes a feast for the pigs. Whereas flying foxes are frugivorous, it is believed that they avoid the jackfruit because the nasty latex could stick to their wing membranes and make flying impossible. Lastly, believe it or not, in Goa if a tree is not yielding fruit at regular intervals, it may be shamed by old shoes, rusty tin cans and broken clay pots tied to its trunk! There is no scientific evidence for why this works – if at all – but it is not an old wives' tale.

Enjoy the fruit if and when you can.

AN OLD-TIME FUNERAL IN GOA

Morbid as the subject may be, not many of us can claim to remember what a typical funeral was like, in Goa, years back. Some may have been too young to remember, and others may have missed an opportunity as they were abroad.

Money was always the first concern when anybody passed away. Neutral as Goa may have been, the war meant that money and the necessities of life were in short supply. Also, very few people kept money in a bank and, in any case, the solitary bank anywhere around was in town, which was several kilometres away. So, if you did not have enough funds hidden in your almirah or mattress, you had to borrow from the neighbours, and deposit some items of jewellery with the lenders, as surety.

Funeral homes were unheard of, and so related survivors had to attend to every facet of the funeral themselves. A trusty elder would be hastily despatched to the village church to make arrangements with the parish priest, the gravedigger, the sacristan, the choirmaster, the candlemaker, the confraternity leader and the village crier. Simultaneous arrangements were made to ring church and chapel bells in the village, to signal the death. One ding and two dongs, in repetition, sounded the knell. Another messenger would be sent to the nearest town to fetch a pine-wood type of coffin draped with black cloth and maybe some frilly lace. One size fitted all. A band to play mournful funeral dirges, and marches to accompany the funeral procession, also had to be hired.

A quick inventory had to be made of friends and relatives in other villages. Runners were then sent off in all directions -- mainly on bicycles -- to notify them. Word of mouth was the only way. And woe betide a family that may have unwittingly omitted to inform a relative. Close relatives abroad were notified by telegram, sent through the nearest Post Office.

Families usually had enough rice, but fish, meat, spices and liquor had to be purchased in bulk and immediately. Large metal pans and clay curry-pots had to be borrowed. If the domestic pig was not fattened enough and ready for the table, one had to be bought. Likewise, chickens. (Those were the days when a "Papal Bull" permitted families that had paid for it, to eat meat on forbidden days) There was no telling how many people would stay for any given meal or drop in after the interment. Of course, nobody in the village had a fridge.

More often than not, suitable clothing for the deceased had to be made right away. There were no ready-made clothes. To save on expenses, it was not unusual for a man's jacket and shirt to be backless.

People of the same gender would help wash and dress up the corpse. The coffin would be placed in the hall or else in the largest room in the house and be straddled by benches for the mourners. This arrangement and candlelight vigil could last for a couple of days without the advantage of proper embalming. Flowers would come from neighbours' gardens or be picked in the wild. The activity and wailing in the front of the house would only take second place to the incessant din and clatter in the kitchen in the rear. And the aromas wafting through the house compensated for any offensive odours that lingered on.

For the funeral itself, the band would play melancholy pieces outside the house and then accompany the foot cavalcade, with sombre march music, to the church. The coffin would be carried by members of the confraternity to which the deceased belonged. From the church, there would be a procession to the cemetery. The actual interment called for everybody to cast some soil on the lowered coffin.

Back at the house, the kitchen would be a frantic hive of activity. From the cemetery, all would wend their way back to where it all began, to drown their sorrow in copious potions of the potent local brews, and to commiserate with the kith and kin of the dearly departed. Dinner would follow and take on the semblance of a feast, considering that times were lean otherwise. The proceedings would go on well into the night.

All sorrow dissipated, and thirst and hunger satiated, people would gradually start making for home. Batteries for flashlights were simply not available. A burning torch, made of palm fronds, lighted the dark path ahead and also helped keep at bay the demons and evil spirits lurking in the shadows.

Until next time, normalcy then returned to mundane life in a pastoral setting.

R.I.P.

RICE PREVAILS IN THE VEGETABLE KINGDOM

Goans wax euphoric when it comes to rice. Some of us abroad may have forgotten that our staple food in Goa was and is rice. Most of the fields in Salcete yield two crops a year, whereas in Bardez the norm is one. This anomaly is simply because Salcete is low-lying, unlike Bardez where the soil is drier and the terrain rockier as it lies on the foothills of the Western Ghats. In Salcete, other than the monsoon rains, water is saved in large man-made reservoirs for planting the second crop. From times immemorial, rice in Goa was the thick brown variety with part of the bran still on. Then, in the 1940s the Government opted to experiment with Japanese rice. The yield was much higher although the "old" rice was voted as much tastier.

Rice has featured in breakfast, mid-day "canjee", lunch and dinner in Goa. Each has been an entire meal. "Canjee" was accompanied by go-with appetizers such as yesterday's curry, pickles, dried fish, sweet potatoes or bits of coconut. Lunch and dinner had the foregoing extras and/or Goa sausage, pickled fish, fried fish, shrimp, mussels or assorted shellfish. Clay pots gave rice and curry a flavour other type of cooking vessels could not match.

From being a main meal in the Orient, it can be a side-dish in many parts of the world. The Chinese might like it sticky or as fried rice. The Japanese use it in sushi. The Hungarians stuff it in their cabbage rolls. The Italians have plenty of ways to use rizzoto which is rice and cheese. Spaniards have paella with lobster tails, shrimp, calamari, and mussels. The Portuguese and Goans have pulao, sometimes cooked in a fish broth. A sweetened version called pilau is popular in the East and West. Cajun and Creole cooks in Louisiana use hot peppers, herbs and red beans in their rice dishes.

So do some people in the Caribbean. In India lentils are the add-ons. Biryani in Pakistan and India may include chicken, mutton, raisins and almonds. Rice pudding has to be added to the mix. And who has not heard of rice-balls, croquets and rice-crispies? The cooking possibilities are endless. Rice is universally popular and is one of the least expensive foods in the market.

Rice is a cereal belonging to the grass family. Wild rice is not rice as we know it. It is an aquatic grass. India was the first to cultivate rice. China started in 2000 B.C. Cultivation has not changed much over the years. In most of the East rice is grown in paddy fields, by hand, in the form of transplants. As the plants grow, the marshy fields are flooded and kept water-logged at all times. When the sheaves turn a golden-yellow they are harvested by hand using a sickle. The threshing is usually by hand and under foot by humans and animals. After the threshing the grains have to be winnowed to remove the chaff and residual granules of clay, stone or sand that may be in the mix. In Goa the un-husked rice is dried on large bamboo mats. In China it is quite common to see rice being dried along a quarter of a paved road's edge. Special mills exist for de-husking rice. The husk is added to the slop for pigs.

In the U.S.A. rice is planted by spreading seeds from a low- flying 'plane. Artificial irrigation is the norm. In about 150 days the sheaves are harvested mechanically and then processed. We have long-grain, medium-grain and short-grain rice. Within these three categories we have thousands of varieties. Almost all rice today is the long-grain type which is milled and polished to become white rice. Only a small quantity is "brown" rice.

After all is said and done, it is fitting to imbibe some good old Japanese rice-wine called "Sake", with the rice dish in front of us!

RISKY FORAYS INTO WILDLIFE HABITATS

A salient component of my job in Uganda entailed safaris across the 90,000 square mile expanse of the country.

Diversions across the famous National Parks always appealed to me because of their variety of flora and fauna, and I seldom wasted an opportunity to get off the main road and cut across a park. Narrow, one-way tracks – essentially fashioned by elephants – came with the territory. Flanking the tracks would be 10-foot-tall elephant grass.

Time and time again, I was held up by elephants with their hindquarters on the track, grazing on the tall grass on both sides, back-to-back. A couple of times I quickly found myself surrounded by them! Egress was impossible until the pachyderms sated their enormous appetite and sauntered away. For up to an hour or two, the risk of real danger to life was palpable. I was the intruder, and a U-turn was impossible. No humans were anywhere near or expected. And a VW Beetle was no match for a spooked elephant.

On one occasion, I suddenly found myself nose-to-nose with a huge hyena dominating the middle of the track. It simply refused to budge. I accelerated towards it, gunned the engine, shouted profanities, yelled at it. All to no avail. All I could do was to stay put until it got tired of the charade.

Then there was the time I was driving along a main road. Out of the blue, a mother boar dashed across the road in front of me. It was a close call. (The thought of a potential pork roast and a missed opportunity crossed my mind later). I braked as hard as I could. Little did I know that a slew of piglets was following her from the dense undergrowth and had now become separated. The furious sow was not happy and came charging towards me. I took off as fast as I could and only received a glancing blow in the rear.

To save time, I had the option of chartering a 'plane for a safari to two or three stations in a day. My favourite pilot was a WW ll Spitfire daredevil now flying a tame Cessna single-engine, two-seater 'plane. At the dual controls, I relished the thought of being a co-pilot of sorts. Needless to say, the upcountry landing grounds or fields were usually bumpy or dusty, with the potential hazard of an animal in our path.

As the hills in Uganda had magnetic properties, the compass would go berserk and become useless. Visual flying was the only alternative. On one occasion, we could not see any familiar landmarks and lost our bearings. As was customary in such situations, we flew till we cut across some railway tracks. We then followed the railway line until we reached a station. The pilot circled the station, then tilted the plane 45 degrees to the right so that I could read the name of the station while lying sideways on the door. Another time we were caught in a violent tropical hailstorm, being tossed around like a kite, and with low visibility. We had a close shave when we suddenly found ourselves skimming treetops and an ominous mountain looming ahead! Evasive action was second nature to this wartime pilot.

Best of all, we liked to fly over the National Parks to get to our destination, sometimes doing a dogleg rather than flying as the crow flies and getting an aerial view of the wildlife below. For a close-up, the pilot would turn off the engine and nose-dive silently towards herds of buffaloes, elephants, wild boars or zebras. This flushed the animals out of their wooded habitat and created a stampede. Hippos in the river snorted their displeasure and ducked for protection. In retrospect, we were performing an illegal flying manoeuvre to the distress of the animals. Come to think of it, if the single engine did not re-start in time, we would have been dispatched to eternity in pieces, and the animals would have had the last laugh.

Throwing caution to the winds, ceased to be an option many, many moons ago.

OLD TIME FUNERALS IN GOA

Morbid as the subject may be, not many of us can claim to remember what a typical funeral was like, in Goa, years back. Some may have been too young to remember, and others may have missed an opportunity as they were abroad.

Money was always the first concern when anybody died. Neutral as Goa may have been, the war meant that money and the necessities of life were in short supply. Also, very few people kept money in a bank and, in any case, the solitary bank anywhere around was in town, which was several kilometres away. So, if you did not have enough funds hidden in your almirah or mattress, you had to borrow from the neighbours, and deposit some items of jewellery with the lenders, as surety.

Funeral homes were unheard of, and so related survivors had to attend to every facet of the funeral themselves. A trusty elder would be hastily despatched to the village church to plan with the parish priest, the gravedigger, the sacristan, the choirmaster, the candlemaker, the confraternity leader and the village crier. Simultaneous arrangements were made to ring church and chapel bells in the village, to signal the death. One ding and two dongs, in repetition sounded the knell. Another messenger would be sent to the nearest town to fetch a pine-wood type of coffin draped with black cloth and maybe some frilly lace. One size fitted all. A band to play mournful funeral dirges, and marches to accompany the funeral procession, also had to be hired.

A quick inventory had to be made of friends and relatives in other villages. Runners were then sent off in all directions -- mainly on bicycles -- to notify them. Word of mouth was the only way. And woe betide a family that may have unwittingly omitted to inform a relative. Close relatives abroad were notified by telegram, sent through the nearest Post Office.

Families usually had enough rice, but fish, meat, spices and liquor had to be purchased in bulk and immediately. Large metal pans and clay curry-pots had to be borrowed. If the domestic pig was not fattened enough and ready for the table, one had to be bought. Likewise, chickens. (Those were the days when a "Papal Bull" permitted families that had paid for it, to eat meat on forbidden days) There was no telling how many people would stay for any given meal or drop in after the interment. Of course, nobody in the village had a fridge.

Often, suitable clothing for the deceased had to be made right away. There were no ready-made clothes. To save on expenses, it was not unusual for a man's jacket and shirt to be backless.

People of the same gender would help wash and dress up the corpse. The coffin would be placed in the hall or else in the largest room in the house and be straddled by benches for the mourners. This arrangement and candlelight vigil could last for a couple of days without the advantage of proper embalming. Flowers would come from neighbours' gardens or be picked in the wild. The activity and wailing in the front of the house would only take second place to the constant din and clatter in the kitchen in the rear. And the aromas wafting through the house compensated for any offensive odours that lingered on.

For the funeral itself, the band would play melancholy pieces outside the house, and then accompany the foot cavalcade, with sombre march music, to the church. The coffin would be carried by members of the confraternity to which the deceased belonged. From the church, there would be a procession to the cemetery. The actual interment called for everybody to cast some soil on the lowered coffin.

Back at the house, the kitchen would be a frantic hive of activity. From the cemetery, all would wend their way back to where it all began, to drown their sorrow in copious potions of the potent local brews, and to commiserate with the kith and kin of the dearly departed. Dinner would follow and take on the semblance of a feast, considering that times were lean otherwise, the proceedings would go on well into the night. All sorrow dissipated, and thirst and hunger satiated, people would gradually start making for home. Batteries for flashlights were simply not available. A burning torch, made of palm fronds, lighted the dark path ahead and helped keep at bay the demons and evil spirits lurking in the shadows. Until next time, normalcy then returned to mundane life in a pastoral setting.

R.I.P.

The Bandits and the Alvarez boys

These guys, you all amongst them, Jessel, Joffre and Joe (Boy) were a life-long inspiration to my brothers (Maurice-Vocals, Morgan Rhythm Guitar, Michael – Bass and myself (Mervin Alvarez - Drums). That musical journey began for us began in the compound in Nairobi, Kenya where we were open-mouthed (in awe) neighbours of Jessel and Joffre. My first memory was when Jessel sat me on his drum stool and my legs did not find the ground and I burst into tears. We as kids (totos) truly admired your musicality and variety of genres, which, to this day, inspires us to experiment with musical notes, beats, arrangements and vocal overtones. We went on thanks to your inspiration in particular, Joffre and Jessel, to seek new musical influences such as Steely Dan, Cosby, Stills and Nash, Earth Wind and Fire and The Doobie Brothers amongst 1000's of others. We also get together and have a jam as recently as last week in South London.

We would love dearly to hook up with any of the band to share our love and experiences of what was to this day, the best times of our lives. We also wish to extend our blessings to their dear parents who to this day we know as Aunty Tecla and Uncle Joe Manricks.

The last we heard of these amazing people and musicians was when they visited our place in Tooting, South London and Jessel and Joffre played on our very basic instruments (in my case similar to the old

Bandits (large coffee tin covered with balloons and cello tape and painted to look like the pearl finish on one of Jessel's kits and with a lamp stand spring as my cymbals). Morgan had an old acoustic nylon strung and Mick a basic bass. Jessel and Joffre used those to make music in front of us and we just stood there as ever, open-mouthed and smiling in fond memory of those inspirational old days in Nairobi. They played a special rendition of *Till There Was You* (Beatles) still a fond favourite of ours. Later, we also recalled that Jessel played at Maurice and Elma's wedding.

-- Mervin Alvarez

The BBC and me, a beautiful love affair

By CYPRIAN FERNANDES

I must have been four or six years when I first listened to the BBC World Service's Sports Round-up. My next-door neighbour, Mr Pinto (Peter, Francis, Jenny and seven or eight other children's dad), also a tailor, used switch his radio on to listen to the British racing results and from Day One I used to be sitting on the floor with my ears pricked. After a week or so I tried very quickly noting down some notes and over the next few weeks and months got a handle on the British sports and their seasons. I would then tell my friends after school all about it.

I did not take down the racing results – Lestor Piggot, Scobbie Breasley, Frankie Durr and a whole bunch of other jockeys appeared interesting -- but I did not pay much attention and I paid a somewhat cursory attention to complete results of the football matches on Saturday nights delivered in a sort of funeral tone, with an equally funeral rhythm ... but I did get to know the names of all the teams, first in Division I, then in II, III and eventually III.

I also got to know some of the players, especially those who made the headlines regularly, the big goal scorers of the day: Stanley Matthews, Stanley Mathews, Bobby Charlton, George Best, Bobby Charlton, Len

Shackelton, Russian Lev Yashin (in the internationals and after whom I would wear a full black outfit the little time I played football) Billy Wright and many others.

Football, of course, always dominated the news in the English winter and Rugby Union appeared to come a sort of by-the-nose second. Further in the year, Ascot and the Aintree Grand National and that is when I began getting a little interested. Especially in the Epsom Derby.

Summer brought what was going to be the great joys of my life: Cricket. It was not long before I abandoned the radio and turned to a second-hand crystal set and made into my radio thanks to the electrical skills of some Seychellois friends. It was great. Tuck it under the blanket, fix the earphones to the ears, listen to the dulcet tones John Arlott, who became my all-time favourite commentator and when I went to England about six or seven times I tried to meet him but missed him by a few minutes or an hour or two. There were others: the authoritative voice of E.W. Swanton, Rex Alston, Alan Gibson and a rosary-full of others.

In a way, the BBC created a reporter out of me from that early age. I listened and regurgitated parrot-fashion. One of the big handicaps, of course, was trying to figure just exactly where the "covers", "long on" "long off", "mid-on" "mid-off" somewhere halfway down the ground, "square leg" etc ... I did not find until I bought an MMC booklet for cricket trainers from the Smith's Bookstore in Government Road Nairobi. Even at that stage, I was in the dark, as I mentioned in *Yesterday in Paradise*.

What impressed me most, as the years wore, was the complete faith I had in the BBC ... if they said it was so. It was unbiased, utterly truthful and set the standards for the rest of the world to emulate in honest journalism. It also helped that London *Times* and the *Telegraph* were also the guardians of the truth as was *The Evening Standard* and one or two whose names I forget. The *Sun* I got to know for its Page 3 girlies nudies, the *Mirror* for its left-wing stance and the *News of World* no mother or father would allow their child to read or be seen anywhere around the house. Then, of course, there was what became the outstanding tabloid of our time: The London *Daily Mail*: bold headlines, stories crisply told, probably gave birth to the bible-like 25-word opening paragraph: *the intro*: if the Bible can be rewritten on the back of matchbox, then you can surely write your first paragraph, dramatic, brilliant, punch, the essence of the whole story in that one paragraph from which the sub-editor was handed the headline on a plate, any day. Hell, you can tell the whole story in that one paragraph.

The other thing about the *Times* and the *Daily Mail* was that both had brilliant crosswords, both became equally famous and the set the pace for the other newspapers to follow.

Then, of course, there the independent TV stations and independent radio stations which I got to know except for the four short years we lived first in London and then in Leicester.

I sometimes feel that I love the BBC World Service more than anything else that I know since I have entered the twilight zone for the aged for whom companionship is the single most important element in the continued struggle for survival ... that in the absence of a partner. Hence in a strange sort of way, the BBC World Service is my partner. Monday to Friday I listen to it 11 to midnight and if there is anything hot on between 11 to 1 am. Other times I will check in on special features, debates and House of Commons. I must say I have tried to follow the debates on Brexit and my mind feels as if it has been through a mincing machine and I have surrendered myself to the result on December 12, being something of royalist/monarchist I would like the British people to regain control of their country and their services which I am told are going to pot being inundated by legal and illegal migrants, asylum seekers and the like. I had heard it said many times the NHSS is quickly heading for self-destruction yet a friend in the know denies it vehemently.

But my memories keep my heart warm: I was there when Churchill made speeches that were some of the greatest spin invented, the rallying calls were the truth and inspired every many woman and child to take up and fight the enemy on our shores, in the air and on the sea. We shall never surrender. Thank God they never did. As the re-runs were played on-air and in the

I have been preaching change to anyone who would care to listen in my profession and elsewhere. However, I am somewhat in caught in a web of sillydom, wondering what the hell is going by the oversaturation of Indian and other subcontinental accents, some good some better off with a sponge in their mouths. I want to know more about what is going in England, Scotland, Wales, Northern Ireland, the rest of Europe and the USA, the big stories in South America, the Caribbean, Canada (occasionally) and like Canada, India occasionally, just the big headline stories. These days I am often forced to switch off the BBC because whatever is on, I find pretty boring including some of Brexit and lots of Trump. Yet I was completely enthralled by a BBC TV story called the Guardians of the Synagogues of Kolkota. The original Jews came from Baghdad, Iran, and a hundred other places and when Palestine was born, they left. Today there are less than 30 for prayers in two or three world-class living museums, cared for by second and third-generation Muslims who swear they will stay their mission forever. I wonder if the change will drive me to switch forever. Never mind, can always watch the cricket and soccer live on Foxtel which also a pretty pathetical looking compared to its early years. Wish the old Nine would come back from the dead!

Once, when I flicked the switch on for the BBC World Service, I transported into a land of real by magic and I was there in person, real person a witness to real news many thousands of miles away.

Much later in life, I had a regular sport on the British Forces Radio Service in Nairobi with a guy called Keith Skewes who went to become a big bwana on the BBC. When the Voice of Kenya started its entertainment program, I was one of the first presenters with entertainer Julie Laval, Henry Braganza with various bands, Leo Rodrigues, Augie Alvarez and a host of other names I forget. I only quit because I had to travel.

One other claim to fame: I was the first journalist in the world to do live trackside interviews at the Munich Olympics. Spoke to every winner of every medal and some losers too. Got there on crutches provided by the Games doctors as well as unnecessary painkillers in my button and a note saying that I was severely incapacitated bordering being an invalid. I had noticed the day before the Games started that the only people allowed in the inner ring of the track were people who were in wheelchairs or otherwise declared handicapped. The rest as they say is history. Gerald Sinstadt of the BBC interviewed me for radio. Could not do the TV interview because I was passing through.

Throughout my life, I have been blessed in meeting and working with some fine journalistic minds both from the UK and the USA, in sport and general news.

So, you were asking ....

No photographs but Norman Da Costa and lots of others are my witnesses.

-- Cyprian Fernandes

A priest on the run

Denis Andrew and nephew Michael Zammit who raised $10,000 in the Dili Marathon

Picture: Catholic Outlook

Dili Marathon: It was 6 am on a Saturday long ago. My nephew, Michael Zammit and I had gathered along with hundreds of others to run the Dili marathon, half-marathon or 7km fun run. The race began at 6.30 am to try to avoid some of the heat of the day. During the second half of the race, the temperature would climb to 30 degrees. But for the moment it was cool in the pre-dawn at a beautiful harbour-front starting location outside the Governor's Palace. President Ramos Horta (2007- 2012) arrived to inspire us with a speech and to thank us for taking part in such an important event for Timor-Leste. Then he fired the starting gun and we were off. The marathon was two laps of a 21.1km course. The first lap was rather exciting as we were surrounded by participants in the half-marathon and 7km Fun Run. The local Timorese were fantastic in their support from the sidelines, as were our Carmelite students. The second lap was quite another story. The runners in the shorter distances finished and we were left to experience the loneliness of the long-distance runner. The heat, the smog of the dry season and smoke from the nearby cooking fires made conditions difficult.

Then there were the obstacles such as the river crossing (fortunately it was the dry season and the water was low) and the odd dog and pig straying across the path but also the police let a lot of motorbikes and cars on the course in the second lap. And that's saying nothing about our aching legs. Still, the locals were highly excited, especially the children. They ran with us wanting to do 'high fives'. And one group brought my nephew Michael into their soccer game as he passed.

At long last, the harbour approached. A left turn and another kilometre along the waterfront and the finishing line was the most pleasing of sights. It was a slow race. Michael and I were both over 4 hours. But as always with the marathon, it was most enjoyable to finish and a great sense of achievement. The Carmelites steered us to a seat in the shade and poured cold water down us. We spent the next couple of days recovering in our novitiate and student community at Hera. Michael is an optometrist by profession. He had generously brought his equipment with him. He began testing the eyes of around 60 of our Carmelite priests, brothers and students along with the cooks, drivers and all the workers associated with us.

Denis Andrew was born in Melbourne, Vic. Some of his earliest memories, as a very young boy, was living with his grandmother at 22 Silver Street, Malvern. He will never forget sitting on his father's knee or visiting him in hospital. Both memories are when he was around two to two and half years old. His father passed away when he was pretty young.

Denis' siblings are Michael, Margaret, Catherine, Elizabeth (RIP) and Josephine.

His first day at school was probably February 1954 at St John's, Mitcham.

Andrew is a quiet, gentle man. He is man of few words. In his sermons, Denis gets his point across without having to beat his breasts or thump the rostrum. He is also very contemplative and easy to converse with.

We share a mutual interest in running and walking: me as a former sports reporter, he as someone who has been running marathons, middle and long distances and some of the longest and challenging walks around.

Here's are his thoughts in his own words: **Love of running**

I was always a good runner but, at secondary school, there were athletics carnivals and some inter-school with a bit of success.

Then Br Roberton CFC got a few of us to join Box Hill harriers and I competed as a junior.

It was probably only after I had joined the Carmelites and, in 1973, I rejoined Box Hill Athletic Club and loved the competition and the training and came to experience running as a positive addiction. The competition was fierce. I got to know some of the Box Hill distance runners. We socialised, especially after a competition. It was a great outlet from the 'hothouse' of the seminary.

Opponents

The popularity of distance running peaked in Melbourne during the 1970s. This was due to a number of factors: the success of Rob De Castella; Frank Shorter (USA) winning 1972 Olympic marathon in Munich (CF: I was there and became the first journalist in the world to interview the athletes trackside. Frank Shorter told me "he hit a wall" but somehow got to the finish.) and repeating it in 1976 in Montreal; the inaugural Melbourne Marathon which attracted 7000 entrants by the late 70s, Filbert Bayi's 1500m world record at the Christchurch Commonwealth Games in 1974 etc.

Inter-club athletics in Melbourne competition peaked in the 70's. In the summer, track competition was held at about six tracks around Melbourne. Box Hill was a powerful club and won the A grade premiership for nearly 12 years in a row. There were teams of three in each event for each grade. For instance, Box Hill had about seven 1500 metre teams across four levels which means you needed to be able to run about 4 min 12 sec just to get a run in C grade. We had a number of Olympic representatives.

Ditto the Winter cross country/road season. There were many events but there were seven major races open to the whole state and very competitive. Three cross countries: 8km, 12 km and 16km. Three road races: 10km, 15 km and 25km. The cross countries along with the 10km and 15km attracted fields of up to 700 runners. Then there was the State marathon championship. There was a Winter championship. For instance, the first six runners home for Box Hill comprised the A grade team, the next six home were the B grade team etc.

Runners who inspired me

Ron Clarke – blazed new frontiers in the distance running. His 27min 39 sec world record at Oslo on 14 July 1965 was incredible and broke the previous record by nearly 40 seconds. I remember Peter Snell saying at the time that you would have to be a distance runner to realise how good that run was. Ron was inexperienced at the 1964 Olympics in Tokyo and ran quite a slow time for third I think in the 10,000 metres. In 1968 he had no hope with the altitude at the Mexico Olympics. Ron mostly ran on the old cinder tracks which makes his accomplishments even greater – the new style tartan tracks have to be worth a second or two a lap. Lasse Viren was a great runner with memorable feats at 1972 Olympics but always had the blood doping question mark about him. I saw him run in Melbourne, but he was past his prime.

Gordon Pirie (GB) was an English long-distance runner. He competed in the 5000 m and 10,000 m events at the 1952, 1956 and 1960 Olympics and won a silver medal in the 5000 metres in 1956, placing fourth in 1952. Born in Leeds, Pirie grew up in Coulsdon, Surrey, and ran for the South London Harriers.

Herb Elliott: Many athletes have won more gold medals than Elliot but few have ever exercised the authority Elliot did in middle-distance running. In 42 races he was never beaten over a mile or 1500 metres. He won the 1500 metres at the Rome Olympics but his time then would have been good enough to win in Seoul (1968), Barcelona (1962) and Atlanta (1996).

Peter Snell (when I read his autobiography I realised he often did not feel at his best in some of his 800 metre/1500 metre races but he gritted it out and fought to the finish and won).

Brendan Foster (GB) British former long-distance runner who founded the Great North Run. He won the bronze medal in the 10,000 metres at the 1976 Summer Olympics, and the gold medal in the 5,000 metres at the 1974 European Championships and the 10,000 metres at the 1978 Commonwealth Games.

Murray Halberg (NZ) handicapped with a withered arm and won 5000m in Rome Olympics 1960.

Kip Keino (not a fan but an admirer but saw him run in Melbourne and beat Ron Clarke).

Henry Rono a great distance runner. I saw him break the Australian 10,000-metre record at Olympic Park in Melbourne in an incredible time of about 27 min 30 sec, but I think he was sadly troubled with alcoholism later in his career. Mo Farrah, the best. I saw him run 5000 metres on the Olympic Games track in London in 2016.

Walking

I got my first taste of wilderness walking on a three-day walk around Wilson's Promontory National Park in Victoria when I was a seminarian in about 1974. I loved it. The camping, the views, the bush. I did a number of camping trips with my family. But I fell on my feet when I arrived at Park Orchards-Warrandyte parish in Melbourne on 15 August 1998. There was a group of about six men who were into some serious walking and I climbed aboard.

Since then, he as walked some of the toughest all around the world including Walls of Jerusalem/Overland Track Tasmania; Mt Jugungal region in Snowy Mountains, Victorian Alps, Grampians Victoria and lots more.

How did God win against athletics?

It is not an either/or. Both are aspects of my life. In the 70's while a student at Whitefriars Monastery at Donvale Victoria, athletics was an outlet, a sport. I loved the camaraderie of the distance running fraternity at Box Hill Athletic Club, I loved the competition. After Ordination, I have managed to keep competing in Sydney and Brisbane while stationed there. A side benefit of the distance running competition is fitness. Ministry in a parish can be quite demanding and I have always felt that the fitness and health that training brings has helped cope with both the physical and mental demands of ministry.

Memories of days gone by

A look back in time... the Mombasa road sometime in 1963 and four young men are heading back to Nairobi.

Probably the beer we drank was warm – we did not know much about ice coldies back then. Somewhere along the memorable track that was the link between capital to coast we stopped for a pee break and, as someone with a camera, I propped the wonky Waltzflex in a position to capture us all. Call us Kenya cowboys but the hats from some Mombasa market give us a Mexican look! Almost 60 years have passed since that moment but, thanks to the magic of film, it can be looked at again and can recapture memories of youth. Sadly, I am the only survivor. That's me on the left. My Kenya mates have all passed on – Jeff and Vic Baronet and Willie Alexander are gone, but only in spirit. This week marks the anniversary of Jeff's death – a suitable time to remember old friends. Had he lived, and not died in 1997, Jeff would have been 81, which seems rather strange today. He is best remembered by reversing those numbers – to the good-looking teenager of 18. Jeff lived his best years as a young man and it is good to remember him as wild and dashing, fun-loving and kind, as ready for a scrap as he was for a drink. Those heady days would soon be calmed for me with marriage and, with Kenya's independence, most school mates moved from Kenya. I caught up with Jeff in Shropshire in 1985 and had a great night with him and brothers Charlie and Dennis. He drove me to the station the next morning and it was the last I saw of him. But the bond was there. Jeff and I were good mates, Willie befriended me at school at the Prince of Wales and was best man at my wedding. Vic was, let's face it, Vic. Those who knew him have their own stories! Ironically, Vic was also a survivor and while Jeff died early, and Willie within the last eight years, the oldest of the Baronet brothers lived on until he was almost 80 when he died, in Poole in 2015. But it is back to those wonderful days of Kenya in the 50s and 60s that we look today. Hell, we left school and straight into a job. We had money and friends and we absolutely knew we would live forever. Yes, an era long gone but cherished.

It is only now, six decades on, that we realise that time waits for no man or woman. But who is complaining? We had a tremendous time and with friends like these, remembered here, the memories live on.

Nicky D'Mello

Nicky D'Mello and Norman da Costa

IT WAS an innings that ended abruptly. Nicky de Mello was a diehard cricket fan who lived for the game. He would diligently wake up at 2 am to catch the first ball bowled on TV in a Test match (in the comfortable confines of his home in Mississauga). But this was Nicky. There were no half measures about him. As a fan, as a travel agent or as a sports administrator, he stood out. He left an indelible mark in whatever project he undertook.

Back home in Uganda he was the regular scorer and on occasions umpired as well. On a couple of occasions, his finger went up, and he gave the best out leg before wicket, even before the ball had reached the batsman. Few crossed his path. He was knowledgeable enough to dissect India's shortcomings, especially in that World Cup semifinal loss to New Zealand. He was very disappointed that India hadn't advanced to the final, but he accepted the fact New Zealand was the better team on the day. "Well India will bounce back and win the next World Cup," said Nicky, a close friend of mine. Unfortunately, India's biggest fan in this part of the world won't be around to cheer India anymore or need any early wake-up calls. The Entebbe-born Nicky passed away in Mississauga in the early hours of Oct. 24, 2019, at the age of 77.

He leaves behind Cressy, his wife of 49 years, and his three children Evelyn (Peter), Twyla and Olivia and grandchildren Larissa, Samaya and Kierra. He is survived by his sisters Eulalia (U.K.) and Rose (B.C.), and brothers Marcus (U.K.) and Mario (Nova Scotia) and numerous cousins, nephews and nieces. Nick was predeceased by his brothers Felix, Victor, Peter and Arthur.

Cricket may have been his passion, but he followed every sport with the same enthusiasm and, after landing in Montreal following Idi Amin's purge of the Asians, he turned his attention to baseball's Expos and attended every home game in the cavernous Olympic Stadium.

Nicky, like most Canadians, was sure the Expos would land the World Series in 1994-95 after an outstanding season. But, in a cruel twist of fate, their aspirations were crushed by a baseball strike. The Expos forced to abandon Montreal for Washington. Unfortunately, Nicky also missed what would have been a crowning moment for him when the Washington Nationals lifted their very first World Series trophy by beating Houston Astros on October 31, a few days after he passed away.

His love for sports knew no bounds possibly because he couldn't personally pursue any single activity seriously after losing an eye to a freak accident in his early teens.

As an administrator, he had no equal. Who could ever forget his efforts in getting the Horizons hockey team up and running? Horizons proved in a short time that they were a team to be reckoned with.

The Horizons team was born after some players who belonged to Kampala Goan Institute became disenchanted with the lack of playing time due to politics. Enter Nicky, and the rest is history.

The Horizons had a dream start by winning a trophy in their very first tournament. The team was led by Osbert Remedios and included Olympian George Moraes, brothers Jerry and Anthony Braganza, Leslie Sequeira, Charlie de Souza, Effie Rato, brothers Stan, Zenon and Hubie de Souza, Narendra Singh and Edwin Fonseca. Fonseca, a Uganda cricket international, scored the winning goal to stun none other than the KGI 1-0 to win the Bhandari Jaffer Trophy, one of that country's top field hockey tournaments.

Nicky did not stop there. He pulled enough strings to get a decent-sized hall at the Lugogo Stadium that was to eventually become the club's clubhouse, complete with a bar. Then he embarked on a membership drive that peaked at 100. "He was meticulous in whatever he did," said Moraes, the tall full-back who was one of three Goans to represent Uganda in the 1972 Olympics in Munich. "He organised several functions at the place and brought in a few sponsors. He was the brains and worked behind the scenes, working tirelessly for his members and I thank him for my selection to Munich," added Moraes.

Since Nicky and my family shared a long history that included his mom Bella being my godmother, we enjoyed a close bond. In 1967 as sports secretary of the Railway Goan Institute I invited the Horizons to pay us a sports visit and that turned out to be one visit that's fondly spoken about till today. Over the four days our bar did a roaring business. A year later in 1968 after RGI won the M.R. de Souza Gold Cup for the third time and we paid a reciprocal visit to Kampala at Nicky's invitation.

With several Olympians in the RGI line-up, spectators were charged an entry fee. But the visitors failed to live up to their reputation as East African champions as most of the players were tripping over the powdered white lines on the ground because of the many cocktails consumed on a hellish journey that took 24 hours as the bus broke down on several occasions. Not to mention lack of sleep (that's no excuse). But the RGI cricket team made up for that loss by thumping the Horizons at the famous Lugogo Stadium. One of the many highlights of this memorable sports visit were the two Golden Jubilee Variety Shows choreographed by my Daily Nation colleague Cyprian Fernandes.

For our return journey, a happy Nicky loaded 12 bottles of waragi and mixers on the bus. Would you believe that someone on the bus stole all the *waragi,* (Uganda alcohol) but was kind enough to leave the mixers behind for others.

As sports editor of the Nation Group, I hired Nicky to write a weekly column on Uganda sports for the Sunday Nation and it drew a healthy readership as no other East African newspaper had a weekly column dedicated to that country's sports scene. In 1992 Nicky put out a 12-page sports newspaper highlighting achievements of Goan sports men and women and that too was warmly received.

In Montreal, Nicky was responsible for an annual darts tournament. Just as the Gold Cup tournament attracted the cream of field hockey teams to Nairobi every Easter, the tournament in Montreal drew friends and families from across Canada. It was a huge success for several years before running out of steam.

Because of his organisational skills, in 2016 Nicky was called upon by former Uganda hockey star Malkit Singh of London to head a local committee to celebrate a *Jambo and Kwaheri Wazees* (Swahili, hello, goodbye old men/elders) get together in Toronto. In typical Nicky fashion, he helped round up at least 200 of Malkit's buddies from around the world for the celebration that included Kenya captain and three-time

Olympian Avtar Singh from Nairobi. Avtar joined several other former East African men's and women's internationals for a night of partying in Toronto. Malkit also somehow managed to rope in one of the world's greatest sprinters Ben Johnson who, in my opinion, was wrongly banned and made to return his 100 metres gold medal on a doping charge at the Seoul Olympics in 1988.

He was also a brilliant travel agent.

Nicky was one of a kind. He will be missed.

Eugene Pereira

1946-2019

Eugene was the best-dressed individual in his group. He walked to school with his buddies in his neatly pressed shorts. His quietness and naughty smile attracted a lot of attention. His close buddies knew him as Poder (Konkani) - baker in English - no rhyme or reason for that.

A determined young man who at a young age left the comfort of his Nairobi home with a friend Cyril Rebello to join the British Forces and carve a path of his own. Being small in stature, he was turned down but fulfilled his dreams of being in the air by joining Air India. He lived in Muswell Hill on 50th Church Crescent, London, England. He was the king of Muswell Hill and became the President of the Goan community who arrived and left from his home, so much so that the

Immigration Dept questioned his address. Clothing was his passion and attracted a lot of attention. Dressed in a three-piece suit, a copy of a newspaper under his arms, shoes highly polished by his guests, he would arrive at work and on his way home stop at the pub, an English pass time. His mother would say he was a gentleman in the rank with no money in the bank. It was here 48 years ago that Maureen passed the test of washing the dishes, cleaning and cooking, and the rest is history.

Eugene's pursuit for the best for his young family landed him in the land of milk and honey in the 1970s and we renewed our family friendship. Wanting nothing but the best for his family, he worked hard and persevered to obtain his CGA. From looking at figures to working with figures was a natural transition. He established himself as an excellent Accountant and offered his services and kept perfect accounts for our Association.

Family and friends were his joy. Wanting to be with his friends, he made an excuse of craving for Goan Sausage on a bun and went to Viva Goa last year, even though his health was failing. That was the last time he socialized with his school buddies. The next final journey was to the family get-to-gather in New Market for Thanksgiving. I am going, this is my family and I want to be with them. Then began the weekly trips with Maureen to the hospital.

The family values he instilled were evident when he had his first setback and Gavin, who was in University at the time, volunteered to take a leave of absence. Gavin relates it: Eugene would not hear of it and gave him a stern NO and asked him to push forward, and here are is what Gavin has to say: My dad had a zest for life like no one I ever met. He cherished all of his friendships over the years. Dad, I am grateful to you for believing in me, teaching me the importance of hard work, compassion and giving to the less fortunate and instilling in me a strong sense of family values and self- confidence. I hope to continue your legacy by providing the same lessons and experiences to Nicholas and Elise.

Eugene was the life of the party without him wanting to be the centre of attraction. New Year's Eve saw Eugene in his glory. At the end of one New Year's dance after really partying as we did in those good old days, Eugene was leaning on me as I helped him to the car and in his humorous way he said to others as we proceeded - I'm helping Denis as he has gone over his limit". He kept on calling for Maureen who at the time was vacationing in Goa.

New Year was a special time for Karl. Every New Year after the night before had settled down, Eugene would say to Karl "I am proud of you, this is going to be a good year for you. Maureen and Eugene brought in 2019 at home. Karl, as usual, went to see them as he did every New Year, and this is how their interaction took place. "Karl, this is going to be a big year, I'm going to walk again, take my grandchildren to the park and recover from this illness. I turned to him and said "dad I am proud of you" - he held my hand, Karl felt the quiet strength, unwavering faith and comfort in the Lord that gave him calm. He provided unconditional love and support. We are broken now but take comfort in knowing that you are finally resting in eternal peace. We will always love you, dad, you will be in our hearts. Eugene showed disdain for self-pity; he never lost his energy or optimism or zest for life. Cancer did not scare him and he maintained that buoyant spirit to the very end, fiercely devoted to his friends and most of all, to his family. Maureen was his pillar and strength. She was his Florence Night in Gale and tended to his every want and need. He wanted her by his side at all times and she was there with him until he breathed his last.

Maureen Pereira

By PAM GONSALVES

1943-2019

I write the following with a broken and heavy heart. The tears are non-stop as I remember all those early memories. The pain of losing Maureen is so great. Caring friends and relatives from around the globe have called, sent emails and cards. These offer solace for a broken and grieving heart. Maureen was a larger-than-life figure in our lives.

Sisters, sisters

There were never such devoted sisters

When a certain gentleman arrived from Rome She wore the dress and I stayed home.

A song my mother taught us to sing and perform. We became known as the Moniz sisters: You know Pam and Maureen Moniz from Parklands!

Dad was very strict about makeup and nail polish whilst still at school. Maureen, however, would manage to over-look this strict rule. Although we dressed alike until we left school, growing up our interests, our friends, our hobbies and our working lives took different paths. I let her drive dad's car one time after church service. As we got nearer the gate, she forgot to straighten the wheel of the car and we swerved into the bushes. I quickly got out, jumped into the driver's seat, reversed and managed to get the car home safely, with just a few twigs stuck in the front bumper. Dad never came to hear about this incident

Both Maureen and I went to dress-making classes with Mrs Fernandes in 2nd Avenue Parklands. Our first project was making a pair of rompers. She always said the rompers would come in handy in the future. Marriage was certainly not on our minds at this stage. We were more interested in making layers of starched petticoats, the fashion of the 1950s.

I believe Maureen was one of the first trained hairdressers in Nairobi. All our girlfriends, Cicely, Suzanne, Girlie, Claire would come on a Saturday afternoon to have their hair done. We would discuss where we were going out that night and with which boy. It was hard convincing our parents that the boys were also good family friends.

Many happy times were spent at the Goan Gymkhana in Nairobi. We loved dancing and it was a job trying to keep up with booking the boys for dances! Our family and friends, picnics to City Park, the Arboretum on New Year's Day after the all-night party at the Gym. Our parents cooked food and took in large tiffins called ick micks. Clarice organized the games and the boys had to dress in fancy dress.

Soon our lives were to take different paths. I left home to study and later teach away from Nairobi. Maureen left to find her fortune in UK where she met Eugene and later married.

Maureen always supported me in my fundraising ventures. She mobilized all her friends in Canada to contribute to a school in Kitui and the aged-care home in Aldona. And if she couldn't, she would know someone who could.

Maureen darling sister, you will be sadly missed especially all those emails always informing us of various events and giving us first-hand information of deaths, births and marriages and much more. Our time spent in 2nd Avenue Parklands were special and I shall always cherish those happy memories.

ALVIRA ALMEIDA: Eugene and Maureen had been our friends forever. Eugene and I go back to the railway quarters days in Nairobi of the 1950s. My Donald insists he knew Maureen before me in Parklands. Maureen and I shared a bedsitter in London around 1965. We never quarrelled. Maureen was a neat and meticulous and I always in a hurry. Maureen would remind me to keep things tidy. She was kind and forgiving. We went to parties in a big group and eventually, Eugene and Maureen gravitated towards each other. The inevitable happened: they fell in love and got married. Reggie and Vivi, Maureen and Eugene and Don and I spent a lot of time together.

Maureen was always the excellent hostess. And if I was in Toronto for my birthday in January, Maureen usually had a huge feast and shared a birthday date with me. She usually brought a special cake for me when she came to England to visit her mum. Don and I were fortunate to spend time with them.

She always came laden with gifts. A kinder person you would not meet. We missed Maureen and Eugene when they decided to move to Toronto, but our friendship had no boundaries. We always made it a point to visit each other.

Maureen was quite straight forward. Her family was her focal point and she couldn't do enough for them and, of course, they reciprocated. She was very artistic in the presentation of her food. We really couldn't do enough for each other. Eugene drove for miles to pick us whilst Maureen got everything ready.

I think Maureen was the only one who told me off when I was in the wrong. She was also very forgiving, moving quickly as two sisters.

When I visited Toronto in May I was so privileged to spend a day with Maureen. The weather was ghastly but we shared one beautiful sunny day together. We reminisced so much we could not stop talking. However, it was easy to see that Maureen was still hurting because she couldn't come to terms with losing her eternally beloved, Eugene. She said without the support of Karl and Gavin and their families she could not cope. That day I spent with Maureen was wonderful. Once again, she cooked a feast. When it was time to go, we arranged that when Maureen came to England to visit her siblings Pam and Cajie and their respective families, Maureen and I would visit Malta.

Little did I know that that was the last time I would hug my best friend. Her loss was too hard to bear even with the wonderful support of the children and the grandchildren.

The gardener was there that last day I saw her, and Maureen tried to supervise her in vain because we were so engrossed in our conversation. I was not to know that that was the last time I would see my darling friend alive.

Yes, we emailed and spoke on the phone but I did I know that your life had been shattered beyond repair and you could not carry on without your beloved Eugene.

Donald and I will miss you forever. Rest in peace.

Justin Dourado

1942-2018

Justin was born in Kitale, Nairobi, Kenya. He was the eldest of 6 siblings. When he was 12, his father passed away and he had become the man of the house. He helped his mum to look after his four brothers, Aklin, Tony, William, Johnny and baby sister Joyce. He had to grow up fast and helped his mum, Maria, provide for them, educate them and shower them with the love and support that a father gives his children. After finishing St Teresa's boys' school in 1961 at the age of 18, Justin joined East African Airways in Nairobi. His work colleagues described him as hard-working, pleasant and very helpful. He took care of the family and made sure that they all completed their education.

Whilst in Nairobi, he played football for the Young Goans and hockey for the Railway Goan Institute. He also took part in athletics, in particular the 100m and 200m sprints. His house was full of sporting trophies that he won. In 1964, he took a transfer and promotion to Mombasa, and whilst there played hockey for the Mombasa Institute. He made many good friends whilst in Mombasa.

In 1967, East African Airways, Mombasa, promoted Justin to a senior officer. His boss said he can still picture his face lighting up when he got told the news.

During the late 1960s, most of the brothers started to move to England. Justin's mum and sister moved in 1970 and Justin moved over to the East African Airlines branch in London in 1971. A few years later he bought a house in Walthamstow and continued to work for East African Airways, later named Kenya Airways until his retirement.

Justin was a father figure to his siblings and the greatest Uncle to his nieces and nephews, we couldn't have asked for anything more. He always optimistic about his job, and through it, he travelled the world, met many great people along the way, and made sure he learnt about their cultures and food. I always remember the picture he had of him shaking hands with Prince Edward on his mantlepiece.

Family values were also important to him. We all looked up to him; he was a legend to others. Some called him the Godfather without the Corleone violence. He was a great cook; no one in our family could beat his fish curry and chicken curry.

He loved watching *Only Fools and Horses* and could watch them one after the other during the Christmas holidays. Justin was known to be an entertainer, the life and soul of a party and the one who came out with all the jokes, some of which were too rude to repeat.

One of my favourite memories was of Justin wearing his French maid's apron on Christmas day, and watching everyone's reaction when they came to visit. I can't remember if he took it off before the priest came over, but it wouldn't have surprised me if he didn't.

He was known for being the WhatsApp king, always without fail sending morning messages to all, wishing them a nice day, sending them quizzes and jokes.

He always made time to help others in need.

Justin was very meticulous in everything he did. Everything had a place and there was a place for everything. Whether that be at work or at home. I've lost count of the times I'd eat at his house and have to put the correct placemats on the dining table.

My Uncle was a straight up man, saying things how they were as he always felt that honesty was the best way to be. This sometimes upset others, but you could be rest assured he wouldn't say anything behind your back he wasn't prepared to say to your face. He corrected us when he felt it was needed and provided us with the wisdom that he gained over the many years of his life.

No doubt, one person that will miss him a lot will be my mum. As the only girl and the youngest of six she was bound to get special attention. When my grandma came over to England, she came over with my mum and they settled together, here in Leicester. So, Justin had his two special ladies here and was extremely fond of them.

Bill Pagano

Pictured is a Lancia I built in 1958. That's me in the driver's seat. Loved racing!

MINE IS a long story. However, I will try and write a bit at a time. I am 85 years old but thank God my memory is still perfect. My father was born in Italy in 1912 and my mother in 1915. I was born in 1935. My father had to join Mussolini's Italian Army in 1939, just before my sister was born, he was sent to Africa and later taken prisoner in Asmara, Ethiopia.

The British and the Allies captured thousands of Italian soldiers in North-Eastern Africa and elsewhere. Of these, some 55,000 Italian POWs were sent to 11-camps (all built hastily) in Kenya. He was held captive in Naivasha, in the Rift Valley, around 90 km from Nairobi (beautiful area). At the end of the war, he had managed to get a job with a Mr Taylor in Kinangop, in what is today Nyandarua County. (The county is located on the northwestern part of the old Central Province and contains the Aberdare Ranges).

While my mother and I were in Italy, for six years, we did not know if our father was alive or dead. The last time we heard from my father was at the end of 1939. He was away fighting for the Duce (Mussolini) My sister was born in June 1939 and, according to my mother, he was sad for not being there to see his new-born daughter. It was 1946 when we eventually heard from him. A Mr Taylor wrote through the Red Cross,

We did not know what the letter said because none of us could speak, read or write English. My mother had to walk 10 miles to find a gentleman who could read the letter. He had lived in America and spoke good English. It was a Mr Taylor said in the letter that my father was OK and in Kenya and that he would be coming home soon. Mr Taylor said in the letter that he was sorry to lose my father and he hoped he would return to Kenya to work for him again.

As soon as my mother returned home, she ran to the priest to cancel the funeral arrangements she had for my father. My father came back in June 1949. He was a carpenter and knew a lot about construction and buildings. By then, Mr Taylor's daughter and son-in-law, Mr Durie, had bought a farm and wanted my father to be in charge and take care of their farm. The Duries were looking after Mr Taylor's farm.

Two years later he applied for a Government job with the Public Works Department and was sent to Eldoret. I followed him and got a job with Cooper Motors. My father and his road crew took care of the repairs to the road from Eldoret to the Equator (there is still a sign advertising the Equator). In the end, he got a big job. He had to build a big, big bridge with railway tracks underneath. There was a significant camp of Mau Mau detainees nearby and, every morning, he would send three lorries to pick up the detainees to work on the bridge. He had to hire four white people, including my uncle. Three years later, I went back to Italy on vacation for six months, all paid for by Cooper Motors.

When I came back, my father finished building the railway bridge and decided to start building contractor business, with me as a sleeping partner. However, by then, he needed a vacation and went back to Italy for six months, all paid for by the PWD.

Dad got a big contract to build around ten dormitories with new toilets, a sewer system and a Catholic Church at Kitale. My uncle joined him full-time and he continued working for the P W

D. He sent an SOS to relatives in Italy to help with the building work. Soon we four relatives arrived. We soon had a two-storey building of our own. The second storey housed a bar and restaurant called Pagano's and it soon became popular. On the first floor, I had a grocery store in partnership with an Indian friend. I also had a transportation business with three lorries working almost 24 hours a day.

I was 23 years old with too much on my young shoulders. The weekend was my time off if I did not have to do police duty to give the full-timers a break. Otherwise, I would go dancing on Saturday nights. On Sundays, I would love to play tennis.

Finally, I need a break. There was an opening for a Service Manager in Tanzania. My boss, Mr Sparrow, recommended me for the job. After a month, much to my father's disappointment, I got engaged to a Scottish girl and took off for Dar es Salaam.

I went to Dar es Salaam because I needed a break from my father's businesses. In Dar I was very well-liked and I lived with a Maltese family. After a month, I was more like a son to them. I met my General Manager who was German but spoke fluent Italian. I was happy about that and thought we would get along very well. He gave me the bad news that he had already hired a service manager. However, he said, I was more than welcome to stay and straighten the place, as they were losing money at the workshop and the spare parts department.

I told him that I was more than happy to stay and would try to straighten things out. It took me three months to do just that. I hired new people and couple a stealing from the parts department. I went back to Kenya for Christmas and officially got engaged to my girlfriend. Meanwhile, in Eldoret, from April to December our lorries lay idle in the parking lot. My brother-in-law was supposed to take care of the repairs when needed. So many things were not same anymore.

My father told me that he planned to return to Italy to start a business over there. I told him I would return to Kenya but could only do so after I finished my contract with Coopers. I left Dar in April on good terms with the Manager.

My father was Pasquino Pagano and my mother's maiden name was Ida Maria de Santo. We arrived in Kenya on my 14th birthday on October 1, 1949, from the Port of Brindisi to Mombasa. A year later, my mother and two sisters and an uncle joined us.

Leaving my little hometown of 800 was very hard on me. We were just one big family, especially during the war. We were occupied first by German soldiers followed by the Africans, the Indians, the English and finally the Americans. There was some fighting. The Germans were in my town, Liscia, and the English in Palmoli where my father was born with the River Trieste dividing the two towns. So, I was not a stranger to people from other countries.

On the Lloyd Triestino, my father met a fellow POW who was going to be working on the farm next to us. My father's boss, Mr Durie, had paid for three train tickets in advance as he also knew my father's friend's boss. We went to the train station only to learn that there were no tickets. For three days we at a hotel in a single room as we did not have much money. We lived on the bread and cheese we had brought from home. Finally, the tickets arrived, and we were on our way to Nairobi. My father's friend's boss came to get us and took us to the Duries' farm in Kinangop

My uncle went to work for a Mr Nightingale. In Naivasha, my very first job was as an apprentice mechanic, also on a farm, and I lived with an Italian, Mr Petrarca, who was in charge of the repair shop. Mr Hughes, who owned the farm, was a Major serving in India. He was a terrible man, as I remember. The first thing he told me was not to talk or have any contact with black people. Otherwise, I would be fired. He used to whip black people every day when they made a mistake. Three months later, I had an accident on a wood planer. I chopped off the tip of the left middle finger and a little off the sides of two other fingers. Mr Nightingale took me to a hospital in Nairobi and his son took me to my father's place. Dad did not have a car and could not come to see me at the hospital.

Three months later, I went to work in Naivasha in Gordon's Garage and stayed with Mr and Mrs Brown. As mentioned, after two years in Naivasha, we moved to Eldoret.

I won the first Mount Elgon motor car rally in 1957. Earlier I lost out in the first Coronation Safari (later East African Safari, Kenya Safari) driving a Volkswagen. I won the rally with a friend of mine and when we arrived at the finish, there were no English people to welcome us. There were only a few Indians and Africans. That was because I was of Italian prisoner of war stock. There was a lot of discrimination in those days.

They even announced an Englishman as the winner of the race in the *East African Gazette*. They did send a little cup as the winner of the race. I still have it. They misbehaved again when the Queen Mother came to Eldoret. I was to drive the Land Rover I had prepared for Her Majesty, as I was also a part-time police officer. They took me off that detail. I loved what I did, and I would do it again. Sorry, excuse my grammar, never did go to an English school.

(Discrimination in Kenya in those days should not have come as a surprise to anyone. However, as far as the Italians are concerned, it was not that long ago that they were killing British soldiers and their allies. The colonial government and settlers were angry that their paltry funds were spent to meet the ongoing costs of caring for the POWs. The British government in London was otherwise engaged.)

The settlers did not want to see white men working with Africans on the farms as menial labour. They did not want the Italians loose with their womenfolk who were in charge of the farms while they were away fighting for Queen and country. After all, most Italians had the reputation of womanisers. Most of them were pretty handsome and charming to boot. Still, if there was a white settler around, there were no problems. Italians were normally good dressers and stylish dancers. However, they were racist too because they did not actually treat their Indian and African camp guards with any kind of decency.

I am being neutral and have been all my life! When the Italians were in Somalia, the Mussolini army-built roads, a railway, schools and much more for the Somalis. Not like the British, they ruled half of the world, Africa, India, Australia and a lot more. They built nothing. Remember the old saying, empire on which the sun never sets because somewhere in the empire, the sun was shining.

When the Italian ships went through the Suez Canal on route to Mogadishu, Somalia, they had to pay in gold. The Mussolini army did not cross over to Kenya, Uganda and so on. The British did cross over in wanting to take over Somalia. There was killing on both sides. The Italians soldier were taken to camps as prisoners to Kenya. The African Guards were well trained by the British to maltreat the prisoners by ransacking their tents, looking for unusual items, like radios etc. Some of the POWs were beaten regularly beaten by the askaris, my father told me, amongst other things.

A fellow prisoner found a roll of wire and pretended to have a radio. He ran the wire from the inside of the tent to the roof. The askari saw it and reported to a senior officer. When they pulled the wire from the ground, they found nothing. When they pull it from the roof, they found a big carrot attached to the end of the wire! As if to say, you are nothing but a carrot!

It is a known fact that Italians are womanisers as you put it! The ones who worked on the farms were too scared to approach the English Ladies. Because their husbands were away in the army, it was the ladies who made the first move. Some of the husbands found out and those innocent Italians were marched to a different camp with more punishment from the specifically trained askaris. You also forgot to mention all the good the Italians did just for some food and a place to sleep. As I said, they built the only stretch of good road from Naivasha to Nairobi (on the Rift Valley escarpment). Two Italian prisoners were killed by lions in the process. They also built a beautiful little Catholic church on the escarpment. Still there today.

We had an Italian soccer team in Eldoret and played against the army team from Gilgil. We lost and I ended up with a black eye. Never played soccer again preferred tennis because that is where the girls were.

I went to Dar es Salaam because I needed time off from my father's businesses. I Dar, I was very well liked and boarded with a Maltese family. After a month, I was more like a son to them. In Dar, I also met my General Manager, a German who spoke fluent Italian. We got on very well. He told me that he had already hired a service manager, however, I was more than welcome to stay and straighten out the place. It took me three months. I went back to Kenya for Christmas and officially got engaged to my "wife".

From April to December, my father's lorries were idle in Eldoret.

My brother-in-law should have looked after their maintenance and other work. Things were not the same anymore. My Father was planning on returning to Italy. I told him I would return to Kenya, but I had to finish my three-year contract first.

For the next six months, I took over as Service Manager at the Nakuru Branch, as the German Manager was going back to Germany on vacation. On my way to Eldoret, I stopped to meet my new boss, a Mr, Reynolds and the Service Manager. I could tell, I wouldn't get along with Mr Reynolds, and we didn't. HE DIDN'T LIKE ITALIANS! I did take over for six-month and then left to be with my family and fiancé in Eldoret for two weeks.

I had many friends in Nakuru, and stayed with M. and Mrs Lamb, (Frank Lamb's brother was a teacher at Hill School). They were nice. As I had lots of free time, I rejoined the Kenya Police and I was able to give the locals a break on weekends, or I would go back to Eldoret. I met Daniel arap Moi through a friend, played billiards with him a few times, later he became Kenya President...

I eventually left Coopers and returned to Eldoret. My "wife" and I got married in February 1961. We had a lovely reception at our restaurant (now called Black Bamboo Bar) for about 150 guests, with great food. My wife and I went on our honeymoon to Nairobi and stayed at the Equator Inn. Six months later, Dad sold the building and was anxious to return to Italy. My Mother went by plane and my Dad went by ship as he had seven trunks of stuff to take. He and my wife went to Mombasa. My wife was delighted to visit Her Mom and Dad. Her father, Mr Clark was the first Railway Master in Eldoret and later the Port Master in Mombasa. Dad left, and I had to take over to finish some work and sell the remaining property we had. In September, my wife left for Italy by plane and a month later I went by ship. On November 22, 1961, we were at my uncle's doorstep in East Hartford, Connecticut, USA.

My wife's maiden name was Irene Clark. Next February (2021), we will have been married 60 years. Our daughter was born in 1966. She has two grown children. My son, who was born in 1968, passed away in 2019. I worked for a Jaguar dealership for 22 years. In 1981-82, I had two lower back surgeries and, a few years later, I had a quadruple by-pass. My doctor advised me to give up mechanical work and I went to work in a bank as a security guard, because of my Kenya Police experience. Three years later, I was in charge of the bank's security. I retired at the age of 62 in 2007 and moved to Florida, where we enjoy the sun just as we did in Kenya.

Me and a teacher from Hill School. Bill in the US. Part-time policeman and Bill's wedding in Eldoret Celebrating 66 years of wedded life soon.

"Time*" at the Kilindini Bar!

IN AN English pub when the bell is rung or the "gov'nah" calls "time" it means the end of the day's business. English law, however, used to allow 20 minutes of finishing your drink time. When they call "time" on Kenya's old pub, the Kilindini Bar in Mombasa, the curtain will come down in 2013 on one of the most written about watering holes in Africa, it will be akin to the final parting at a funeral. Many who have known the bar for many decades will surely shed a tear or two as the bulldozers and demolition crews smash it out of existence and out of living history.

The Kilindini Bar must go to make way for a new Likoni Bridge which will replace its iconic self. The old bridge has outgrown itself.

Thus, more than 100 years of Goan entrepreneurship will be rendered dust-unto-dust. The bar was founded by the late Alexio

Caetano De Souza. He was born in Anjuna, Goa in 1896. The bar was originally part grocery store and it as the first such venture by a Goan. He was among a batch of early Goan pioneers who made the perilous Indian Ocean journey by Arab dhow. More of then not, one would have to get to Oman first from India to catch a dhow heading for East Africa.

According to our current host, Maura De Souza Abranches: "The Kenya National Highways Authority / J I CA Project of the Mombasa Gate Bridge is in the pipeline. However, we have not been given any date when the project will start.

"We are saddened that the bar and the adjoining property will be demolished as the Government has requisitioned the property to make way for the construction of the Mombasa Gate Bridge project. Having been born and brought up in our home, which is adjacent to the bar, it will remain in our memories in our lifetime.

We hope that this iconic and historic establishment will remain in the archives for future generations to know that it one of the longest operating Goan establishments in Kenya's History."

According to one writer, "When the Kilindini Bar was first opened at the turn of the century, it stood alone, for part of the island had yet to feel the impact of development. It was hardly inhabited and those were the days of kerosene lamps, well water and rough tracks, often frequented by wild animals.

"Customers arrived at the bar by railway trolley railway, which then pursued its leisurely course to the port and passed within a few hundred yards of the bar. At that time there was no brewery in Kenya and the only beer available was imported from South Africa, Europe and Japan. (Ivan Fernandes).

Mr De Souza ran the bar/grocery store until his death in 1918. His sons John and Ambrose ran it until 1940 when Ambrose took over sole ownership. He and wife Catherine ran it until his death in 1989 when his daughter Grace took charge of the business. Catherine passed away in 2013. Between 2013-2019, the bar was run by the devoted staff. Today, it is being run by Catherine's daughter Maura and her husband Clarence Abranches.

The first time I went there was in the early 1960s. My host was Francis Rafiki (Raymond) who was one of the journalists and eventually went on succeed Adrian Grimwood as Editor of Coastweek. I remember it as mostly down-to-earth as were most of its customers. It was a friendly place, especially if you spoke good Swahili. It seemed to me that everybody knew each other. Besides solving the problems of the Coast, the problems of independent Kenya, loud arguments about the shortcomings of the Feisal and Liverpool football teams, the banter was generally friendly. One thing I missed was the local food. The bar did not serve any. We had to head out to a "hotel" (it as really a poor man's café) where they served impressions of Indian curries but the prize on the menu was the super-large mince-egg-chappatis and several lamb and beef dishes, including a version of Kenya's favour, nyama choma (charcoal grilled pieces of tender beef).

Back to the Pub. Sure guys got drunks and made utter asses of themselves. Sure, they argued and threatened each other with all sorts of things. Sure, it got a little loud sometimes. There was always Francis Kilatya to calm thing. He never lost his cool and the quiet way he went about bring order to the pub earned him respect of all the familiar faces, even those who sometimes made fools of themselves.

It was much loved as these messages say:

"Old is gold," the late Franklin Pereira, Mombasa.

"Sad to lose these iconic premises," Gabriel Ngala, Mombasa. "Good to meet the third generation running the bar," Linda

Pereira, Goa.

"Amazing oldest Goan Bar," Tony Pereira, Goa.

"Of great merit more than a life experience," John Kilonzo, Kenya Ports Authority, Mombasa.

"Feeling honour drinking in the oldest bar in Mombasa," Jodie and Ian McGucken, Georgetown, Ontario, Canada.

"Unforgettable experience," Johnny and Matilda Fernandes, San Francisco, California.

"Amazing history. Great space, lovely people," Alan Lo Bue, Illinois, USA.

"An incredible bar. A wonderful place," Daniel Heathcote, Edinburgh, Scotland.

"Fascinating to delve into the history of the bar," Alina Oswald, Berlin, Germany.

"This place i9s WOW!" Glenn Egala, Kenya Highways Authority, Coast Region.

"The history is superb," Njeru Njue.

"Great to have been at this historical place," Wachira Mwangi, Mombasa.

"A history of generation well kept," the Hon, Nicholas Mochorwa, Nyandarua County.

"Amazing part of the history," John Fernandes, GI Nairobi.

"Great recreation of the generational history. Very warm reception from the proprietor former headmistress of Loreto Msongari. Will come back," Hon. Rundikiri Mugambi, MP Meru County.

"Fantastic. May they never destroy this historic monument," Inge Thomesen, Norway.

"The history is rich. The best historical gem I have been to," Albert

Mamburi, Pwani Tribune.

As long as it there, as long as people are able to read about it in books, magazines, in libraries and where else the written word is available, the Kilindini Bar will live on the hearts, minds and memories of those who visited and enjoyed a drop or two of a drink or two and revelled in the history of the place the generations of De Souza who were its guardians.

Njuguna Mutonya once wrote: "The Kilindini Bar is a worthy monument which in its centenary year plus its existence as a public house in Mombasa has continued to be a melting pot of cultures having survived the apartheid days when only whites could partake of its services.

"To see the well-heeled socialites who gather there regularly break out in song, sometimes the oriental renditions of Lata Mangeshkar and many-a-times the 60s rollicking tunes of the Beatles, Elvis or the Rolling Stones is to a have glimpse of the Kenya we aspire to.

"The clientele has only one thing in common, their love for heritage exemplified by the smoothly worn mahogany seats and the ancient adverts adorning the walls, some going back to 1927."

And so, say all of us.

Maura and Clarence Abranches, just hoping for a miracle that the Kilinidini Bar, once called The Railway Bar, will avoid extinction by demolition.

St Francis Xavier Chapel, Malindi

An interior view of the St Francis Xavier Chapel in Malindi

Now under the National Museums of Kenya, the historic St.

Francis Xavier Chapel is one of Kenya's most popular worship sites: a reminder of centuries that have come and gone, a vanguard of the Christian faith in Kenya. It will always remain a favourite of local and visiting Goans who make the pilgrimage whenever possible.

The Arrival Of Vasco Da Gama

On July 8, 1497, three ships left a dock in Lisbon, Portugal, led by prime navigator, Vasco da Gama. His expedition was intent on sailing the fastest route to Calicut, India where they purposed to trade items and eventually spread Christianity in the race for religious dominion. It took them more than nine months to reach Mombasa harbour where they were not welcome and the fleet was denied port.

The Kenyan Coast In The 15th Century

Desperate to anchor ship for a few days for provisions before resuming their journey, the three ships continued to hug the coastline, as they sailed north. Eventually, a welcome was found in the settlement of Malindi, in what is today Kilifi county.

The inhabitants of 15th-century Malindi were ruled by Sheikh al-Bauri, who saw the Portuguese as potential allies in continuing feuds with their neighbours to the south, in Mombasa. It was an era of survival through alliances.

When it was time for da Gama's crew to set sail for Calicut, the Malindi Sheikh offered two of his best sailing pilots to ensure the Portuguese arrived at their destination safely. But it is said that the Malindi residents had no knowledge of Christianity, and one of the pilots abandoned ship as soon as he realised this. Vasco da Gama successfully arrived in India in May and, on his return voyage, anchored yet again in Malindi on January 8, 1499. On one of the trips, the group established a small chapel surrounded by trees not far from the shoreline. With thick walls and a modest frame, the chapel has one small window that opens onto the entrance of the gate. This concept was designed for

Christians of another time to spy outside, on anyone approaching the building. More than 500 years later, the nondescript building, with its thatch roof, stands on Riversand Road in Malindi town, surrounded by larger buildings. Visitors are immediately welcomed by the ancient stone pillars which host the names of some of those buried in its grounds.

St. Francis Xavier

The chapel is named St. Francis Xavier Chapel, after one of the founders of the Jesuit Francis Xavier of Spain, who visited in 1542 on his way to India. St Francis who had been commissioned as a missionary to Asia and was later beatified by Pope Paul V on October 25, 1619 and canonized as a saint by Pope Gregory XV. On his saint day – 3 December, many Catholics and other faithful gather in the small chapel to celebrate his works. Its small interior is able to accommodate at least 60 people and is occasionally used from time to time for worship and other celebrations. Despite being abandoned between 1593 and 1893, the chapel and its history have withstood the test of time.

St. Francis Xavier sailed up along the East African Coast on his way to Goa in 1542, and, in a letter to his Jesuit superiors in Rome, he describes his stop over there in April of that year. "We visited a city inhabited by Moors (i.e., Arabs) who are at peace with us", he writes. "We learn that Portuguese merchants were usually found there, and that the Christians who died there were interred 'in tombs of great size with crosses on them'"

He mentions the Vasco da Gama cross "gilded and very beautiful". It is with great pride that he writes: "The Lord God knows what comfort it gave us to see it, conscious as we are how great is the virtue of the cross, standing thus solitary and victorious in a Moorish land".

St Francis buried a sailor who had died on board and said that the Muslims were greatly edified with "...the way we Christians have of burying the dead". Before continuing his journey, he had lengthy discussions with some of the leading members of the Muslim community, at the end of which he tells us that "...their point of view remained unchanged... and so did mine".

Mosque attendance was a worry for one of their religious leaders. He told Francis that the faithful were attending only three out of 17 mosques in the town, and to those only a handful went regularly. He wanted to know if Christians had the same problem. From Malindi Francis headed north again and describes a visit to the island of Socotra (to which we shall return later on), and then ends his letter suddenly with the words "we reached the city of Goa on 6th May, 1542" (over a year since they had sailed from Lisbon).

Francis was only 36 years old and had but another ten years to live. This great pioneer missionary to the East Indies and Japan, signed his letter with the utmost humility: "Your useless brother in Christ". "Useless" as he may have been in his own estimation, he remains today patron of missionaries; and on a more modest scale his feast is celebrated with special devotion in Kenya by his spiritual children, the Goan Catholic community.

The Portuguese Period

As far as Christianity is concerned, the first stirrings seem to have been in the island of Socotra in the northern part of the Indian Ocean. We have alluded to a description of St Francis Xavier's visit there. Christianity was brought there by Christian Arabs as early as 524 AD, when Cosmas Indicopleustes visited the island. We cannot say why missionary activity did not radiate from there, nor is there any trace of any penetration of Christianity further south on the well-defined trade route along the East Coast of Africa.

What Christianity remained on the island itself was in a sorry state when St Francis Xavier called there. There was no longer a bishop or an ordained clergy; the inhabitants "...are Christians in their own opinion", according to Francis, "and pride themselves on having Christian names to prove it; they have churches and crosses and lamps; their 'clerics' do not know how to read or write; they know a lot of prayers by heart; they go to church at midnight, in the morning, at the hour of Vespers and in the evening at Compline time; the people are followers of St Thomas; these clerics do not baptise nor do they know what baptism is". Many of them implored Francis to remain with them and to introduce them to baptism and the Mass, but the Governor would not allow him to remain for fear of the Turks who used to come to this island, and who probably would make Francis prisoner. So, he set sail and left behind him what we might call only a vestige of Christianity.

An excerpt from Mombasa Mission: The growth of the church in Mombasa 1888-1990 Father Edward Corcoran, the author, died in 1997

'HALF CRACK' in TRACK and FIELD

By Mel D'Souza

In any sport, the names of gold medal winners go down in the annals of history and are remembered by fans all over the world. Memories are short when it comes to silver medalists and almost lost when it comes to platinum or bronze.

On the other hand, many athletes never make it to the winner's podium but readily come to mind for a spectacular feat against all odds. Examples of such athletes are Eddie the Eagle, the British ski jumper, and the Jamaican bobsled team of the 1988 Winter Olympics. We may not know the names of some of these individuals, but their feats will be remembered for posterity.

In the 1960s, when I was in my twenties, the hero of every Goan in East Africa was Seraphino Antao. He had won the 100- and 220-yards Gold medals in the Commonwealth Games in Perth, Australia. There were other good athletes in East Africa, but they did not make it on the international stage as prominently as did Seraphino.

Two decades earlier, however, when I was about ten years old and schooling in Dar es Salaam, my hero was a young Goan athlete named

Francis Xavier D'Souza who was popularly known as "half- crack". Back in those days, 'crack' was slang for 'not of sound mind'. So, one would assume that 'half-crack' meant having the proverbial 'screw loose'. But Francis certainly did not fit the bill. He was a good-looking upright young man, always neatly dressed, soft- spoken, and a man of few words. Everybody referred to him casually – but without malice – as 'half-crack', and I am sure that they, like me, did not know why… until I found out a few years later.

In 1947, I moved to Goa with my mother and started the first of five years of my schooling in the village of Saligao.

One day I was having my hair cut by the village barber, a Hindu Goan, in his wood-and-corrugated iron shop when a newspaper cutting pinned to the wooden stud next to the mirror caught my eye. It featured a photograph of an athlete standing in front of another athlete doing the pole vault. As a young boy, I had a sports scrapbook and I was looking for a picture of a pole vaulter. I asked the barber if I could have the cutting, but he would not part with it.

"He was Goa's champion" the barber exclaimed in Konkani, adding "and nobody could beat him in any sport!"

That is when I decided to take a closer look at the picture. "Hey," I said to the barber, "I know this fellow. He is Francis Xavier from Dar es Salaam!"

I asked the barber for more information about Francis' sporting achievements, and he went euphoric as he told me the rest of the story.

"Tho amcho champion!" (he is our champion) he said with great pride and affection. "Nobody could win against him".

Apparently, the barber then began to highlight Francis' prowess in track and field events. Francis participated in any athletic event without a break to catch his breath between events. The barber recounted a particular sports day in Arpora. "After winning the mile, he walked over to the starting line for the 100 yards dash, outran his competitors, then did the high jump... and won that event too! He just won every event in which he took part."

The reputation of Francis' sporting prowess followed him to Tanganyika (now Tanzania) when he moved to Dar es Salaam to seek employment before WWII.

In the sporting field, he displayed feats that astonished his teammates who would, today, describe them amusingly as 'crazy'. But back then, they used the word 'crack' to describe an individual as 'out of this world'. Hence the moniker 'Francis Xavier Half- Crack'.

I witnessed one of his crazy feats during a football game in Dar es Salaam in the early 1940s. When I was about seven years old, Francis was the goalie for the Goans team playing against the side from the British Gymkhana.

The Gymkhana forward had taken a shot on goal which Francis blocked in mid-air. He bounced the ball on the ground about three times as the players moved forward to receive his pass. The players of the other team also turned around and started moving back. However, instead of kicking the ball to his forwards, Francis tossed the ball sideways, stepped out of the penalty box, and ran at top speed, kicking the ball along the sideline, past the centreline, before taking a shot at the Gymkhana goal!. The spectators cheered!

Nobody expected this move and I am sure that the Goan team were caught by surprise just as were the players of the other team. I remember the game well because the goalie of the other team was Mr Branch who was also one of my favourite football players.

Fast forward to Goa around 2008 – 2010. My sister, Avita D'Sa, is invited to a wedding and takes me along to the reception held at the A'lua – a restaurant with an outdoor dance floor located in a coconut grove on the outskirts of Panjim off the road leading to the village of Santa Cruz.

"Come here, Mel," says my sister, "I'd like you to meet somebody".

She introduces me to the owner, saying "This is Andrew, the son of Francis Xavier Half Crack".

"Nice to meet you," I say and hasten to explain that "Half- Crack" was not uttered in a derogatory way but rather as a nickname by which his dad was affectionately known and admired by his many young fans of which I was one.

Kenya honours John Gomes

We are proud to announce that Mr. John Piedade Gomes has been conferred with **The Order of the Grand Warrior of Kenya** by His Excellency the President and Commander in Chief of the Republic of Kenya, Uhuru Muigai Kenyatta, in recognition of his service to Education in the Country.

THE KENYA GAZETTE
Published by Authority of the Republic of Kenya
(Registered as a Newspaper at the G.P.O.)

Vol. CXXII — No. 226   NAIROBI, 18th December, 2020   Price Sh. 60

John and Annie Gomes

Sheer dedication

John Gomes left his home Goa in 1956 at the tender age of 22, as a lay Consolata missionary to head to the Port of Aden in Yemen to teach at St Anthony's boys. In 1959, at age 25, he was asked to come and teach in Africa, and this appealed to him very much.

When he arrived in Kenya, the then Bishop who liked him very much told him he would send him to Rome to become a priest. John fondly knowns as 'Mwalimu' replied to him 'I will do the work of the priest without wearing a cassock' and hence began his illustrious career as a teacher and headmaster that spanned over 32 years in Kenya. He married Annie Gomes fondly known as Mama in 1965. Together they created the family atmosphere at each of the schools they were posted to, with 'Mama' being the mother, the matron, the counsellor, the nurse, the cook and Mwalimu being the father, the teacher, watchman, driver and the man with the 'kiboko' (whip or cane in Swahili). They were loved and revered by all their students.

These are a list of the schools they taught in: 1960 Mugoiri Girls

1962 Karima Boys, Othaya

1963 and 1965 Gaichanjiru Secondary School, Muranga 1964 Nyeri High School, Nyeri

1966-1970 St Mary's Karumande Boys, Gichugu Division, Kirinyaga

1970 to 1972 Kiburia Girls, Kirinyaga 1972 to 1991 Moi Equator Girls Nanyuki.

Bishop Ceasar Gatimu was impressed with this young man who was changing so many lives that he then posted him to St Mary's School Karumande in Gichugu Division of Kirinyaga District in 1966. In 1970 Mwalimu and his wife Annie took over the running of Kiburia Girls School, where they completed building six classrooms, an administrative block and staff houses before he was transferred to Equator School in Nanyuki in 1972. Equator Secondary School was working from a primary school and the immediate problem was to build infrastructure for the secondary school to run. As the then Vice President was passing the school and stopped for a brief visit with the girls on the roadside, Mwalimu decided to ask him to come and visit the school and, with his support, he built the Administration Block after which the school was named Moi Equator High School.

From 1972, with 39 students working from the sacristy of the school church, he single-handedly built 12 classrooms, four dormitories, five laboratories, seven staff houses, a well-equipped library and a hall that could accommodate 500 students. Mwalimu then went on to build a school farm with over 1000 chickens, 56 cattle, 65 pigs, 70 goats and 60 sheep amongst others.

Mwalimu was on call 24 hours a day counselling the girls. He and Mama would also double up as the ambulance driver and nurse and rush girls to hospital in the middle of the night if there was an emergency. John Gomes was also nicknamed Ghost, as he could catch any girls who by chance had got out of the boarding school and gone to a disco in town. Somehow, he would be driving into town and would catch them and bring them straight home. Mwalimu was concerned about his girls and always made sure they were on the straight and narrow. Discipline was high on the agenda.

Mama made sure that the girls got a special treat every week over and above the average food they ate. At school, the girls would get special treats every week including beef, chicken, pork, eggs, loaves of bread and bananas. However, every time the girls had a sports visit or a study trip, Mama would get up at 4 am and make traditional Goan 'roast beef' sandwiches for the girls along with eggs and bananas. They were the envy of many schools. Mama also was the nurse and counsellor for the girls, teaching them many skills. Just like any mother.

Between them, in the many schools they had been too, they came up with an empathic and vital way to deal with teenage pregnancies. While most schools would expel the girls, some of whom committed suicide due to rejection by both school and their parents, John and Annie would allow these girls to carry on studying until the last day when they were about to give birth. They would then talk to the parents about acceptance of the child, and then as soon as the girl gave birth would bring her back to school to complete her education to support her child. The girls and their parents never forgot this.

By 1990, the student population had reached 520 girls from all over the country. The cost of constructing the school was entirely from the savings of the school and four Harambees (fundraisers). At that time, the fees were only Shillings1,350 per year for boarding, tuition fees, exercise books, pens, pencils and erasers and yet Mwalimu managed to build the infrastructure of the school.

These schools have produced many talented individuals, celebrities, ministers, philanthropists, politicians, successful businessmen and women, teachers, doctors, lawyers, social workers, civil servants. The list is unending. Mention names like the no-nonsense politician Martha Karua, Senior Advocate of the High Court Waweru Gatonye, Geneva-based Diplomat Dr. Stephen Karao and Equity Bank Group Chairman Peter Munga and his name duly crops up.

After teaching in some of the remotest parts of Kenya, Mwalimu retired. He and Mama returned to Goa. When it was time to leave, 600 girls held them tight and refused to let them go. After many tears and promises that they would try and come back, they finally left. That night the girls for the first time in the history of their tenure, marched to the Chief's office and insisted that they should be brought back to Moi Equator Girls School, there had never been a strike during Mwalimu's tenure

Before departing for Goa, Mwalimu He asked the Bishop he there was any form of pension for lay missionaries. The Bishop put his hand on his shoulder and said to him "My dear Son, your reward will be in Heaven".

John Gomes returned to Kenya in 2010 and has been living with his daughters in Kenya. Today, almost 50 years later, the alumni of Moi Equator Girls, Gaichanjiru Boys, Nyeri High that he founded, still get together every year to honour Mwalimu John Gomes and the Mama the late Annie Gomes. Moi Equator Girls School's dining hall is named after him. The dormitory of Gaichanjiru Boys' School built by one of his students in his honour is also named after him.

At the age of 86, he still carries on his duty of educating children and sponsors many children to finish their secondary education through his foundation.

John Gomes with his extended family.

Tony D'Costa, Tony Reg D'Souza and Gilbert Fernandes at a Goan Institute Nairobi function.

Polly Fernandes

Nation Journalist

From left: Polly Fernandes, Phoebe Munene, Norman da Costa (late) Alfred de Araujo, (late) Sultan Jessa.

POLYCARP FERNANDES, the journalist who died in London on November 17, 2020, was a minor martyr of sorts. Fernandes was 74. The man he was named after, the

> Christian martyr Polycarp was burned at the stake (AD 156) for speaking his mind and sticking to his faith. He was unpretentious, humble and direct. Polycarp, the reporter, was no saint but he was honest, humble and straightforward. He was also hilarious with a permanent smile. He was not a liar, nor was he a sensationalist.

Polly was deported from Kampala, Uganda after reporting on the football tournament, the East African Challenge Cup in October 1969. The Challenge Cup, between Kenya, Uganda, Zanzibar and mainland Tanzania, replaced the unforgettable old Gossage Cup.

Hence, all who knew him (and even those who did not know him in person but followed his stories in the *Daily* and *Sunday Nation*, Kenya's leading newspapers) were shocked by his deportation.

No one paid too much attention to Tanzania or Zanzibar. Neither side featured in too many finals. Like any other time, the focus was all on Kenya and Uganda. Both teams played hard, unrelenting, never giving an inch, tough-tackling man-to-man football. Both sides had their light-touch players, too, but it was the gladiators in both teams' the fans loved. The supporters were also gladiatorial in the stands. Loud, abusive and sometimes physical, they would quite happily invade the pitch regardless of the police, the police dogs and other security personnel.

Both teams had a philosophy, in Swahili: "Damu kwa damu." Blood for blood, and "no surrender."

Most players, administrators and match officials recognised in Polycarp a reporter of integrity, fair and unbiased. A visiting Russian football team were so delighted with his match reports that they presented him with an honorary Order of Lenin, a Lenin badge. Polycarp called it as he saw it, that was his job, nothing else but the facts. There used to be banner on *Nation* newspapers which said, "the truth shall make you free." A lot of *Nation* pioneers made it their mantra.

On October 1, 1969, Kenya met Tanzania, and against all odds, lost 3-0. Worse, it meant that Uganda, Kenya's eternal rivals would keep the trophy on goal difference even if they failed to beat Kenya. Uganda had already scored 10 goals and conceded none.

Here is how the *Uganda Argus* reporter saw events unfold: "Kenya's centre-forward William "Chege" Ouma was sent off the field two minutes before the end by referee Kizito-Mubanda after he was hit with the ball. The same player had earlier been booked by the Kizito-Mubanda for a similar foul.

"Police were forced to use dogs to disperse a large crowd which invaded the field. Ouma refused to leave the field."

It was a hard-fought match but Tanzania stood tall and defended brilliantly.

The *Sunday Post* in Nairobi said: "No official statement has been given but Fernandes' match report contained a reference to about "10 Ugandan policemen rushing to a Kenyan player after a row with the referee. Sections of the crowd also joined in the melee.

"Other reasons for his (Poly's) deportation were that the anti-Kenya feelings displayed by the Police and the crowd might have embarrassed the Ugandan Government which has close relations Kenya as partners of the East African Community which also includes Tanzania."

On behalf of Polly, the British High Commissioners in Kampala and Nairobi made representations to the Ugandan authorities.

The relations between Kenya and Uganda have always been dicey. Like two country cousins, this relationship had conflicts and co-operation as the key components. Professional envy was part of the reason the seeds of which sown by the colonial government by the uneven development of the two countries, Kenya, of course, was the apple of the British eyes.

Hence, there was no love lost between the two countries. Even with the East African Community which was supposed to unite Kenya, Uganda and Tanzania, it was a matter of choosing the lesser of two evils, remain united under protest or disband (which happened in 1977, only for the EAC to be born again much later).

So, what did Polly write to get him deported (probably was the first-time ever that a sports journalist was deported for writing the truth). Norman da Costa, *Nation* Sports Editor said, "The match between Kenya and Uganda for the championship turned into a wild, rough encounter in which the referee appeared to lose control of the game. A full-scale riot ensued with police using tear gas and charging onto the field and into the stands."

"Polly, of course, captured this drama in his report. The following day we got a call that Polly was being deported -not to Kenya - but the United Kingdom since he was a British subject. The case was dealt with by the higher-ups at the Kenya Embassy and the British High Commission while the *Nation* tried to get him returned home. In the meantime, I had to console his Dad Darmel and Mum Carlota and keep them posted on a near daily basis as we were neighbours behind *Mlango Kubwa* (the big gate) in Pangani.

It was a traumatic time for the whole family, as his brother James recalls: "I got home that evening (can't remember the date or month) and that there was a lot of commotion in the house. My family were all distressed and devasted by the news that Polly had been deported. We did not know what to think and we feared the worst. In the next day or two we heard that Polly was being put on a flight to London.

"My brother Jacinto contacted our sister Sarita in London and asked to meet Polly on arrival. He stayed with Sarita and her family until his return to Nairobi six months later."

The Nation carried a brief report about Polly's deportation: "His deportation follows two reports he made in connection with the Kenya-Uganda match which contained allegations about the conduct of the Uganda Police.

"Mr. Fernandes was interviewed by police several times on Friday morning and afternoon but was allowed to return to his hotel." He thought the whole matter was over but he was detained in the evening and told he would be deported. He was put on a flight to London which did not stop over in Nairobi.

Here is what Polly reported:

FROM POLLY FERNANDES IN KAMPALA

In one of soccer's most disgraceful scenes, Kenya reserve Peter Ouma was pounced on and manhandled by about 10 policemen when he went on to the field in the 58th minute after the game was interrupted following a scene when a section of the crowd ran on to the field because Kenyan players argued with the Ugandan referee Kizito Mubuganda. Referee Mubuganda had just ordered off Kenya centre-forward William "Chege" Ouma after the Kenyan had deliberately hit (sic) the ball to the referee in this Challenge Cup match.

The trouble started at the Nakivubo Stadium when Kenya were awarded a corner kick. Outside-left John Nyawanga gave a short pass to Ouma but the referee ordered it to be retaken because he had signalled for the kick to be taken.

After Ouma was sent off, Kenya players crowded around Mubuganda protesting. Police ran on to the field after the crowd joined the altercation, but for reason best known to themselves Peter Ouma was singled out and manhandled till Kenya football officials ran in and rescued him.

Polly Fernandes was temporarily sacrificed by the Uganda authorities on the altar of political expediency.

True, and Polly was not to know this, it happened at a time when there was consternation in the political cabinets of the three East African countries about the future of the East African Community. Kenya feared the growing shift towards Communism or socialism by Uganda and its partnership with the Socialist Tanzania. I chased the story until the three heads of states met in Nairobi in an attempt to thrash out their differences and concerns. I also got a chance to ask Presidents Milton Obote, Julius Nyerere and Jomo Kenyatta a few questions at an Embakasi Airport press conference. The last question was to President Kenyatta: "Mzee, will the East African Community survive." His answer was: "Everything is good." But he did not look happy at all. Angry, really.

KENYA'S CUP HOPES TAKE A NOSE-DIVE

KENYA .... 0 TANZANIA 3

IN ONE of soccer's most disgraceful scenes Kenya reserve Peter Ouma was pounced on and manhandled by about 10 policemen when he went on to the field in the 58th minute after the game was interrupted following a scene when a section of the crowd ran on the field because Kenya players argued with Ugandan referee Kizito Mubuganda.

Referee Mubuganda had just ordered off Kenya centre-forward William "Chege" Ouma after the Kenyan had deliberately hit the ball to the referee in this Challenge Cup match.

The trouble started at Nakivubo Stadium when Kenya were awarded a corner kick. Outside-left John Nyawanga gave a short pass to Ouma but the referee ordered it to be retaken because he had not signalled for the kick to be taken.

After Ouma was sent off Kenya players crowded round Mubuganda protesting.

Police ran on to the field after the crowd joined the altercation but for reasons best known to themselves Peter Ouma was singled out and manhandled till Kenya officials rushed and rescued him.

Uganda, the Challenge Cup holders, are now virtually certain of retaining the trophy. They have the maximum four points from two matches and having scored 10 goals are the

FROM POLLY FERNANDES, KAMPALA

disorganised and there was no co-ordination between the forwards and the halves.

A 10-minute goal burst had Kenya reeling and they were so badly shaken up that they never moved as a team after this. Instead they made sporadic, half-hearted bursts and their attack was so mediocre that Tanzanian goalkeeper Mbaraka was hardly tested.

Inside-right Luo, who was left out for the first half in the match against Uganda, was one f the stars who earned this with two goals.

In the eighth minute Luo beat Kenya goalkeeper John Ogutu with a neat ground shot. Two minutes later outside-right Jundu lobbed a ball into

the Kenya penalty box and centre-forward Lukongo beat Ogutu with an acute angle shot which Ogutu should have saved.

Ogutu was replaced by Mohammed in the second half but that did not stop Luo from getting his second goal after a deft Tanzanian move between Jundu Lukongo and Luo.

GOLF DATES

THE Kenya Golf Union has applied for the dates April 30 o May 3 for the Kenya Open golf championships, of 1970.

It is understood that B.A.T Kenya Ltd., will again be sole sponsors but there is every probability of co-sponsors in 1971.

NORMAN DA COSTA: Early morning telephone call on Thursday, November 12, 2020, sent a chill down my spine. At the other end of the phone was Joan do Rosario asking me to find a chair and take a seat as she had terrible news to share. There was no need for that as I was still in bed. Then, between sobs, Joan floored me with what felt like an uppercut to the jaw by Mike Tyson. My longtime buddy Polycarp Fernandes was no longer with us. My dear and close friend, a classmate, hockey teammate, workmate at East Africa's premier newspaper, the *Daily Nation*, and best man at my wedding to Delphine, had unexpectedly died of a massive heartache. He leaves behind his wife Vanessa and son Malcolm, his brothers Jacinto and James, sisters Sarita and Tina, their spouses and families.

During this pandemic that is sweeping the world, this sad news compounded matters and comes on a string of recent losses. Polly was the third close classmate of our class of 1963 to die in the last two years. Alfred de Araujo left us in 2018 and Eugene Pereira in 2019.

Many knew Polly as a thorough gentleman, a first-class field hockey goalkeeper and a top-notch sports reporter who made world headlines of his own in 1999. No obituary would be complete without mention of his love for food. He sported a perpetual smile and was never easily flustered despite being the brunt of so many jokes. Like nearly every student at Dr Ribeiro Goan School in Nairobi, Polly had his share of nicknames. He was called Darmel as he bore a strong resemblance to his father; Marabu since he had a curly mop of hair and Corned Beef because of his love for corned beef sandwiches. The man credited for christening him Marabu was our late teacher Michael Britto.

During one vacation to Malindi, a whole bunch of friends sought refuge from a fierce rainstorm in a dark empty hut and Britto had no idea who he was in the room. So, he went around touching each one's head until he got to this curly head. "This must be Polly," he said.

Then there was Corned Beef. On a Hornets hockey team visit to Mombasa, Polly and his teammates Steve Fernandes and Hygino Vaz leapt off the slowing train as it was inching its way to a dead stop in Voi.

On the journey to Mombasa, finger food provided the various mothers was stored away in one of the carriages. There was music, card games and various other activities to keep everyone occupied. However, when they stopped for dinner, there was none to be found in the carriage where the food had been stored. Laughing from ear to ear, the trio admitted their crime. On the way back, Fernandes arranged for a kind lady to pack a box of finger foods and it was stored on the train with a guard of four to keep the three food robbers at bay. When dinner came, they asked for some food. No! No food for the trio because they had eaten all the food the last time. So, as we approached a train station, they wanted to be first in line for their sandwiches. Jumping off a moving train is forbidden and as luck would have it, they were nabbed by the local police. As there were no available cells, the two had to crouch under a police officer's desk. It must have been pure agony for Polly dreaming of that sandwich.

Another teammate Hilary Fernandes went to the police station to enquire about their whereabouts. "I could not see them but heard a faint cry for help. They were under the desk," Hilary laughed.

"Our manager Cyprian Fernandes rushed to see the station master who turned out to be Menino Viegas, a fellow Goan but he was not paying any attention to Fernandes' pleadings. "They have broken the law".

Fernandes asked Hilary to see if he could convince Viegas and get him to release the "starving" prisoners.

"After pleading with Menino Viegas (a hockey player himself) for what seemed like an eternity, they were allowed out. We will never forget that day," said Hygino, who now lives in Mississauga. "We can all laugh about it now but it wasn't funny then." Polly's love for food was legendary.

Once at an Indian restaurant in Pangani, Polly, Octavio (Pereira) and I were handed four gulab jamuns (Indian sweets) following our meal. We tossed a coin to see who would win the extra gulab jamun. Polly was the winner but before Polly could get his hands on it, Octavio quickly stuffed it into his mouth. The next minute we saw the confectionery fly out of Octavio's mouth and on to the floor. A furious Polly had punched him in the face.

Polly was a superb hockey goalkeeper in school and went on to play for the Railway Goan Institute. He was a member of the RGI team that won the M.R. de Souza Gold Cup and several other local trophies. He also represented Nairobi in the Tata Cup and went on to play against the touring Pakistan national team led by incomparable Gen. Mansoor Atif.

Also, on the RGI team was his younger brother James, who was an excellent left-back. Polly's older brother Jacinto was Kenya's badminton champion and represented the country at the Commonwealth Games in Edinburgh in 1970.

At the *Daily Nation* Polly assumed the soccer and field hockey beats from me after I became sports editor. He was a dedicated reporter who knew his sports well. After earning his stripes, his first overseas assignment was covering the world field hockcy championships in Barcelona followed by the East African Challenge Cup soccer tournament in Kampala in October 1969.

The boat builder of Eastleigh

Louis Fernandes had a naval architect's degree from India. He worked for some time with the Kenya Police. Later, he went into business for himself, Ferns Industries, Art Treasures. Their landlord was Carmo Rodrigues. Pictured are his children Sandra, Audrey and Evelyn (who married Walter Fernandes, the classical musician). I can't remember the family or Carmo Rodrigues. There were two houses in front of the church, one Romolus and Remus (named after the two boys who died in Big Doom, the larger of the two derelict quarries on the same hillside as Mathare Mental Hospital. The other was Rodrigues' home, Eddie, Manu, etc.

Printed in Great Britain
by Amazon